Economics of Healthcare

An approachable beginner's guide to health economics that brings the economist's way of viewing the world to bear on the fundamentals of the US healthcare system. The conversational writing style, with occasional doses of humor, allows students to see how applicable economic reasoning can be to unpacking some of the sector's thorniest issues, while accessible real-world examples teach the institutional details of healthcare and health insurance, as well as the economics that underpin the behavior of key players in these markets. Many chapters are enhanced by "Supplements" that offer how-to guides to tools commonly used by health economists, and economists more generally. They help form the basic "economist's toolbox" for readers with no prior training in economics, and offer deeper dives into interesting related material. A test bank and lectures slides are available online for instructors, alongside additional resources and readings for students, taken from popular media and healthcare and policy journals.

Andrew Friedson is Director of Health Economics for the Research Department at the Milken Institute. Prior to this he taught undergraduate and graduate health economics at the University of Colorado Denver for over a decade. He has received numerous teaching and research award nominations, and won the 2015 National Tax Association's Richard Musgrave Prize, as well as an Impact Award as part of the University of Colorado Denver's 2021 Pandemic Research and Creative Activities Awards. His research on public health insurance, cost of care provision, medical malpractice, risky health behaviors, and public health regulations has been covered in media outlets such as *The New York Times*, *The Wall Street Journal*, *Newsweek*, and *The Economist*, as well as academic publications including *Health Economics*, the *Journal of Human Resources*, and the *Journal of Health Economics*.

"This is the book health economics instructors and students have been waiting for! The real-world examples immediately draw in readers and provide a foundation for looking at important issues in health care from an economic perspective. Dr. Friedson's approach to examining complex topics is both intuitive and hilarious."

Professor Elizabeth Munnich, *University of Louisville*

"A captivating tour of the economic foundations of modern healthcare. With practical examples and delightful humor, this book effortlessly breaks down complex concepts, making health economics accessible to diverse readers. A must-have resource for students seeking a comprehensive grasp of healthcare markets and the challenges they entail."

Professor Sarah Miller, *University of Michigan*

"This is a book on the economics of healthcare that is well organized, comprehensive in its coverage, and actually fun to read! It is well suited for a diverse audience, including undergraduate and graduate students from different degree programs, practitioners, and policy makers."

Professor James H. Marton, *Georgia State University*

"The hallmark of this book is its dedication to practicality. Demanding no prerequisite economics background, Friedson's "Health Economics" is ideal for students and professionals in public health and healthcare management. Rich with insights into the economics of the healthcare industry, it occupies a unique space in the health economics literature."

Professor Natallia Grey, *Iowa State University*

Economics of Healthcare
A Brief Introduction

Andrew Friedson   The Milken Institute

CAMBRIDGE
UNIVERSITY PRESS

Shaftesbury Road, Cambridge CB2 8EA, United Kingdom

One Liberty Plaza, 20th Floor, New York, NY 10006, USA

477 Williamstown Road, Port Melbourne, VIC 3207, Australia

314–321, 3rd Floor, Plot 3, Splendor Forum, Jasola District Centre,
New Delhi – 110025, India

103 Penang Road, #05–06/07, Visioncrest Commercial, Singapore 238467

Cambridge University Press is part of Cambridge University Press & Assessment,
a department of the University of Cambridge.

We share the University's mission to contribute to society through the pursuit of
education, learning and research at the highest international levels of excellence.

www.cambridge.org
Information on this title: www.cambridge.org/highereducation/isbn/9781009258456

DOI: 10.1017/9781009258463

First published 2024

Printed in the United Kingdom by CPI Group Ltd, Croydon, CR0 4YY

A catalogue record for this publication is available from the British Library

*A Cataloging-in-Publication data record for this book is available from the Library
of Congress*

ISBN 978-1-009-25845-6 Hardback
ISBN 978-1-009-25843-2 Paperback

Additional resources for this publication at www.cambridge.org/friedson.

Contents

Preface

It is incredibly uncommon for an individual to go through life without somehow touching the healthcare sector. In every year since 2010, the US has spent over 17 percent of its gross domestic product (GDP) on healthcare. Thus, it is no surprise that understanding the healthcare sector has become central to business, policy, and citizenship. To match the expansion of the healthcare sector there has been an expansion in course offerings for studying the economics of healthcare. This book is meant to serve as an introduction to both the healthcare sector and the economist's way of viewing the world simultaneously. If you want to get your students (or your in-laws) up to speed quickly, this is a book written to do just that: help people become competent with the core logic and concepts that drive the healthcare sector.

Why *Economics of Healthcare: A Brief Introduction*?

There are many textbooks on health economics. My first course on the topic (which had a fantastic textbook) opened my eyes to a field of study that has held my interest and imagination for the better part of two decades. But, by the time I took that course, I was already an economics major with several years of training under my belt. The textbook I used, and many of the existing textbooks are made to slot into the usual progression of coursework for an economics major: first you learn the language of economics, then you learn the tools of an economist, and then you finally get to put it all together and apply your skills in a field course such as health economics. I think that this keeps a lot of people from learning economics, because they stop before they get to see (what for them are) the most interesting applications.

Someone interested in healthcare, for example, might be better off learning price elasticities at the same time they learn what causes individuals to go to (or not go to) see a doctor. There are potentially large benefits to students from seeing the applications up front and learning the tools that they need as they need them. That's what this book does: it teaches the economics tools as you need them to understand a specific area of study.

There is no need for a student to have a prior background in economics, the book is a one stop shop.

Intended Audience and Level

Given that this book teaches economics tools at the same time that it teaches the economics of the healthcare sector, it is a great fit for students in programs such as Master of Public Health (MPH), Master of Public Administration (MPA), or Master of Business Administration (MBA) where courses with titles such as "Health Economics" or "Healthcare Economics" or "Economics of the Healthcare Sector" are commonly the only economics course that the students have ever taken (or will ever take). When I taught "Healthcare Economics" for the MPH program at the Colorado School of Public Health, this was exactly the case: the course included students with medical, public health, and social work backgrounds (as well as a few with backgrounds in the social sciences, including economics) and was for many of them their first and only exposure to economics.

This book also works well for a "no prerequisites" field course in health economics offered by an economics department as part of an undergraduate degree. Recruiting into economics majors can be difficult, and we lose many students along the way who start with introductory macroeconomics or introductory microeconomics and never get to see applications such as are seen in a health economics course.

It is also important to note that along with requiring little prior knowledge of economics, this book also requires a much less rigorous base of mathematical knowledge than a typical economics textbook. That's not to say that there is no math present, but that all math used beyond high school level concepts (and even some of the high school level concepts) are explained as they arise. Given the large differences between healthcare sectors across nations, this book focuses in on the United States specifically.

Structure

The book is broken into four parts. The first part of the book deals with fundamentals of consumer choice theory, looked at from the point of view of the consumer of healthcare (i.e. the patient). This section covers topics such as what drives decision-making (how individuals account for benefits and costs, and the concept of optimization), production of health (a simplified version of the Grossman model), demand for medical care, demand distortions due to insurance, and how to evaluate evidence. This lays the groundwork for much of the logic and economic intuition that will be applied in later chapters.

The second part of the book focuses on the production side of the health-care sector, covering topics such as firm behavior, the makeup of the labor force, provider responses to incentives (some of this is an application of personnel economics), and hospital structure and behavior. Also in this section of the book is the basics of markets under perfect competition, a topic which tees up the remainder of the book: the healthcare sector is full of features that cause the logic (and benefits) of perfectly competitive markets to not always apply, and the rest of the book largely explores these areas.

The third part of the book deal with health insurance, health insurers, and the consequences of having these actors in the sector. Part three begins with a chapter on health insurance as a product, and then moves on to topics such as adverse selection in the health insurance market, how prices are distorted by having insurers as intermediaries, managed care organizations, and public insurance programs.

The final part of the book deals with parts of the sector that require understanding of behavior of buyers, sellers and insurers to truly unpack. These chapters are largely self-contained, giving instructors some additional flexibility in course design based on their individual pedagogical priorities. Topics in this part of the book include pharmaceuticals, externalities, medical malpractice, inequality, and comparisons of different healthcare systems.

Features

- Health economics content that is appropriate for a novice economist, no prior economics is needed to pick up and dive in.
- Casual, conversational writing style. This book is meant to be a relatively easy read as compared to traditional "dry" texts. Topics are introduced with intuitive examples, and a dose of humor when appropriate.
- Non-technical explanations of both economic fundamentals and health economics. Mathematical proficiency is not a requirement for understanding and using the text.
- Many chapters have end of chapter supplements that provide "how-to" guides on common tools used by health economists and economists more generally. These include how to use price indices, how to calculate measures of market power, and how to do a benefit–cost analysis. The supplements are slightly more technical than the rest of

the text but will still be simplified relative to traditional texts. They will help form the basic "economist's toolbox" for readers with no other training in economics. Other end of chapter supplements will provide deeper dives on interesting tangential material.

- End of chapter assessment questions. These are meant to get students thinking about and applying the material.

Online Features

- Test bank of questions that can be used for homework or exams
- Lecture slides
- Bank of related readings in popular press and accessible journal articles, as well as related podcasts.

Acknowledgments

There were many people who made this book possible. I owe thanks to the Teaching Health Economics working group, as well as specifically Anaka Aiyar, Priyanka Anand, Joe Benitez, Michael Darden, Melanie Guldi, Matt Harris, Beth Munnich, and Yulya Truskinovsky for early stage interviews that helped solidify the purpose and premise of the book. I also owe special thanks to Emily Dubansky, Stephen Dubansky, Arthur Friedson, Steven Medema, Laura Wherry, and many anonymous reviewers for feedback on specific chapters, as well as to Seth Freedman who piloted early versions of chapters in his class. A very special thank you to Monica Aswani who did all of the above, including very detailed and helpful feedback on the majority of the book.

On the production side, this book would not have been possible without my editors Sean Fabery and Melissa Shivers at the Cambridge University Press, as well as Peter Buckles, Balaji Devadoss, Lucy Edwards, and Judith Shaw. I also wish to thank my graphic designer Coleman Conley who is responsible for all of the figures in this book looking considerably better than the original versions that I created (poorly) in a drawing program.

In terms of encouragement, I have very generous research collaborators who picked up slack on projects to allow me to meet book deadlines. I also received a tremendous amount of support from the Economics Department at the University of Colorado Denver. Finally, my family: parents, brother, in-laws, kids, and my wife Molly, all of whom encouraged me to pursue and complete this project. Molly, I could not have been able to do this without your support, thank you for everything.

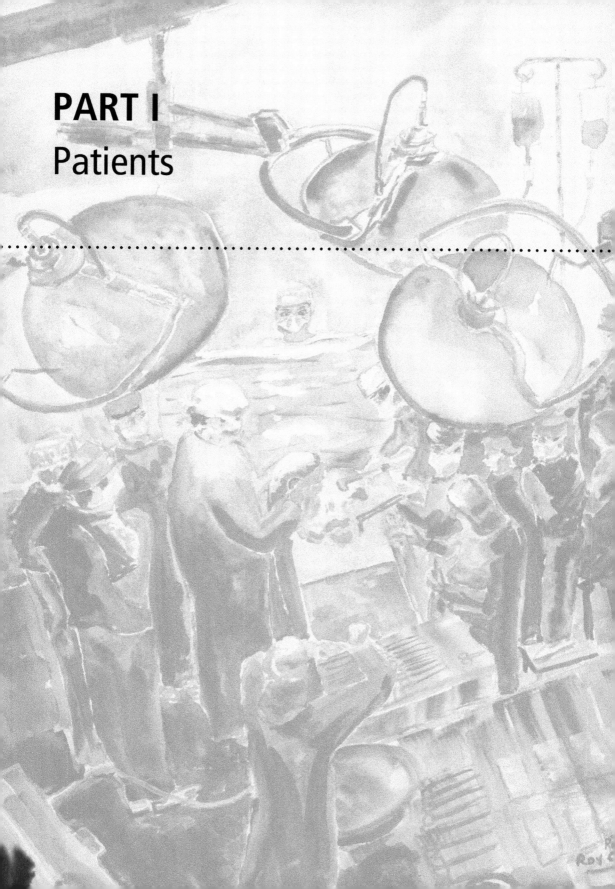

PART I
Patients

1 How Economists View Human Behavior

One feature shared by the actors within the healthcare sector is that they are humans or entities run by humans. If you are human, you have likely wanted medical care at some point in your life. If you are human, you have likely wanted other things too, like food, or companionship, or really cool pants.[1]

Humans exist in a world where they have things that they want and limited resources to spend to get them. At the center of economics is the idea that humans will look at the resources that they have, and the things that they want, and will do their best to use those resources to acquire the mix of things that they believe will make them the happiest.

So, the economist's point of view is that each time you make a decision, you are answering the question "given my resources what is the choice that will make me the best off?"[2] A person's answer to this question will depend on three factors:

1. the person's preferences over possible goods and activities,
2. the costs of the goods and activities, and
3. the resources that the person has to spend.

Doing your best given these factors is called *optimization*, and following the *optimal* (i.e. best possible) decision given the information that you have is called behaving *rationally*.

Things Humans Want

Humans value a great many things: tacos, naps, watching sunsets, socks, and the list goes on. Every person places different values on things, whereas I love tacos and naps, you may also love naps but only be lukewarm on

---

[1] To be fair, if you are a dog then you also have wants, like food, or companionship, or a really cool ball. Also, kudos on being able to read.

[2] Given mathematical representations of preferences, prices, and resources (i.e. your budget) this question is mathematically solvable, which is a subject covered in most microeconomics textbooks. This is the basis for the branch of economics known as "consumer theory," the study of consumer choices.

tacos. Each person will have their own set of *preferences*, or list of which things they like more than others.

While it may not be feasible to write down every single preference you have in every situation that may arise, economists generally believe that these preferences exist somewhere within your psyche. They use a concept called *utility* to create some general rules about preferences and how people behave. Utility is the abstract happiness or satisfaction that you derive from something that you value. The more you value the object or activity, the more utility you get. So, given any two options that cost the same, a person will pick the option that gives the most utility.[3]

For the purposes of understanding how people behave with regards to health and medical care, we can identify a few categories of things that people value. The first is your health. People value their health and, given the same amount of everything else, would prefer to be healthier. Would you rather have (A) some ice cream, or (B) some ice cream and the flu? The answer is clearly A. Given the simple choice between being more healthy and being less healthy (with no other strings attached to the decision), people will pick to be more healthy.

Humans also value a wide array of goods and activities. Let's put them into three groups:

1. goods and activities that have no bearing on your health,
2. goods and activities that are good for your health, and
3. goods and activities that are bad for your health.

The amount of utility that a person gets from the first group is based on how much happiness a person gets from that good or activity. If I like black T-shirts, then the more black T-shirts that I have, the happier I am. There is no tradeoff between the number of black T-shirts and my health.

The latter two groups are a little more complicated, because humans get direct utility (or happiness) from the good or activity itself, but also indirect utility from the good or activity's impact on their health. The overall satisfaction that an individual gets will then be the combination of the direct and indirect components.

An example of a good or activity that is good for your health is kale. Kale gives little in the way of direct utility, but because it has a positive effect on health, which people value greatly, it has become a somewhat popular vegetable. An example of a good or activity that is bad for your health is chocolate cake. Chocolate cake gives a lot in the way of direct

---

[3] Utility is expressed in units called *utils* which are completely arbitrary and do not mean anything beyond "more of these are preferred to fewer of these."

utility, but because it has a negative effect on health, which people value greatly, it is eaten sparingly.

Decisions will depend on how much direct satisfaction a good or activity gives, as well as any health ramifications, and the costs of the goods or activities. It is important to underscore that individuals care about *all* of these things. A person may rationally choose to smoke marijuana, eat a lot of chocolate cake, or engage in unprotected sex with many different partners. All of these activities are risky from a health perspective but may also provide a great deal of direct satisfaction.[4]

Costs

This brings us to one of the most obnoxious, but also true, economist sayings, "there is no such thing as a free lunch." Everything humans want costs something. The most commonly discussed cost is money, and keeping track of money costs is what accountants do, which is why the money cost of something is often called the *accounting cost*. But there are lots of other costs that may apply as well, such as costs to your time, your mental well-being, or your social standing. These costs need not be concrete in the sense that you give up something tangible, they just need to be felt enough to influence your behavior. If you count up all of the costs that could influence the behavior of a human then you have what economists call *economic cost*.[5]

Accounting Costs

Accounting costs are important for keeping track of finances, but do not always influence your decision-making. The difference has to do with timing relative to the time the decision is made: are you thinking about money that you have yet to spend, or money that has already left your pocket?

Sunk Cost
Money that you have already spent at the time you are making a decision is a type of accounting cost called a *sunk cost*. Economists do not consider

---

4 This is not to say that everyone gains direct utility from these activities, just that some people do.

5 Accounting costs and economic costs are both important, but in different ways. Accounting costs are vital for keeping track of finances and accurate budgeting. Economic costs on the other hand are costs that are relevant to choices.

these costs to be part of your decision-making, and do not count them as economic costs. If you go to buy ice cream, then it only matters how much money you have to spend at that time: having $100 available to spend and having spent $20 the week before is the same as having $100 available to spend and having spent $1,000 the week before. The money spent the week before is *sunk*, and is no longer recoverable, as such it has no influence on your ability to buy things at that moment.

This is important when thinking about how health insurance will influence how a human decides how much medical care to purchase. The price of the health insurance plan itself (the *premium*), is a sunk cost by the time that person decides how much care to get. When you ask yourself, "should I go to the emergency room?" you likely consider how much the emergency room is going to cost you as a direct result of your visit, but do not likely consider how much you already spent to buy your health insurance plan that year. The health insurance premium is sunk, and while the money spent on the premium is important for accounting, that expenditure is not important for the decision-making process in the moment.

Cash Out-of-Pocket

An accounting cost that does matter for the decision-making process is any cash spent out of your own pocket due to your decision. To go back to the example of "should I go to the emergency room?" the price of the emergency room visit is extremely important to decision-making. The details of your health insurance plan, such as whether you have to pay $50 or $250 out-of-pocket, has a large bearing on whether or not you ultimately decide to go to the emergency room. Cash spent out-of-pocket is both an accounting cost and an economic cost.

Economic Costs

There are several types of costs that influence your decision-making but that do not require money to change hands. These costs would not show up on an accounting balance sheet but are relevant to human behavior.

Time Cost

The time you spend on an activity carries a time cost, sometimes referred to as a waiting cost. An easy example is to think about choosing a food truck from among several available. One thing that will help you decide which one to buy from is how long the lines are. The food is going to cost you both money and time spent waiting.[6]

Time costs can be a barrier to obtaining medical care, and can pop up at several points in the process of obtaining care. There can be time costs when trying to schedule an appointment (e.g. waiting on hold if you call to schedule your appointment), time spent traveling to the appointment, and time spent physically waiting in a waiting room or examination room.

Travel Cost

If you do not have a car (or a friend or family member with a car who will help you) and need get across a city to get to a medical appointment, then the travel cost of obtaining medical care might be quite large, and may prevent you from getting care at all. Travel costs include time spent traveling (which is a time cost), but also include things like bus fares, tolls, gas, or other expenses related to traveling. Note that any cash spent on travel could rightfully be considered an accounting cost as well.

Travel costs become particularly important when thinking about policies for getting care to disadvantaged populations who may have limited travel options: policies that push down the out-of-pocket price of care but that do not help with transportation may not be as effective. Free care is attractive to those with little income, but is irrelevant if they are incapable of getting to the location where the care is being delivered.

Discomfort

Physical or emotional discomfort is another cost that can influence decision-making. Many people avoid going to the dentist because of the cost of discomfort. Think right now about having your teeth scraped by the dental hygienist. Chances are you just physically cringed, I did writing this.[7] Desire to avoid physical discomfort can prevent individuals from seeking care, such as those who avoid the dentist because they do not like getting their teeth scraped.

Physical discomfort is not the only form of discomfort cost that can influence decisions: fear and anxiety are also discomfort costs. I dislike roller coasters. This is not because I dislike riding them, once I get on, I usually have a good time. But I often have anxiety about the roller coaster

---

[6] Economists often roughly approximate a cash value to the cost of time spent waiting using a person's wage. The idea is that the wage is how much money you could have been making if you weren't stuck waiting. So, if your wage is $15 an hour, and you were waiting 30 minutes, that wait cost you approximately $7.50 worth of time.

[7] Some of you might have instead thought, "getting my teeth scraped, now that's what I'm talking about!" and smiled. This book is not here to judge you.

while waiting in line to get on the ride. I usually decide that the discomfort I experience during the wait is not worth it. Fear and discomfort can keep people from seeking medical care as well. Many individuals will avoid therapy for traumatic experiences due to a desire to avoid the discomfort associated with reliving those experiences.

Social Status

Some behaviors carry costs that are felt within one's social group. For example, certain religious communities do not allow for some forms of medical treatment, so, for a member of that community, utilizing a forbidden type of medical care can carry with it the additional cost of paying a social penalty in terms of lost status within the community.

These social costs need not be extreme to be effective at changing behavior. As a society, we use social norms to impose the social cost of being labeled as "gross" to make many types of disease-spreading behavior costly. Behaviors such as spitting, picking your nose, or using your hands to serve yourself at a buffet are considered to be gross, and individuals avoid these behaviors in order to avoid the cost of being labeled as a gross person.

Social status costs can also come from breaking social norms within your immediate social group as individuals do not want to deal with the judgment of others for non-conformity. This is sometimes referred to as "peer pressure." A new mother, for example, may find it to be more costly to choose to formula feed if all of the mothers in her social group breast feed (or vice versa).

Opportunity Cost

Opportunity cost is the cost of giving up your next best option. One way to think of opportunity cost is as a quantification of fear of missing out (sometimes called "FOMO"). If you choose to stay home and study on a night that your friends are going out together you incur a larger opportunity cost of studying than on a night where none of your friends have any social activities planned. Every activity has an opportunity cost. You can only be in one place doing one activity at any one time. So, the other options that are available at a given time will dictate an activity's opportunity cost.

Opportunity cost is the reason why it is more difficult to decide what to order at a restaurant with many enticing menu options. If the menu has only one appealing option and everything else on the menu is essentially fried tree bark then the opportunity cost of that single appealing option is low and the decision is easy to make. When a menu has many enticing options then the decision becomes much more difficult, that is because choosing any item means that you do not choose to order the next most delicious looking thing and incur a larger opportunity cost.[8]

Optimizing

With the above concepts, we can now understand the economist's view of human behavior. Given a choice, a person will look at the options presented to them, and choose the option that they like the most subject to the resources that they have available and the cost of those choices. A human will try to do the thing that they believe will make them the best off.

This is not to say that choices are always easy. There are complications to deciding that can arise and make it difficult to be completely sure what the best option is. It is also possible that what an individual believes to be their best option at the time of a decision may not in truth actually be a very good choice.

Perception and Choice

The value that a person places on goods and activities, as well as the costs that person assigns to choices, are based on that individual's perceptions. A decision-maker need not be correct in their perception for that perception to influence their behavior, they need only believe it to be true. If I believe that a medicine will taste bad (even if it in truth tastes fantastic), my incorrect belief about the taste will still have some influence on my decision. This means that incorrect information (or worse, active disinformation) about the benefits or costs of a given choice can greatly alter individual decisions.

Misinformation

Problems can arise when individuals are misinformed about the benefits or costs of medical treatment. A classic example of this problem is incorrect beliefs surrounding the costs of vaccines. In 1998, the *Lancet* published a study linking the Measles, Mumps and Rubella (MMR) vaccine to among other things, childhood autism (Wakefield et al. 1998). This study was later shown to be fraudulent and was retracted (Godlee et al. 2011). However,

---

[8] You may then ask, "why not order both?" In that case you are trading off an opportunity cost for a larger cost in the form of cash out-of-pocket, and perhaps an additional cost to your social status for gluttony. You would also incur the opportunity cost of not ordering the next best item on the menu. There is still no free lunch, and even more so at a restaurant.

the false story that the MMR vaccine causes autism may have caused many people to worry about vaccines carrying additional costs in the form of health risks, lowering vaccine utilization in some populations.

This cuts the other way as well. If people are convinced that a product is beneficial for their health, even if the product is not, then they may be willing to purchase said product. False advertising of medicine was a huge problem in the United States prior to the 1912 Sherley Amendment to the Pure Food and Drugs Act, which prohibited false and misleading claims about medicines. Prior to this amendment, false advertising of inert (or sometimes dangerous) medicines was common, and profitable (Parascandola 1999). For example, a best-selling treatment for tuberculosis prior to the Sherley Amendment was "Radam's Microbe Killer," a purported medicine that was 99 percent water with trace amounts of acid and red wine (Hemmingson et al. 2015).[9]

Uncertainty and Risk

Perception of costs and benefits is also important when dealing with decisions around uncertain outcomes. If the cost or the outcome of an activity (such as a surgery) is uncertain, then individuals will make their decisions based on their best guess of what the outcome will be.[10]

That said, humans tend to dislike risk, a trait economists refer to as *risk aversion* or being *risk averse*. Risk aversion means that when given two options, one that on average gives you some money (say $100), but sometimes gives less and sometimes gives more, and another option that gives you the $100 for certain, the risk averse person will prefer the certain option. People are not risk averse in all situations: under some circumstances such as gambling, uncertainty is considered fun. In other situations, such as uncertainty around whether or not you will develop a life-threatening illness, uncertainty is rarely desired.

The Future

The future is by definition uncertain. When individuals make decisions that impact their future, they also make their best guess as to outcomes. If you are trying to decide whether to go to school to become a doctor or

---

[9] False claims of efficacy in medicine still exist, but are more aggressively pushed back against in the United States. In 2020, televangelist Jim Bakker sold a colloidal silver solution as a cure for COVID-19 (it is not a cure for COVID-19) on his television program. He was promptly sued by the State of Missouri (Schwartz 2020).

[10] The mathematical concept commonly used for this best guess is "expected value," which can be calculated when the possible outcomes and their probabilities are known. This concept is important for understanding insurance and will be discussed in greater detail in Chapter 10.

to become a lawyer, you make you best guess as to which of these future career paths will make you better off and choose that one.

The future has an additional property of not being right now. Humans dislike waiting for things and place less value on something the longer that they have to wait for it. Economists call this *discounting*, and the *discount rate* (or rate of time preference) is the rate at which something loses value the longer you have to wait for it. So if you have a larger discount rate, then that means you are more impatient. This is a useful concept when thinking about policies aimed at avoiding health costs in the future: if smokers on have high discount rates, then an anti-smoking campaign that highlights benefits to quitting in the future, such as lowered risk for future illness, may be less effective at its goal than an anti-smoking campaign aimed at highlighting more immediate benefits to quitting such as that smokers tend to get paid less (Hotchkiss and Pitts 2013; Darden et al. 2021).

Making decisions about the future can be tricky. You may have to compare one value right now with another value that is off in the future. You could get a job now and get a going market wage, or you could go to medical school and lose money now (go into debt), but get a much higher wage later. To do this comparison, economists use the concept of *present value*, which scales a value obtained in the future to what it is worth to you right now using your discount rate.[11] The rational decision about the future is made by comparing the present values of different possibilities and picking the one that is the most valuable.

Self-Assessment

1. Consider the statement "Smoking is bad for your health, therefore nobody should ever smoke." What is correct about this statement? What is incorrect? Write a more accurate statement.

2. Would the money that you spent on a gym membership last year influence your decision whether or not to purchase a gym membership next year? Why or why not?

3. Give an example of a situation where out-of-pocket cost does not limit who has access to medical care, but ...
   (a) time cost is a limiting factor that prevents some people from accessing care.

---

[11] The present value of a cup of coffee a year from now is what the guarantee of a cup of coffee in one year is worth to you right now. It is not the value of giving you that coffee right now. The mathematics of present value calculations are covered in most economics textbooks.

(b) physical discomfort is a limiting factor that prevents some people from accessing care.

(c) costs paid via social status are a limiting factor that prevents some people from accessing care.

4. Imagine you have an illness and there are three different medications that can treat it. Each medication works, but has a different set of side effects. What is the opportunity cost of taking any of the given medications?

5. Public education campaigns can be seen as correcting misinformation. If you were going to launch a public health education campaign, what information would you try to get to the general public? Would this correct a misperception about the value of something? Would this correct a misperception about the cost of something? How would this correction ideally influence behavior?

6. Some choices, such as whether or not to eat junk food for dinner give direct utility immediately (when you eat the food) but give indirect utility with a delay (when you deal with any health consequences). Explain how it is possible for two people who have the same preferences with regards to health and junk food, the same beliefs about how harmful junk food is, and the same resources to spend, to rationally make different decisions with regards to whether or not eat junk food for dinner.

Supplement. Practical Economist Skills: How to Use Price Indexes

· ·

One other concern when dealing with the future is that a dollar today is not necessarily worth the same as a dollar a year from now (or a year ago). This is because the amount that a dollar is capable of purchasing changes over time. Usually, the amount that a dollar is capable of purchasing decreases over time, meaning that you need more money to purchase the same item. This is known as *inflation* (the opposite, money becoming more valuable over time is called *deflation*). For example, $1.00 in the year 2000 purchased roughly as much as $1.50 purchased in the year 2020.

This creates an important distinction when dealing with dollar amounts over time between *nominal* dollars, or the amount of money, and *real* dollars, or the value of said money in terms of purchasing power. To keep the same example as before, $1.00 in 2000 and $1.00 in 2020 have the same nominal values but different real values. The $1.00 in 2000 has a real value of $1.50 in 2020 dollars (or the $1.00 in 2020 has a real value of $0.67 in 2000 dollars).

Typically, when comparing values over time, we want to compare real values to real values, because, when making decisions, what we ultimately care about is the value of the goods and activities money can buy us, not the money itself. To convert to real dollars, economists use something called a *price index*, which follows the same goods over time and tracks their prices. The most commonly used price index is the *Consumer Price Index (CPI)* which follows a standard group of consumer goods. A price index is calculated such that the ratio of price index values at any two points in time is the ratio of a dollar's purchasing power at those two points in time. So, using our above example:

$$\frac{CPI\,2000}{CPI\,2020} = \frac{Value\,in\,2000}{Value\,in\,2020}$$

To turn nominal values into real values, one need only cross multiply and solve the for the value of interest. So if I want to know the real value in 2020 dollars of $1.00 in 2000 the expression would be:

$$Value\,in\,2020 \times CPI\,2000 = Value\,in\,2000 \times CPI\,2020$$

or

$$\text{Value in } 2020 = \frac{\text{Value in } 2000 \times \text{CPI} \, 2020}{\text{CPI} \, 2000}$$

and we can plug in the actual values[12] to get

$$\text{Value in } 2020 = \frac{\$1.00 \times 258.8}{172.2} = \$1.50.$$

---

[12] These values were taken from a historical CPI table kept by the Federal Reserve Bank of Minneapolis, www.minneapolisfed.org/about-us/monetary-policy/inflation-calculator/consumer-price-index-1913-

2 Where Does Health Come From?

Health is something that humans value greatly. However, unlike many (but not all) things that humans value, health is not something that can be bought or sold directly. You can walk into a restaurant and say, "one hamburger, please!" and exchange money for a hamburger. In real life, you cannot walk into a health store and say, "one health, please!" and exchange money for health. As such, no market for health exists. What do exist are markets for goods and services that impact health, and humans will attempt to adjust their health by purchasing these goods and services.

One of the most common things that humans will purchase to attempt to adjust their health is *medical care*, which is a catch-all term that encompasses a wide array of goods and services. Examples of medical care include, but are not limited to, physician visits, prescription drugs, surgeries, and diagnostic tests.

Medical care is not the only thing that impacts one's health. There are many goods, activities, and natural phenomena that can change your health. We have already discussed several examples, such as diet and use of illicit drugs in the previous chapter and will explore determinants of health more broadly in this chapter.

The Health Production Function

To organize all of the things that impact health, I will use some simple mathematic notation and write:

$$H = f(m,...)$$

This is what we will call the *health production function*. All that this notation is saying is that your health (denoted by the letter H) is some function (denoted by the letter f) of medical care that you consume (denoted by the letter m) and of other things (denoted for now by "..."). This notation is shorthand for the sentence: "Medical care (m) impacts health (H) in some way, and some other stuff (the "...") also impacts health in some way."

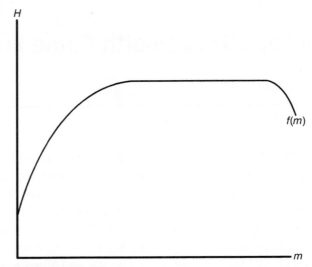

Figure 2.1 Medical care and health

One of the interesting things about medical care is that humans tend to purchase it solely because of its impact on health. In fact, many of the features of medical care are considered undesirable: these are features one would usually be willing to pay to avoid. Consider the following experience: you are knocked unconscious with chemicals and put on a table where other humans cut you open with knives and then sew you up. If this experience had zero health benefits whatsoever, would you be willing to pay for it? Or would you be willing to pay to avoid it?

Medical care has the general relationship with health shown in Figure 2.1. Broadly, the relationship between medical care (the "*m*" or horizontal axis in Figure 2.1) and health (the "*H*" or vertical axis in Figure 2.1) follows this rough pattern: at first, more medical care will improve health, but each unit of medical care used will be less effective than the last, and at some point, additional units of medical care will make no improvement in health. At some later point, additional units of medical care could actually harm one's health – a phenomenon referred to as *iatrogenic illness*.[1]

Marginal Changes

When medical care is used to increase health, each unit is less productive than the last. This is a property that economists refer to as *diminishing*

---

[1] The term "iatrogenic" comes from Greek (as do many medical terms). In this case, the Greek word *iatros* means "physician" or "healer" and -genic is a suffix that means "came from" or "generated by." So, iatrogenic illness refers to illness caused by your doctor.

marginal returns, or *diminishing marginal productivity*. The idea is that each *marginal* unit, that is to say the next unit to be used, is less effective that the one before it.[2] Economists like to use the term "the margin" to refer to potential increases in utilization (or consumption) of a good or service. So, if we were to think about "the margin" of your medical care utilization we would be considering increasing or decreasing your medical care use from the amount that you are currently using.

The concept of marginal changes actually covers two distinct margins, or two distinct ways to change your amount of care utilization. The *extensive margin* refers to changes between not using something at all and using it in any amount. There are a large number of choices that can be made on the extensive margin, all of which can be phrased as "yes or no" questions. Going from not taking a medication to taking a medication is a change along the extensive margin, and can be phrased as "are you taking any medication, yes or no?" Similarly, the choice between visiting a doctor and not visiting a doctor is a choice along the extensive margin.

The *intensive margin* refers to changes in intensity of use provided that one is already consuming any amount of the good or service. There are also a large number of choices that can be made on the intensive margin, all of which can be phrased as "how much" or "how many" questions. Going from taking two pills a day to taking three pills a day is a change along the intensive margin, and can be phrased as "how many pills are you taking each day?" Deciding how many times to see your doctor (provided that you see them at least once), and deciding how many chocolate candies to eat (provided that you eat at least one) are choices along the intensive margin.

To return to the concept of diminishing marginal productivity of medical care in producing health, medical care generally follows the pattern of decreasing marginal returns when increasing along either the extensive or the intensive margin. Let's start by thinking about a routine screen for a common form of cancer: a colonoscopy. Suppose that a person starts by getting a colonoscopy once every 10 years. Increasing use along the intensive margin would be increasing the frequency of testing. Once every

---

[2] The concept of a "marginal" or "next" unit of something can be counterintuitive. To cement the concept, I suggest the following exercise: put a number of small snacks (chocolate candies, pieces of popcorn, chocolate chips, etc.) on a table in front of you. Start eating them one at a time. Which snack is the marginal unit? It is the one that you are about to eat. Notice that you will likely get diminishing marginal satisfaction from these snacks: each will be good, but not quite as good as the one you just ate.

10 years could be increased to once every 5 years, or once every 2 years, and so on. Each additional colonoscopy in the 10-year timeframe increases the overall likelihood of catching cancer early and saving that person's life which increases overall health. However, each additional test is less likely to be the specific test that catches the cancer. The marginal effectiveness of each test has decreased, even though the overall benefit of testing is larger when tests are done more frequently.

One notable exception to diminishing marginal productivity along the intensive margin is pharmaceuticals. The exact relationship between the amount of a pharmaceutical used (i.e. the dose) and the returns in terms of health depend on the biochemical properties of the drug in question. Some drugs may have increasing marginal productivity for changes between lower and higher doses. That said, any drug will eventually have diminishing marginal productivity, as any drug will eventually have a point at which increasing the dose is either no longer as effective, or is outright dangerous (i.e. an overdose).

There is also diminishing marginal productivity of medical care along the extensive margin. At first glance, this may seem impossible as the extensive margin is a single switch from not using care to using care. But, if you consider *population health* and extend care to different subpopulations in the order of greatest benefit, then medical care has diminishing marginal productivity along the extensive margin.

An example of diminishing marginal productivity along the extensive margin is the initial rollout of COVID-19 vaccines. The vaccines were safe and effective at preventing infection and serious illness. That said, there was a large difference in the health benefits of the vaccine from person to person based on (1) how likely COVID-19 was to make that individual seriously ill, and (2) how likely that individual was to contract COVID-19. To be clear, the vaccine provided health benefits to almost everyone, but it provided larger benefits in the forms of: (a) a worse fate avoided to those who were more likely to die from COVID-19 (older individuals and those with certain comorbidities), and (b) a larger decrease in infection risk to those who were more likely to come in contact with the disease (such as healthcare workers). So, when the vaccine was first approved for emergency use, it was made available to healthcare workers and the elderly: those who would have the largest benefit from the marginal vaccination. Then it was offered to those with risky comorbidities and those in professions with elevated infection risk, and finally it was offered to the general population. Each group saw large benefits from vaccination, but the marginal improvement in health as new groups were added along the extensive margin was smaller with each addition.

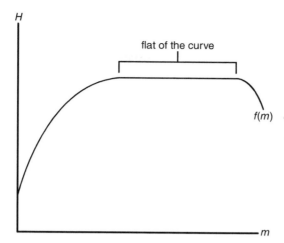

Figure 2.2 The flat of the curve

The Flat of the Curve

There is a point with medical care where additional care will do little to nothing to improve health. This is the portion of the health production function highlighted in Figure 2.2.

What has happened is that the value of the marginal unit of medical care has diminished to the point where the improvement in health is negligible. One way to think about the flat of the curve is to think about medical treatment when there is no problem to be treated. Drilling a tooth and putting in a filling improves health when the tooth has a cavity, but a drill and fill procedure makes no improvement in health if there is no cavity.

The flat of the curve does not just apply to treatment, it applies to all types of care. Consider again the example of increasing the frequency of colonoscopy to screen for colon cancer. With each additional colonoscopy in a fixed span of time the marginal benefit of a colonoscopy decreases. At some point, perhaps an annual screening, or a monthly screening, or maybe even a weekly screening, the added information from the additional screen is negligible as it is unlikely that a person's colon has changed meaningfully over the time that has elapsed since the previous screening. At this point, additional colonoscopies are on the flat of the curve.

Flat of the curve medical care is problematic as medical care is not free to produce and is not free to purchase. If the only reason that people want to purchase medical care is because of its benefits to health, then spending on the flat of the curve represents wasted resources. An individual who purchases medical care when they are on the flat will pay the costs and reap none of the benefits. This includes not only any cash out-of-pocket, but other relevant economic costs such as time spent and physical discomfort.

Illness and Injury

Medical care is by no means the only thing that impacts health. Illnesses that you develop and injuries that you sustain also profoundly and directly impact your health. As such, I can update the health production function to include a term for illness and injury.

$$H = f(m, d, \ldots)$$

In this case illness and injury will be represented by the letter d as in *diagnosis* or *disease*. Why not use the letter I to stand for illness and injury? Economists (and this book in later chapters) reserve the letter I to stand for income, and I'm not looking to start a fight. As before, the mathematical notation is saying is that medical care (m), illness and injury (d), as well as other stuff (the "...") all impact your health in some way.

Another point about the functional notation used above is that how this is written leaves open the possibility that different determinants of health can interact with each other. The type of illness or injury that an individual suffers from can impact how effective medical care is at impacting health. We have different medical technologies for treating different diseases, and these technologies change (usually, but not always, these changes are improvements) over time. For example, the effectiveness of medical care at influencing health when an individual is afflicted with a bacterial infection was very different before the discovery of antibiotics.

Lifestyle Choices

As discussed in the previous chapter, goods that individuals consume and activities that individuals engage in can influence health as well. This allows us to, once again, update the health production function:

$$H = f(m, d, X, \ldots)$$

X represents goods and activities that an individual engages in which have an impact on health. These can be referred to as *lifestyle choices*. Lifestyle choices can either positively or negatively impact health, depending on what those choices are. Use of tobacco products, such as cigarettes, is an example of a lifestyle choice that negatively impacts health, whereas use of a pair of running shoes is an example of a lifestyle choice that positively impacts health.[3]

Genetics

Another thing that impacts your health is your genetic makeup. Individuals might be born with a genetic illness such as cystic fibrosis or sickle cell anemia which will directly and powerfully impact their health. Also, family history of disease can be predictive of elevated risk of developing certain illnesses later in life such as heart disease, stroke, and certain types of cancer. We can update the health production function to include individual genetic characteristics, g:

$$H = f\left(m, d, X, g, \ldots\right)$$

It is also important to note that g has become particularly important with regards to how it interacts with other terms in the health production function. For example, there are now therapies for some cancers that are targeted to individuals based on their particular genotypes – meaning that carrying certain genes makes medical care (m) more effective at promoting health. Likewise, individual genetic characteristics such as your personal metabolism can impact how different lifestyle choices (X), such as diet impact your health.

Age

As you age, your health is affected. This manifests in several different ways. During childhood, a person grows bigger and stronger as they reach adulthood. Then as individuals reach more advanced ages, they gradually lose the vitality of their youth. Over time, individuals will both carry a smaller baseline level of health and may also be hit harder by any health shocks (such as illness and injury). As such, age can also be included in the health production function, as shown below:

$$H = f\left(m, d, X, g, age, \ldots\right)$$

---

[3] To be clear, I am referring to using a pair of running shoes to run. Sadly, simply wearing running shoes does not itself make you healthier.

Environmental Factors

There are also numerous factors that impact your health which are determined by the environment in which you live. For example, exposure to pollution is bad for one's health. We can include external factors as the letter e in the health production function:

$$H = f(m, d, X, g, age, e)$$

At this point, I have removed the "..." from the function to say that what is listed are all of the things that impact health. This may not be true, there may well be others that are not included in these categories, but these are all of the factors that will be discussed in this book. The point here is that the equation written above is meant to be a tool for organizing your thinking about where health comes from and not dogma. Mathematical models can and should be adjusted to represent new information as appropriate.

Interestingly, many environmental factors that impact your health such as pollution are determined, at least in part, by the decisions of other people. This is what economists refer to as an *externality* or a *spillover*: where the decisions of a party impact the outcomes of another party who is not part of the decision-making process. This is a major topic in economics, important to both individual health and the healthcare sector, and is the focus of Chapter 16.

Interactions within the Health Production Function

As mentioned before, the health production function not only includes factors that may impact health, but also leaves open the possibility that these factors may influence each other's impact on health. Figure 2.3 shows a slightly more concrete (but still somewhat abstract) example of medical treatment for different illnesses or injuries.

Figure 2.3 shows how medical care impacts health for three different illnesses or injuries: d_1, d_2, and d_3. It also introduces two new concepts: H_0, which is the minimum amount of health that you need to stay alive, and H_1 the healthiest that you can possibly be at a given time. If you drop below H_0, then you are dead. The most important takeaway is that the effectiveness of medical care is highly dependent on the type of illness or injury being treated.

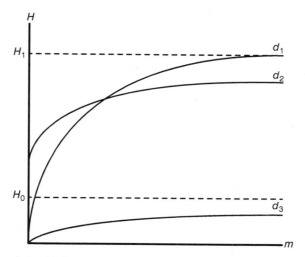

Figure 2.3 The relationship between medical care and health influenced by illness or injury

Each illness or injury shown has a different responsiveness to medical care. Consider d_1, this is an illness that if left untreated (no medical care is used) the individual will die, but with only a small amount of medical care the individual is restored to a high level of health. An illness represented by d_1 might be a serious bacterial infection which can be life threatening if left untreated but is easily curable with antibiotics.

On the other hand d_2 is an illness or injury that medical care can do a little to help with, but even with appropriate care the individual will never completely recover to H_1. This is something like the loss of a limb or a stroke, medical care can help with recovery with tools such as prosthetics or physical therapy, but it is possible that the individual will never fully recover.

Finally, d_3 represents a serious illness or injury that is beyond the ability of current medical care to treat other than possibly providing comfort and is fatal. Examples of this include incurable terminal diseases such as late-stage Alzheimer's disease or injuries such as getting sucked into a jet engine. It is important to note that the relationship between m, H, and d is based on current medical technology, and as medical technology changes over time, treatments may improve and diseases or injuries considered terminal may no longer be so.[4]

---

[4] It is possible that in the future, diseases such as Alzheimer's disease may become curable due to technological advancement. I am less optimistic about being sucked into a jet engine.

Connecting Back to Individual Decision-Making

The mathematical notation introduced in this chapter also allows us to easily observe different components of decision-making process from Chapter 1. Recall that economists generally believe that individuals pick choices that they believe will give them the most *utility*, and that utility depends on both health (*H*) and goods and activities (*X*). This allows me to write:

$$U = u(H, X)$$

This is mathematical notation claiming that utility (*U*), is some function (*u*) of both health (*H*) and goods and activities (*X*). People like their health, and they like most goods and activities, so I'll put little plus signs over them to remind me that the relationship between these inputs and utility is "more is better:"

$$U = u\left(\overset{+}{H}, \overset{+}{X}\right)$$

Now I have the tools to think through the question "would you like some free cake?" I like cake, and cake is a good I can eat, so *X* increases (in this case I get some cake) and so does my utility.

However, at the same time, I am adding an unhealthy good to my health production function: I am increasing the amount of an unhealthy *X*.[5] So, I'll put a little minus sign above the *X* in the health production function to remind me that cake is unhealthy and harms my health:

$$H = f\left(m, d, \overset{-}{X}, g, age, e\right)$$

To connect this back to decision-making and the utility function, eating cake increases *X*, which I like, and decreases *H*, which I don't like. I get *direct* utility gains from enjoying eating the cake, and *indirect* utility losses from the cake harming my health. In the end, my choice will depend on the relative size of the direct and indirect effects of the cake. If the direct utility gain from eating the cake is larger than the indirect utility loss from the cake harming my health then I eat it, and if the direct utility gain from eating the cake is smaller than the indirect utility loss from the cake harming my health then I do not.

---

[5] For simplicity's sake I am using a single *X* for all types of goods and services in the equation and keeping track of whether I am dealing with something that is good or bad for your health. It is also correct (and common) to split *X* into groupings such as X_B for things that are bad for your health and X_G for things that are good for your health. It's just a matter of which notation works better for your mental accounting.

In this case, the mathematical notation serves as a shorthand that allows us to cleanly see how a lifestyle choice and health are connected, and how that in turn impacts individual decision-making.

End of Chapter Notes

Much of the material in this chapter is a simplification (and in some sections of the chapter an extension) of parts of the Grossman Model of Health Demand (Grossman 1972) which has been a workhorse model for economists thinking about individual decisions with regards to health and medical care consumption over the lifecycle. The Grossman model is at its core a dynamic model, meaning that it considers how things change over time, and as such the full model requires more advanced mathematics to properly solve. What is presented in this chapter is meant to be an introduction to some of the insights of the model. Deeper discussions of the Grossman model can be found in more advanced texts or the original article itself.

One of the largest simplifications that I have made is worth pointing out explicitly. The Grossman model treats health as an investment that delivers healthy days to you over time. In this chapter, I treat health more as a durable good that you enjoy directly. While much of the intuition is similar (and simpler) in the framework used in this chapter, the more complicated investment framework is much more appropriate if you want to do work that thinks about how health is valued (and invested in) over time.

Self-Assessment

1. If health could be purchased directly (i.e. you could walk into the health store and say "one health, please") would you expect a unit of health to cost more or less than an amount of medical care that gives you the exact same amount of health? Why?
2. You can treat being unable to see (or being unable to see well) due to darkness by using a light. The brightness or intensity of the light can be adjusted – this is an adjustment along the intensive margin. Explain diminishing returns to your ability to see along the intensive margin in this context. Explain iatrogenic illness in this context.
3. A mosquito net is a net that goes over a sleeping area to prevent mosquitos from biting you while you are asleep and transmitting illnesses,

such as malaria. If you were giving mosquito nets to an area that would benefit from them but had a limited supply of nets, how would you decide who got them first? Second? Explain how this creates diminishing returns to mosquito nets along the extensive margin.

4. Recall from Chapter 1 that beliefs and perception of benefits can strongly influence decision-making. Give an example of a situation where someone would consume medical care on the flat of the curve due to incorrect beliefs about the benefits of the care.

5. The health production function allows for multiple inputs to interact with each other. Give an example of a situation where the age of an individual will influence how another input in the health production function (other than age) influences health.

6. Using both a utility function and a health production function, explain the tradeoffs a person considers when deciding whether or not to exercise. Will this tradeoff be same for everybody?

Supplement. Apples to Apples Comparisons of Health

The conceptual models presented to this point in the book treat health as something that can easily be represented by a single unit, when in reality this is unlikely. There are numerous different metrics that can be used to measure health, from relatively easy to observe metrics such as "is this person dead?" or "can this person walk?" to biometric measures such as blood pressure or resting heart rate. It may thus be easy for a person to spot an improvement in health such as "this person has less difficulty breathing now" or "this person can see when previously they could not" but difficult to tell which gains or losses in health are "bigger" or "smaller" than others. In other words, it is difficult to make "apples to apples" comparisons between changes in health along different dimensions.

This becomes important when considering alternative courses of treatment, or different investment or spending patterns due to the presence of *opportunity cost*. Using one form of treatment often means foregoing another, and spending funds on one social program may mean that those funds are not available for other programs.

Obviously, when possible, we should simply use the same measured units for making comparisons. For example, if I am going to decide between two blood pressure medications with the same side effects and the same cost, I would want to see which medication generates the largest reduction in blood pressure (to a point). But what if the drugs have different sets of side effects? Now the comparison is no longer along a single dimension of health.

Or, what if I have a single $10 million grant to allocate and the options are a program that can provide X cochlear implants (a device that allows people with certain forms of deafness to hear) to a needy population or a program that can provide Y custom fitted leg prosthetics (allowing people with missing limbs to walk more comfortably) to a different needy population? This is not as simple as comparing X to Y as the benefits of each intervention are potentially quite different in terms of health improvements.

The answer is to use a common unit. For the purposes of health comparisons these units are called Quality Adjusted Life Years (QALYs) or Disability Adjusted Life Years (DALYs). These are units that put all health situations on a common scale to allow for apples to apples comparisons. QALYs scale a year in perfect health to 1 and death to 0 and give a year under any health situation a value between 0 and 1. So in the problem above, it is simply necessary to look up the QALY gain from a cochlear implant (we can call this A)

and the QALY gain from a better prosthetic (we can call this B).[6] Then the decision above comes down to comparing X times A to Y times B.

DALYs function similarly to QALYs but scale in the opposite direction (i.e. 0 is perfect health and 1 is death). The method for calculating these common units is beyond the scope of this book, but resources such as Hyder et al. (2012) help explain the general methods used to calculate these units and some of the more technical differences between them. QALY and DALY adjustments for different illnesses are estimated a published by many different parties. An example of a large, publicly available, and easy to access set of estimates are the Disability Weights (i.e. numbers used to convert to DALYs) published by the Institute for Health Metrics and Evaluation based on the Global Burden of Disease Study. These can be accessed for free here: http://ghdx.healthdata.org/record/ihme-data/gbd-2019-disability-weights

---

[6] The comparison would not just use gains for a single year, but would count up the health gains over the remaining life expectancy of the treated individuals.

3 | Demand for Medical Care

One of the primary tools used by economists to understand how humans behave is the *demand curve*. A demand curve is a representation of how individual or group preferences play out when it comes to actually purchasing goods or services. It represents the relationship between the *price* of a good or service and the *quantity* that a person wants to buy. Figure 3.1 is shows a demand curve for medical care (m).

To walk through the picture, the price per unit of medical care (P_m) is shown on the vertical axis, and the amount of medical care purchased (m) is shown on the horizontal axis. The demand curve represents a list of the *quantity demanded* or amount a person would be able and willing to purchase at any given price. So, when the price of medical care is high, for example P_{m1}, the quantity demanded (or the amount that a person would want to purchase) is smaller, in this case m_1. Similarly, when the price of medical care is low, for example P_{m2}, the quantity demanded (or the amount that a person would want to purchase) is larger, in this case m_2.

The demand curve in Figure 3.1 (and most demand curves) has a downward slope. This means that there is a negative relationship between price and the quantity demanded: when an item has a higher price, people buy less of it, and when an item has a lower price, people buy more of it. The idea that "the lower the price, the more people will buy" is referred to as the *Law of Demand*. Another way to think about the Law of Demand is if the price of something is raised (and nothing else is changed), people aren't going to say, "oh yeah, give me more of that stuff!"[1]

You can also think about demand as representing *willingness to pay*. Any given point on a demand curve answers the question "how much are you willing to pay for a given quantity of a good?" How much are you willing to pay for m_2 units of medical care? In Figure 3.1, the person is willing to pay P_{m2}.

---

[1] Goods that violate the Law of Demand and have upward sloping demand curves are called "Giffen goods." Giffen goods either do not often or never appear in the wild, depending on which economist you ask. Many economists find it fun to fight about whether or not they exist. Giffen goods are a lot like the sasquatch of economics.

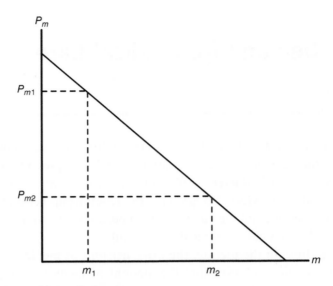

Figure 3.1 Demand for medical care

Why Not Study Demand for Health?

Individuals are certainly willing to pay for health. The problem with using demand curves to study health is not that there is no demand for health, but that there is no market in which you can exchange money for health directly. Instead, individuals can spend resources such as money (but also time and effort), on goods and activities that enter into the health production function discussed in the previous chapter. As a consequence, the markets where people actually spend their resources to impact their health have become primary areas of study for health economists (e.g. the market for medical care, the market for illicit drugs, the market for not living next to a toxic waste dump, etc.).

Elasticity

Price Sensitivity
In Figure 3.2, we can see two different demand curves for medical care. One is far flatter, and one is far steeper. The steepness, or slope of the demand curve represents how sensitive to prices people are for that particular good or service. The demand curve for medical care A is fairly flat, so when the price of care changes, the amount of care purchased changes a fair amount. The demand curve for medical care B is much

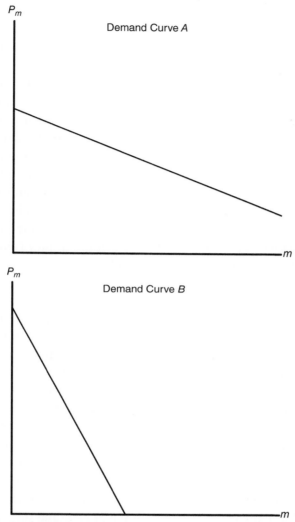

Figure 3.2 Demand curves with different slopes

steeper, so when the price of care changes, the amount of care purchased does not change nearly as much. This is most easily seen by
looking at the same change in price for both demand curves: if the price
decreases by the same amount on both curves the corresponding change
in the amount of medical care purchased will be larger for curve *A* than
for curve *B*.

There are many factors which can impact people's price sensitivity for
purchasing goods and services. When it comes to medical care, one of the
biggest determinants is the urgency or importance of the care desired. If
you are shopping for over-the-counter pain medication (such as ibuprofen)

to stock a home medicine cabinet and are not currently in pain, then you may pay more attention to price when deciding how much to buy. If there is a sale (such as a two-for-one coupon) you will likely purchase more of the pain medication. In this case, you would be rather price sensitive.

However, if you are sick with major sinus congestion and want relief, then you are going to pay less attention to the price for nasal decongestant than you would have for the over-the-counter pain medication. Price may still matter for the amount you purchase, just less so than in the case of the over-the-counter pain medication. In this case, you would be less price sensitive.

You could even imagine a case where price matters very little (if at all), for example in the case of a life-saving drug such as insulin for a diabetic. In this case, an individual will want to purchase the insulin at any price that they can afford. They might even go to extreme measures (such as taking on debt with bad terms) to purchase the insulin if they could not afford it, because without it, they could literally die.

What Is Elasticity?

How price responsive people are is important for businesses such as health insurers or hospitals as well as for policymakers. If the price of a good is going to be changed either by a business or via regulation, then it is incredibly useful to have some idea as to how much sales of that good will change. However, the slope of a given demand curve is not necessarily useful when trying to compare demand for different goods (or different types of medical care) to each other. This is because prices and quantities may not be on comparable scales. A $100 drop in price of a doctor's office visit being associated with one more visit a year is not the same thing as a $100 drop in the price of a surgery being associated with one more surgery a year. The change of $100 may be the majority of the price of the office visit, but only a small fraction of the price of the surgery. Likewise, a change of one encounter (an office visit or a surgery) may make up a different fraction of the yearly total depending on the encounter type.

To get around this, economists use *elasticity* to measure responsiveness of one thing to another. Elasticity is a measure of slope expressed in terms of percentage changes. So instead of "a $100 decrease" or "a 10 visit increase," elasticities express changes in terms of "a 5 percent decrease in price" or "a 2 percent increase in quantity." An elasticity is a ratio of the two different percent changes. The formula for elasticity is:

$$\text{Elasticity}_{a,b} = \frac{\%\Delta A}{\%\Delta B}$$

which simply states that the elasticity is the percentage change in A divided by the percentage change in B. Elasticities can be positive or negative numbers. A positive number means that the two things move together (both increase together or both decrease together), and a negative number means that the two things move in opposite directions (when one increases, the other decreases and vice versa).

Elasticities are just shorthand notation for the relationship between the two things. So, an elasticity of 0.1 is shorthand for "when A increases by 1 percent, B increases by 10 percent." Likewise, an elasticity of −2 is shorthand for "when A increases by 1 percent, B decreases by 0.5 percent."[2] If I flex my muscles 10 percent more during the day and rip through 5 percent more of my T-shirts, then there is a muscle-flexing to T-shirt ripping elasticity of 2 as:

$$\text{Elasticity}_{\text{flexing,ripping}} = \frac{\%\Delta\text{flexing}}{\%\Delta\text{ripping}} = \frac{10}{5} = 2$$

Price Elasticity of Demand

In the case of a demand curve, the most commonly used elasticity is the *price elasticity of demand*, or

$$\text{Elasticity}_{q,p} = \frac{\%\Delta\text{quantity demanded}}{\%\Delta\text{price}}$$

which is the percentage change in quantity divided by the percentage change in price. The price elasticity of demand brings back the idea of the slope, or price responsiveness of the demand curve, but instead expresses it in terms of percentage changes.

So, a price elasticity of demand of −1 means that any percentage change in the price will see the same (but opposite direction) percentage change in quantity demanded. A 10 percent increase in the price of medical care with a −1 price elasticity of demand would see a 10 percent decrease in quantity of care demanded. Numbers with a larger absolute value (bigger numbers if you ignore the negative sign) mean that the good is more price responsive. A price elasticity of demand of −2 would mean that only a 5 percent increase in the price would be needed to get the same 10 percent decrease in the quantity demanded. If eyeglasses that cost $150 have a 10 percent price reduction to $135 and see a 5 percent increase in sales then those eyeglasses would have a price elasticity of demand of −0.5 as

$$\text{Elasticity}_{q,p} = \frac{\%\Delta\text{quantity demanded}}{\%\Delta\text{price}} = \frac{5}{-10} = -0.5$$

---

[2] Notice that the exact numbers used can vary but still give the same elasticity. An elasticity of 0.1 represents "when A increases by 1 percent, B increases by 10 percent" but also represents "when A increases by 2 percent, B increases by 20 percent." For elasticities, only the ratio matters.

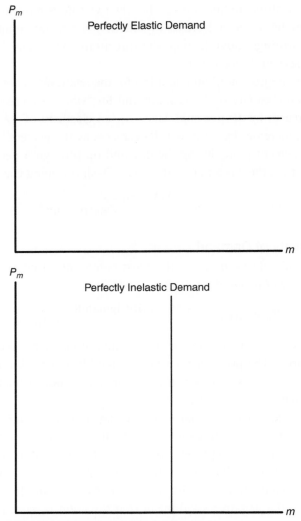

Figure 3.3 Perfectly elastic and perfectly inelastic demand

Price elasticities of demand are not positive numbers, as that would violate the Law of Demand. Demand that is more price responsive is referred to as *more elastic* demand, and demand that is less price responsive is referred to as *less elastic* demand or *more inelastic demand.*[3] There are two special cases, shown in Figure 3.3. First is demand that is *perfectly elastic* (i.e. is completely horizontal), and second is demand that is *perfectly inelastic*

---

[3] My father, who also taught economics, used to help his students remember that elastic means "more horizontal" by saying that when you want to shoot an elastic band (a rubber band) off of your finger at someone, you would stretch it horizontally. So, if you want to shoot my father with a rubber band, I suggest you attack from above, he won't expect it.

(i.e. is completely vertical). These are the extremes for what most economists consider to be reasonable demand curves.

Perfectly elastic demand is a situation where there is a price that an individual will pay, and will purchase any amount at that price and only at that price. The key idea is that if the price goes up by a single cent then they will not buy it – this is extreme price sensitivity. Perfectly inelastic demand is a situation where a person will purchase a fixed amount of a good and will pay any price for it. The key idea is that price is no object here, the person wants that much and will pay any price to get it – this is extreme price insensitivity.

Are these special cases realistic? No. But are they close enough to realistic to be informative? Yes. Perfectly elastic demand is very close to a situation where there are many identical products from different brands on the shelf (e.g. BAND-AIDS® and similar bandages). If one of them is pricier, then I am going to buy zero of that type. Perfectly inelastic demand is very close to a situation where there is a single life-saving drug that you need to survive, and will pay almost any price to get it.

Demand Shifters

Demand curves are also helpful for thinking about how changes in underlying conditions might impact a person's willingness to pay. There are a great many factors that can change how much you are willing to pay for a hamburger other than its price: how hungry are you? How much is it for ketchup? How much is it to purchase something else that you would like to eat more than a hamburger? All of these underlying conditions (a) can change from moment to moment, (b) are not the price of the hamburger, (c) are not anything about the hamburger itself, and (d) influence how much you want the hamburger. Anything that changes how much you want something without changing anything about that good or service itself (including the price) is called a *demand shifter*. This is because changes in these conditions shift the entire demand curve outward or inward.

Changes that make you want the good or service more shift the demand curve outward, something called an *increase in demand*. Changes that make you want the good or service less shift the demand curve inward, something called a *decrease in demand*. These are shown in Figure 3.4.

Shifters for Demand for Medical Care
In order to shift demand for medical care, something would need to change that would make you want medical care more or less. As the only reason

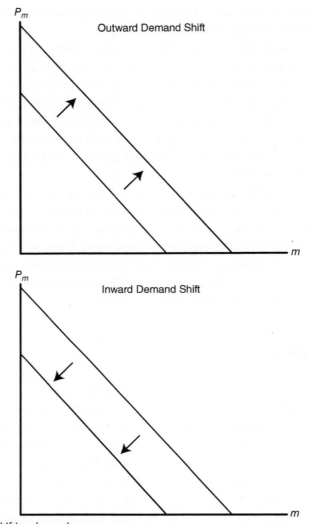

Figure 3.4 Shifting demand curves

that people want medical care is because they desire health, all of the shifters for the demand for medical care (with one notable exception that we will return to in a moment) are found in the health production function.

$$H = f(m, d, X, g, age, e)$$

We can run down the list, and ask: if this health production factor changes, will it also change how much I want medical care (*m*)?

Consider illness or injury (*d*). When you are healthy you have a certain amount that you are willing to pay for cough medication such as guaifenesin, commonly sold as Mucinex®, which helps break up mucus and relieve chest congestion. What happens to your willingness to pay for cough medication when you have a chest cold? Your demand shifts outward. Then, once your cold is resolved and you no longer need relief for chest cold symptoms, your demand shifts inward again.

Similar stories exist for the other variables in the health production function. Age, for example: as you age, you become more susceptible to illness and injury, making your demand for medical care shift outward – either in response to those illnesses and injuries or as a preventative measure given their increased likelihood.

Complements and Substitutes

There are special types of demand shifters referred to as *complements* and *substitutes*. Complements, sometimes referred to as *complementary goods*, are goods or services that are consumed or used together. A complement may have natural synergy, or cause increased desire for the good that it is complementary to. An example of complements is hot dogs and hot dog buns. Substitutes or *substitute goods* on the other hand are goods that can replace one another. If a good or service can be used instead of another good or service, then those goods are substitutes. An example of substitutes is eyeglasses and contact lenses.

Demand can be shifted by a change in the price of a complement or the price of a substitute. If hot dog buns get more expensive, then by the Law of Demand, I will buy fewer hot dog buns, and, as I typically use hot dog buns and hot dogs together, I will also buy fewer hot dogs. In this case, an increase in the price of a complement will shift a demand curve inwards. If the price of the complement instead decreases, that would shift the demand curve outwards. Likewise, if contact lenses get more expensive, then I will buy fewer contact lenses, but, as I still want to see well, I will instead spend more on eyeglasses, a substitute. When the price of the substitute increases, demand shifts outwards. If the price of the substitute instead decreases, demand shifts inwards. There are many complements and substitutes within the larger umbrella of medical care. The aforementioned eyeglasses and contact lenses are medical care substitutes. Surgery and anesthesia are medical care complements.

There are also things that are not medical care, which may exhibit complementarity or substitutability with medical care. The most common of these are lifestyle choices. Goods or behavior that are bad for your health can be seen as complements to medical care. For example, if the price of cigarettes increases, individuals may smoke fewer cigarettes (or be less likely to take up smoking in general) and be healthier – thus needing less medical care. On the other hand, other types of lifestyle choices may substitute for medical care. Condoms reduce the likelihood of needing medical care for a sexually transmitted infection and also reduce the likelihood of needing pre-natal care and, as such, are a substitute for these types of medical care.

Cross-Price Elasticity

The complement or substitute relationship between different goods and services can be of varying strength. Some goods are *perfect complements* meaning that they are always used in exactly the same combination: one flu shot dose and one syringe are perfect complements. Some goods are *perfect substitutes*, meaning that they always sub in for one another in exactly the same way: a dose of a name-brand pharmaceutical and an identical dose of a generic version of the same pharmaceutical could be considered perfect substitutes.[4]

There are also weaker complements and substitutes. Tissues are a weak substitute for nasal decongestant. Tissues do not perfectly replace nasal decongestant, but are useful when decongestant is not available or not working completely. Bandages and antibacterial ointment (such as Neosporin) are weak complements. Sometimes they are used together, but not always.

We can measure the strength of complements and substitutes using a *cross-price elasticity*.[5] Cross-price elasticity is a measure of the price responsiveness of one good to changes in the price of a second good.

$$\text{Elasticity}_{qA,pB} = \frac{\%\Delta \text{quantity demanded of } A}{\%\Delta \text{price of } B}$$

A cross-price elasticity < 0 shows that goods are complements. The price of one good decreasing (increasing) is associated with the quantity of the second good increasing (decreasing). The price of one good moves in the opposite direction as the quantity of the complement. If the price of heartburn medication increases, then individuals with acid reflux may purchase less spicy food.

Similarly, a cross-price elasticity > 0 shows that goods are substitutes. The price of one good decreasing (increasing) is associated with the quantity of the second good decreasing (increasing). The price of one good moves in the same direction as the quantity of the substitute. If the price of a routine check-up office visit with a nurse practitioner decreases, then individuals might purchase fewer routine check-up visits with a medical

---

[4] A perfect complement or perfect substitute relationship need not be 1:1, for example one car is a perfect complement with four tires.

[5] The price elasticity of demand is sometimes called "own-price elasticity" to help contrast it to cross-price elasticity.

doctor (substitute care). The larger the absolute value (the size of the number ignoring whether it is positive or negative) of the cross-price elasticity, the stronger the complement or substitute relationship.

So, if the price of nasal decongestant increases by 15 percent and the amount of tissues sold increases by 3 percent then these goods would have a cross-price elasticity of 0.2, as:

$$\text{Elasticity}_{q(\text{tissues}), p(\text{decongestant})}$$
$$= \frac{\%\Delta\text{quantity of tissues}}{\%\Delta\text{price of decongestant}} = \frac{3}{15} = 0.2$$

This is a cross-price elasticity > 0, meaning that the goods are substitutes.

Income

The only shifter for the demand for medical care that does not show up in the health production function is income. Income shifts any demand curve. Increases in income generally shift the demand curve outward, and decreases in income generally shift the demand curve inward.

One reason for this is because income can be seen as a scale by which we judge how expensive a given price is. Is $100 a lot for an office visit? If I make $10 a day, then yes. If I make $2,000 a day, then much less so. Thus, when income increases, every price *feels* less expensive, even though the number hasn't changed, shifting demand outward. Likewise, when income decreases, every price *feels* more expensive, even though the number hasn't changed, shifting demand inward.

However, there are certain goods, where increases in income cause demand to shift inwards. These goods, which you consume less of as income rises, are referred to as *inferior goods*. In contrast, goods that you consume more of as income rises are referred to as *normal goods*.

A single good may be normal at some levels of income but inferior at other levels of income. For example, taking public transportation may be normal (more income, more rides on public transportation) up to the point where a person can afford a car, at which point it becomes inferior (more income, fewer rides on public transportation).

Income Elasticity

How responsive demand is to changes in income is measured with the *income elasticity of demand*.

$$\text{Elasticity}_{q,I} = \frac{\%\Delta\text{quantity demanded}}{\%\Delta\text{Income}}$$

Positive income elasticities of demand mean that income increasing is paired with an increase in consumption of the good, signifying a *normal good.* Negative income elasticities mean that income increasing is paired with decreased consumption of the good, signifying an *inferior good.* If income for someone making $50,000 a year increased by $5,000 (a 10 percent increase) and that individual changed from consuming one physician office visits to consuming two physician offices visit during a year (a 100 percent increase) then the income elasticity of demand for physician office visits would be 10 as

$$\text{Elasticity}_{\text{office visits}, I} = \%\Delta\text{office visits} \Big/ \%\Delta\text{Income} = 100 \Big/ 10 = 10$$

This is an income elasticity of demand > 0, meaning that office visits are a normal good.

So, is medical care in general a normal good or an inferior good? The answer depends on the level of income for the individual, as well as that individual's lifestyle choices.

Engel Curves

One way to understand how income is related to willingness to pay for a good is to plot an *income–consumption curve* or an *Engel curve.* Engel curves slope upwards (increasing consumption with increasing income) when a good is normal, and slope downwards (decreasing consumption with increasing income) when a good is inferior. Figure 3.5 is an Engel curve for medical care.

At lower levels of income, when income increases so do expenditures on medical care, meaning that medical care is a normal good. However, at higher levels of income there is some uncertainty as to what an individual's Engel curve will look like. This is because as income rises to higher levels, individuals start to have variation on how they spend their money. Let's consider two extreme cases, both of which are potential answers to the question: "if you suddenly had thousands of additional dollars of disposable income each week, how would you spend it?"

One possibility is that you quit your job, and move into a spa. You spend your days eating organic food lovingly prepared by your dietician and doing yoga. In this case you have dramatically changed your lifestyle in a way that will make you less likely to have certain types of negative health shocks. This lifestyle change is enabled by income growth, and is a substitute for certain types of medical care, making medical care an inferior good. This extreme case is represented by the lower dashed line in Figure 3.5.

A second possibility is that you quit your job and move into an apartment above a pub. You spend you days in the pub drinking beer and eating fried

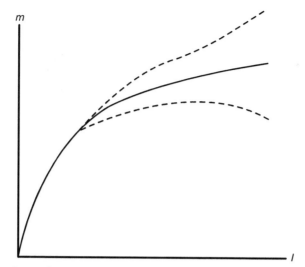

Figure 3.5 Engel curve for medical care

food. At night, you go back to your apartment and use many expensive illicit drugs. In this case you have also dramatically changed your lifestyle, but in a way that will make you more likely to have certain types of negative health shocks. This lifestyle change is again enabled by income growth, but is instead a complement for certain types of medical care, maintaining medical care's position as a normal good, and potentially increasing use of care faster than income is growing.[6] This extreme case is represented by the upper dashed line in Figure 3.5.

These are, of course, extreme cases, but they do help to illustrate that there can be quite a bit of variability in how consumption of medical care responds from person to person as income increases and allows for discretionary adjustments in lifestyle choices.

Consumer Surplus

Demand curves are not just helpful for understanding how individuals will act and react to changing circumstances. They can also be used to understand how much an individual will value a given transaction. This is difficult to do with tools like utility, which is measured in abstract

---

[6] When a good's consumption grows faster than income (in percentage change terms), then that good is termed a *luxury good*, which is shorthand for having an income elasticity of demand > 1.

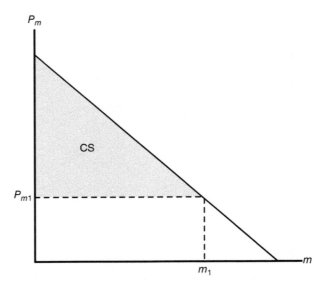

Figure 3.6 Consumer surplus

units. However, once we have demand, we can express how much value an individual gets from a transaction in dollars (or whatever the local currency is).

The amount you were willing to pay for something, minus the amount that you actually pay is known as *consumer surplus*. So, if I was willing to pay $500 to have a painful tooth extracted, and my dentist charges me $100 for the service, then I have gotten $500 – $100 = $400 of consumer surplus from the transaction. If the dentist instead charges me $50 for the tooth extraction? Even better! I have now gotten $450 of consumer surplus.

Consumer surplus can be measured from a demand curve as shown in Figure 3.6. It is the area below the demand curve (the willingness to pay) but above the price of the good (the amount actually paid). So, in Figure 3.6, the price paid is P_{m1}, the amount purchased is m_1, and the consumer surplus is the shaded triangle labeled "CS." Consumer surplus can be negative, this is a case where a person somehow pays more than they are willing to pay for a good or service. Negative surplus is referred to as *welfare loss* or *deadweight loss*.

What is helpful about consumer surplus is that it allows for comparisons across people as to who got a better deal. Saying that one person got more utility than another is meaningless, as utility is only used to rank possible outcomes for a single individual. Cross-person utility comparisons do not mean anything. But saying that one person got $50 in value while another got $100 in value actually means something (and is much easier to understand).

Consumer surplus can also be used to help understand individual decision-making. When presented with a choice between two transactions, rational individuals will choose the one that gives more consumer surplus.

Individual vs. Market Demand

One final point to make is that the demand for an entire market is simply the sum of the demand for all of the individuals in that market at each price. For example if a market has 2,500 people, all of whom would purchase two boxes of tissues at a price of $2 a box, then at a price of $2 a box, the quantity demanded for the entire market is $(2{,}500 \times 2) = 5{,}000$ boxes of tissues. This is sometimes referred to as adding demand *horizontally*, as it only adds the quantities together, which are typically placed on the horizontal axis, but not the prices, which are usually shown on the vertical axis.

Self-Assessment

1. An elasticity is shorthand for a sentence. These sentences take the form "A X percent increase (or decrease) in A is associated with a Y percent increase (or decrease) in B." What does that sentence look like for a price elasticity of demand of -2? Can you write more than one sentence for the same elasticity?
2. Why would a producer of medical care be interested in knowing the price elasticity of demand for medical care? How could it help them in making business decisions?
3. Why would a policymaker interested in health policy be interested in knowing the price elasticity of demand for medical care? How could it help them in making policy decisions?
4. If you were an investigative reporter trying to expose price gouging in health care, would you start your investigation looking at care that has price elasticity of demand that is very elastic or very inelastic? Why?
5. Do you think that the cross-price elasticity of demand between anesthesia drugs (drugs used to numb people or knock them unconscious, used commonly during surgery) and surgeries is positive, negative, or zero? If you are a producer of anesthesia drugs, why would the price of surgeries be important to you?
6. Consider the statement "If you give people more money they will just spend it on junk food and illicit drugs." What is correct about this statement? What is incorrect? Write a more accurate statement.

Supplement. Practical Economist Skills:
How to Calculate Elasticities

Because of their convenience for making comparisons, economists spend a lot of time calculating elasticities. There are two main ways to go about doing this, each yields its own type of elasticity, where the names denote the method used. The first is to calculate using a single point, and a measure of the slope at that point. As such, this is called a *point elasticity*. To see how to get to a point elasticity, I have broken the price elasticity of demand into its components:

$$\text{Elasticity}_{q,p} = \frac{\%\Delta \text{quantity demanded}}{\%\Delta \text{price}} = \frac{\Delta q / q}{\Delta p / p} = \frac{\Delta q}{\Delta p} \times \frac{p}{q}$$

$\frac{\Delta q}{\Delta p}$ is the slope of the demand curve at a given point (for the usual axes this is actually inverse slope). This is usually estimated by econometric analysis of data on transactions. The ratio $\frac{p}{q}$ reflects the two coordinates for the given point (i.e. the price and the quantity). Given the slope and a single point, you simply plug the values into the above formula and, voila!, you have the point elasticity.

But sometimes a slope or an estimate of the slope can be difficult to come by. In that case there is a second method, called an *arc elasticity*, which requires two points to calculate. The benefit of the arc elasticity is that you need simpler inputs to get to it, which comes with the tradeoff that the elasticity only covers the area between those two points, and that it is a rough approximation. To calculate an arc elasticity, you use the slope of the line connecting the two points as the slope, and the average of the two points (or midpoint of the line connecting the two points) as the point in the point elasticity formula.

4 Health Insurance and Demand for Medical Care

Now that we have an understanding of demand curves, we can use them as a tool to predict how individuals will act when they have health insurance. Health insurance is central to the functioning of the US healthcare system, and changes the price that individuals experience when they go to purchase medical care.

When thinking through how health insurance influences decision-making it is important to distinguish features of the health insurance plan such as cost sharing from the price of the plan, also known as the *premium*. Premiums are very important to the decision whether or not to purchase health insurance in the first place, and determine many features of the market for health insurance (which will be the focus of Chapters 10 and 11). However, once health insurance has been purchased, the premium becomes a sunk cost (as discussed in Chapter 1) and does not factor into decisions as to how much medical care to consume.

On the other hand, features of the health insurance plan, which are the main focus of this chapter, directly impact the amount of cash an individual will have to pay out-of-pocket for the purchase of medical care. In some cases, insurance plans may also introduce other types of costs to obtaining care, such as time costs. Both out-of-pocket payments and time costs are economic costs and will impact decision-making.

Cost Sharing

One of the most important features of a health insurance plan is its cost sharing rules. Cost sharing refers to how the cost of paying for medical care is divided between the health insurer and the insured. Not only is the generosity of cost sharing important to a person's decision-making as to how much care to purchase, but how the cost sharing is divided (i.e. flat amounts or percentages) matters a great deal as well. Cost sharing comes in three flavors: copays, indemnity, and coinsurance.

Copays
Copays are a form of cost sharing where the person with insurance pays a fixed amount out-of-pocket for a given amount of medical care, and

Figure 4.1 An insurance card

the insurer pays the remainder of the cost. Copays are very common, and are easy for patients to understand (at least relative to other features of insurance plans). To help illustrate, Figure 4.1 is an (only slightly changed) picture of my health insurance card.

For office visits (which my card abbreviates as "OV"), I have a $30 copay if the office visit is with my primary care provider (i.e. my usual family practice doctor), and a $40 copay if the office visit is with a specialist. I have a $30 copay for a visit to an urgent care, and a $250 copay for a visit to an emergency room. I also have a $250 copay for outpatient surgery.

My insurance card illustrates a few things about copays. The first and most important is that as far as the patient is concerned, the copay is the price. A few years ago, I had outpatient surgery on a toe on my right foot. One toe was gradually bending under another and causing discomfort while walking and running. The orthopedic surgeon cut open my toe, did some work inside, and now I have a carbon fiber rod inside of that toe that keeps it straight.[1] To this day, I have no idea how much was paid in total for that surgery. The surgery included a surgeon, an anesthesiologist, and several support staff each of whom I'm fairly sure was well compensated for their time, but, as far as I am concerned the entire surgery cost me a whopping $250 in out-of-pocket costs. The surgery could have had a total price tag of $500 or a total price tag of $15,000, but from my point of view the price tag would still have been $250.

In terms of understanding how a copay will influence the behavior of consumers (i.e. patients), copays simply fix the price of care at a set level. All you need to do is look at a demand curve, find the copay price, and read off the quantity of care that the individual will purchase. This is shown in Figure 4.2, the copay acts exactly how a price would when interacting with a demand curve.

---

[1] I would go into greater detail as to the specifics of the surgery but, while the surgeon was explaining, I was spending most of my energy trying not to faint.

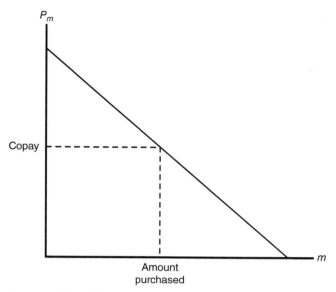

Figure 4.2 Copays and demand

If the copay is lower than the price that a person would pay if they purchased the care directly from the provider (i.e. without insurance), then by the Law of Demand, that person will usually purchase more of that care than if they had no insurance.[2]

One last point to consider about copays is that under this cost sharing arrangement, prices are not set by the interaction of buyers and sellers as is done in a typical market. From the perspective of the buyer, the price of medical care is dictated by an intermediary (the insurance company).[3] It is a situation less akin to a traditional free market and more akin to prices set by a central planner.

Although a copay is usually lower than the true cost (otherwise it's not really "cost sharing," it's "cost is your problem and I'll just stand over here"), there is nothing that says an insurance company can't set prices strategically to serve their own best interests. For example, if in many cases that end up in the emergency room, the patient could have been treated in a more cost-effective manner in an urgent care setting. To try to avoid these cases, an insurance company could choose to drastically raise copays for

---

[2] If demand was perfectly inelastic then that person would purchase the same amount of care, but pay a lower price. That is why I wrote "usually" in the sentence above. If I had implied that in all cases lower prices mean that people buy more, then economic theorists would give me dirty looks at the grocery store.

[3] The price as felt by the seller is also influenced heavily by the insurance company, this interaction is discussed in greater detail in Chapter 12.

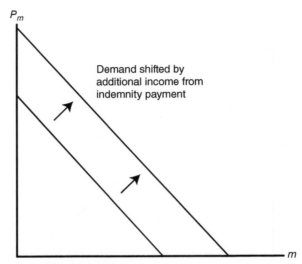

Figure 4.3 Indemnity shifting demand

the emergency room while keeping copays for urgent care low. This would create a financial incentive for patients to go to urgent care rather than the emergency room, steering patient behavior in a way that could help the insurer's bottom line. If you look back at the picture of my insurance card in Figure 4.1, this type of strategy would be consistent with my actual insurance plan characteristics.

Indemnity

Indemnity insurance is the reverse of a copay. Under a copay, the patient pays a fixed amount of the cost of care and the insurer covers the rest. Under indemnity, the insurer pays a fixed amount and the patient pays the rest.

In terms of how this impacts an individual's choices with regards to purchasing medical care, indemnity insurance works as an increase in income. When a person goes to purchase medical care the indemnity insurance kicks in and drops a pile of money in their lap. This additional income shifts their demand for medical care outwards as shown in Figure 4.3.

The individual then goes out into the market and purchases medical care directly with the extra income in their pocket. Unlike with copays, the price is not set by an intermediary.

One form of indemnity insurance is a *Health Savings Account* (HSA). An HSA allows individuals to put money away into a tax-preferred account.[4] Then, when an individual needs to purchase medical care, they are allowed

---

[4] This usually means that unlike traditional income, the money that goes into the HSA is not taxed or is taxed at a lower rate.

to use money from the HSA to pay for it. This is effectively extra income which becomes available when it is time to buy medical care.[5] The key to an indemnity payment is that once medical care that is covered is needed, the insurer pays a flat amount and is done with their responsibility.

Coinsurance

While copays and indemnity are arrangements where one party pays a fixed amount and the other pays the remainder, coinsurance is a situation where the cost of care is split based on a percentage. Under coinsurance the patient pays a fixed percentage and the insurer pays a fixed percentage (and both add up to 100 percent). Usually, coinsurance is represented by some number C, which represents the percentage paid by the patient, where $0 \leq C \leq 1$. So, when the true price is P_m, the price paid by the patient is $C \times P_m$. If $C = 0.2$, then the patient pays 20 percent of the cost and the insurer pays 80 percent of the cost, if $C = 0.5$, then each party pays half. If $C = 1$, then the patient pays 100 percent of the cost of care, and that person should reconsider whether or not they did a good job picking out an insurance plan.

As with copays and indemnity, you can use a demand curve to predict consumer behavior when their insurance uses coinsurance. All you need to do is find the *effective price*, which is the price that the patient actually pays as opposed to the price charged. If $C = 0.5$, then the effective price is $C \times P_m = 0.5 \times P_m$, similarly, if $C = 0.3$, then the effective price is $C \times P_m = 0.3 \times P_m$. Then you simply read off the amount that a patient will purchase given the effective price. Notice that the more generous the coinsurance (the lower the value of C), the higher the quantity that a patient will demand at any given price.

One thing that we can do is plot the amount actually purchased when coinsurance is set at C horizontally from the true price. So, using Figure 4.4 as an example, if the true price is P_m, then the effective price is $C \times P_m$, and this makes m_2 the amount actually purchased at true price P_m. If we do this for all prices, then we have plotted an *effective demand curve*. The effective demand curve is shown in Figure 4.5 and shows how much a person will actually buy at any true price when they have coinsurance that makes them only have to pay $C \times P_m$.

Effective demand helps illustrate a key point about coinsurance. When people pay only a percentage of the true price, their effective demand curve is steeper than their true demand curve. This is a change in the price

---

[5] If you want to get nitpicky, the extra income is actually the portion of the HSA that would have been taken as taxes had it been paid out as traditional income.

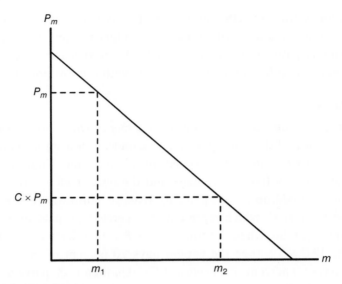

Figure 4.4 The effective price

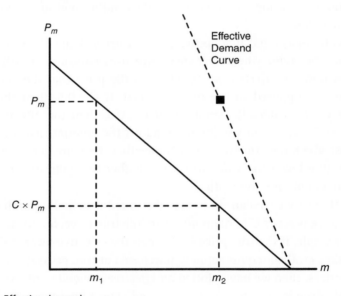

Figure 4.5 Effective demand

elasticity of demand: when given coinsurance people become less responsive to prices, and the more generous the coinsurance (the lower the value
of C), the less price responsive they become. This makes some intuitive
sense: if you have an X percent off coupon for everything in a store, then
price matters less. The better the coupon (the higher the X percent off), the
less price matters to you. In fact, if $C = 0$ then the effective demand curve

would be vertical (perfectly inelastic) as the true price would not matter at all. As far as you were concerned, everything would be free.

Spending Triggers

Aside from cost sharing, insurance plans can also have triggers that, well, trigger, when certain amounts have been spent. These triggers change the features of the insurance plan, usually the cost sharing. The two most common types are deductibles, which make cost sharing more generous once the trigger is activated, and payment limits, which make cost sharing less generous once the trigger is activated. The key concept to understand is that someone, either the patient or the insurer, spends a pre-set amount of money, and then the plan changes characteristics.

Deductibles

One of the most common types of spending triggers is a deductible. A deductible is an amount of money (D) that must be spent before insurance begins paying for things. Once the patient spends the deductible (D) in out-of-pocket costs, then we say that they have "met their deductible." So, when a person has a deductible as part of their insurance, it is as if they face two different prices for the same medical care: a higher price when the deductible has not yet been met, and a lower price once the deductible has been met. This creates a price for medical care as shown in Figure 4.6.

In this case, the higher price P_{m1} is the "true" price, and must be paid for care before the deductible is met. Then, once the deductible is met, which is when the patient has spent $D = P_{m1} \times m^*$, the price lowers to P_{m2}. P_{m2} is whatever the price is after the insurer steps in and begins coverage. P_{m2} could be a flat copay, or could be $C \times P_{m1}$ if the plan is based on coinsurance. The point is that once the deductible is met, the price paid by the patient is lowered.

We can predict how much care an individual will purchase under a deductible using demand, we simply use the two-part deductible pricing and read the quantity off of the demand curve. However, deductibles can create a situation where individuals have more than one point where the demand curve intersects the price, as shown in Figure 4.7.

In this case, there are two potential quantities that the consumer could choose: A or B. It is possible to know whether A or B is preferred by looking at the consumer surplus for each choice. If A is chosen, then the patient gets consumer surplus X, the area under the demand curve (willingness to pay) but over the price (amount actually paid). If B is chosen, then the patient gets consumer surplus $X - Y + Z$. They gain X and Z, where they

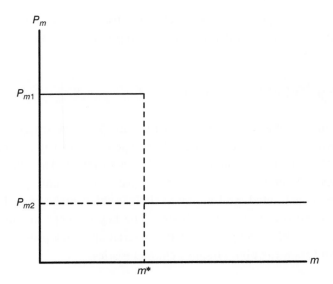

Figure 4.6 Deductible

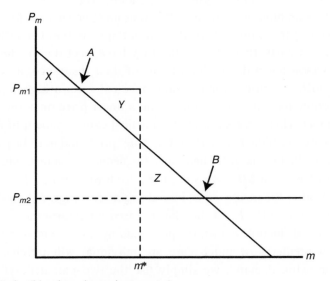

Figure 4.7 Deductible where demand crosses twice

were willing to pay more than they paid, but they lose Y, where they paid more than they were willing to (the price is above the demand curve). So, if $Y > Z$, then A is a better choice and the person consumes less care, and if $Y < Z$, then B is a better choice and the person consumes more care.[6]

---

[6] This is a lot of mathematical notation that boils down to "you pick the amount of care that gives you more value." It's all about what the better deal is based on the patient's preferences.

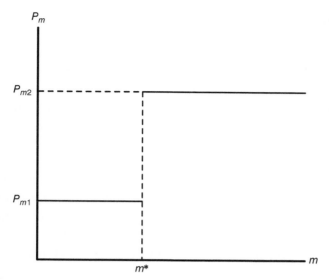

Figure 4.8 Payment limit

Payment Limits

Payment limits are the reverse of deductibles. A payment limit is a spending trigger where once the insurance company spends a set amount of money (M), the cost sharing in the insurance plan becomes less generous, possibly moving to a situation where the insurer no longer pays for things. This creates a price for medical care as shown in Figure 4.8.

In this case, once M has been spent by the insurer, which happens when the amount m^* has been purchased, the price paid by the patient increases from P_{m1} to P_{m2}. Unlike with deductibles, there is no possibility that a demand curve will intersect in more than once place, as demand is downward sloping.

Spending Triggers and Timing

Spending triggers are usually set to cover a pre-determined amount of time, after which they reset. A deductible may be an annual deductible, meaning that at the end of the year it resets and must be met anew for the new year. Likewise, spending limits might be annual, meaning that coverage that has "run out" would be refreshed when the new year begins. These pre-determined amounts of time need not be years. For example, coverage for hospital stays might have a deductible for each time a person is admitted to the hospital. In this case, the pre-determined amount of time is "one hospital admission."[7]

---

[7] This is not unique to health insurance. Auto insurance commonly has deductibles that must be met each time there is an accident, in this case the pre-determined amount of time is "one accident."

If spending triggers reset at known intervals, this can create interesting incentives for patients near the time when their policy is going to reset. Consider the case of a deductible that resets every year on January 1. If a patient needs surgery near the end of the year, but that surgery is nonurgent and can be put off, then the patient may have an incentive to delay (or hurry up) the surgery depending on the state of their deductible. If the deductible has already been met for the year, then the incentive is to do the surgery as soon as possible, because on January 1 of the new year, the price will suddenly increase as the deductible resets. However, if the deductible has not been met for the year, then the patient has an incentive to delay the surgery. Why pay down a deductible now and only be able to take advantage of the lower prices for medical care for a few weeks until the new year hits and the deductible resets? It would be much better to delay until the new year, have the surgery cover the deductible for that new year, and have lower prices for almost an entire year.

Example of Spending Triggers: Medicare Part D

A great way to observe spending triggers and how they work is to look at a health plan that is stuffed full of them: Medicare Part D. Medicare will be discussed in greater depth in Chapter 14, but for the purposes of discussing spending triggers, we will briefly discuss only Medicare Part D, Medicare's health insurance coverage for prescription drugs. Figure 4.9 shows Medicare Part D as it was in 2018. I have made one simplification to the picture: for part of the plan, Part D distinguishes between generic drugs and name-brand drugs, and has different cost sharing for each. I have drawn the picture assuming that all drugs purchased are generics.

Part D had a deductible of $405, so the price of drugs is P_m per unit until $405 has been spent out-of-pocket. After the deductible has been met, the plan changes to 25 percent coinsurance ($C = 0.25$). So, the price that a patient pays then becomes $0.25 \times P_m$, until a total of $3,750 has been spent on drugs. At this point, the plan hits a payment limit, and coverage becomes less generous. Coinsurance changes to 44 percent coinsurance ($C = 0.44$), until a total of $8,418 has been spent on drugs. This portion of the plan was colloquially known as the "donut hole" as there was relatively generous coverage on either side (which to follow the metaphor is represented by delicious donut) with less generous coverage in the middle.[8] At the end of the donut hole, the plan hits a final spending trigger, and the coinsurance changes a final time

---

[8] The donut hole is where there was a difference between name-brand and generic drugs. While the co-insurance was 44 percent for generics in the donut hole, the coinsurance for name-brand drugs was 35 percent. Although this is a little misleading, as the insurer (Medicare) only paid 15 percent for name-brands, with the manufacturer giving a 50 percent discount to make up the difference.

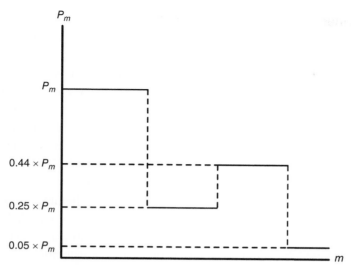

Figure 4.9 Medicare Part D pricing (2018)

to ($C = 0.05$) for any drugs purchased from that point forward. That is, until the whole plan resets back to start at the end of the year.[9]

Other Plan Characteristics

There are other plan characteristics that can influence patient consumption of medical care. Broadly, any plan characteristic that changes an economic cost has the potential to change how much and what type of care a patient consumes.

Direct Payments/Rebates

Health insurance companies can offer direct cash incentives to their policy holders, why they may want to do this will be the topic of greater discussion in Chapter 13. For example, some insurers offer direct payments to policy holders who visit their primary care provider at least once a year. An insurance company also might offer to pay for a gym membership, or for a patient to enroll in a wellness program. These are not incentives to purchase medical care, they are actually incentives to purchase goods and services which influence health, but the insurer might want push patients toward these healthy behaviors in order to save money on medical care.

---

[9] Well, not exactly, the plan has slightly different numbers for the triggers each year, and the donut hole has been "closing" over time (meaning that the plan has been becoming more generous for the patient), but you get the idea.

Red Tape

Insurance plans can also influence the amount of care that people consume by imposing costs in the form of inconvenience. This "red tape" creates a time cost to obtaining care, which is an economic cost. Additional red tape for a given type of care will steer patients away from that care, and less red tape will steer patients toward it. A great example is the red tape of having to make an appointment. Appointments are required for many types of care, but also impose a cost in the form of inconvenience: an appointment isn't always available when you want one, and the scheduling process can be frustrating and time consuming. So, for certain types of care, an insurer can arrange for (i.e. pay for) walk-in care during flexible hours. This is done, for example, with flu shots: many insurers pay for walk-in flu shot clinics. With such a clinic, the red tape of an appointment to get a flu shot is lowered, which encourages more people to get vaccinated.

Self-Assessment

1. There are two different insurance plans. Plan A has a higher premium (price to purchase the plan) and lower copays, and Plan B has a lower premium but higher copays. Would you purchase more medical care in an average year if you had Plan A or Plan B? Why?

2. If you receive an indemnity health insurance payment for $1,000 that must be spent on medical care, does that mean that your spending on medical care will increase by $1,000? Why or why not? (Hint: Think about money that you would have spent on medical care without the indemnity payment.)

3. Gaining insurance with coinsurance typically increases the amount of medical care that a person will purchase. How will the price elasticity of demand influence the size of this increase? Will there be any change if demand is perfectly inelastic prior to obtaining insurance?

4. Would you expect someone to be more likely or less likely to purchase medical care when they are very close to meeting their deductible? How does the time of the year play into your thinking on this?

5. Would you expect someone to be more likely or less likely to purchase medical care when they are very close to hitting a payment limit? How does the time of the year play into your thinking on this?

6. How does the resetting of payment triggers each year for Medicare Part D encourage patients to stockpile drugs?

5 | Evaluating Evidence

"It is a capital mistake to theorize before one has data. Insensibly one begins to twist facts to suit theories, instead of theories to suit facts."

Sherlock Holmes

So far this book has presented a lot of what is referred to as theory. Theory is a way to organize how you think about things, in this case, how you think about human behavior. But should you believe any of it? Only to the extent that the theory does a good job of explaining the world around us. Whenever a scientist (or in our case a social scientist) thinks that they have an explanation for how the world behaves (or in our case how actors in the healthcare sector behave), they need to take their theory into the real world and see how it performs.

To do this, we need to collect *evidence*. Evidence is information taken from the real world which will either support or not support the theory.[1] When evidence supports a theory, then we leave the theory be, and when evidence goes against a theory then we need to adjust the theory to fit the new evidence. The theory might be flat out wrong, or it may need to be adjusted to include exceptions for special cases such as the new information presented. When a scientist goes out to collect evidence, they do this in a systematic way, which is referred to as a *study*. As an economist, I am going to focus mainly on *quantitative evidence*, or evidence that deals with numerical measures of things, but you should be aware that there is also a wide world of *qualitative evidence*, or evidence which deals with more abstract types of knowledge such as feelings, thoughts, and firsthand descriptions.

---

[1] There can also be evidence that doesn't support a theory but also doesn't go against it. This is called irrelevant information. If I am testing a theory about health insurance and the purchase of medical care, then the fact that a horse named Mr. Buckets likes carrots is irrelevant information.

Types of Quantitative Evidence

I am going to put quantitative evidence into three broad buckets:

1. associational evidence,
2. experimental evidence, and
3. quasi-experimental evidence.

Each of these forms of evidence brings something to the table, and each has its drawbacks. The rest of this chapter will focus on how these types of evidence are collected, what you can (and cannot) infer from them, and some ways of evaluating whether or not the evidence should be considered reliable.

Associational Evidence

Associational evidence shows that two (or more) variables are in some way related. Usually this type of evidence establishes that variables move together. Here's an example: in Figure 5.1, I have plotted data from countries in the Organization for Economic Co-operation and Development (OECD) in 2015. Each dot in the picture represents data from a different country. The x-axis shows the average life expectancy at birth in that country in 2015, and the y-axis shows per capita (per person) spending on healthcare in that country in 2015. These data come from OECD Stat and the World Bank. The line is the "line of best fit" for the data, showing the best approximation of the relationship between all the points if we assume that relationship to be linear.

What can we learn from this evidence? Clearly, there is some relationship between the amount of money that a country is spending on healthcare and the life expectancy of their population. This can be considered evidence that supports one of the theories presented earlier in the book: that medical care (m) can be used to improve health (H). The data presented in the above picture are consistent with the story that spending more on medical care improves health outcomes. This is what I would call a *suggestive association*.

Why not say that this evidence demonstrates that the theory is correct? While the data presented can be taken to support the theory, it is insufficient to *prove* it. To be specific, based on the data presented, I cannot say that a country spending more on medical care *causes* increased life expectancy with certainty. While this is one reasonable explanation for the pattern observed, there are other possible explanations that I cannot rule out.

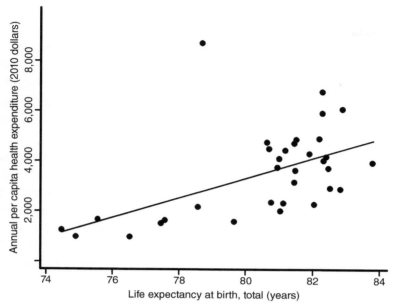

Figure 5.1 Life Expectancy and health expenditures in OECD Countries
Source: Created by author using data from OECD Stat and the World Bank,
https://ourworldindata.org/the-link-between-life-expectancy-and-health-spending-us-focus

Latent Variables

One limitation of associational evidence is that it is difficult to rule out the influence of *latent variables* (sometimes referred to as *omitted variables*) as an alternative explanation for the association observed. A latent variable is a third variable that causes both of the observed variables to move at the same time. An example of a relationship caused by a latent variable would be if I observed that when the amount of ice cream sold increases so do the number of sunburns. I could then (incorrectly) draw the conclusion that ice cream weakens the skin, making it more susceptible to sunburn – as this is a theory that fits the facts presented of ice cream sales and sunburns moving together. The latent variable here would be the weather. On hot, sunny days, people buy more ice cream. On hot, sunny days, people are also more likely to get sunburned. The latent variable of weather created a relationship between ice cream sales and sunburns that was non-causal, but that could be mistaken for causal.

For the example of OECD countries' healthcare expenditures and life expectancy shown in Figure 5.1, a potential latent variable is income. Countries with a higher-income population may spend more on healthcare, but may also spend more on other goods and services that lengthen life, such as better food distribution or water sanitation. It is possible (but also not certain) that income could be what is causing the observed relationship between healthcare spending and life expectancy.

Here is one more example of latent variables. This example has been giving healthcare researchers headaches for decades. If I was to look at the relationship between hospital spending on things like medical staff and equipment, and patient outcomes at that hospital (measures such as patient mortality), I might find that hospitals which spend more tend to have worse health outcomes for their patients (or at least worse than one might expect). The reason for this is the latent variable of how sick the patients are that go to each hospital. If you are a patient who is not very sick, then almost any hospital will probably do. However, for riskier patients, where every little extra bit of new technology or physician expertise might be the difference between life and death, it is quite valuable to search around for the most technologically advanced and well-staffed hospitals. This creates a situation where the latent variable of patient risk makes better hospitals look worse than they really are in patient outcome data.[2]

Reverse Causality

Another limitation of associations is that it can be difficult to tell which way causality runs. To return to the example in Figure 5.1, national healthcare spending and life expectancy move together. If the relationship is indeed *causal*, that is to say that one of these variables moving causes the other to move, it is hard to say with certainty which one causes which. It could be the case that more spending on healthcare causes people to live longer. However, it could also be the case that people who live longer (perhaps due to better lifestyle choices, or due to better infrastructure such as clean water) spend more on healthcare (because you spend more on healthcare at advanced ages). So, causality could run in either direction. Life expectancy could influence spending or spending could influence life expectancy.

The fundamental trouble with associations is that it is very difficult to show an association that rules out all possible latent variables and reverse causality. In fact, it is quite possible that for a given association, both directions of causality are happening at the same time. It is also possible that latent variables are acting at the same time that a causal relationship is also happening. So, to be able to answer questions such as "what is the effect of increasing variable X on the value of variable Y," we need to use a type of study that can effectively rule out these alternative explanations.

---

[2] Healthcare researchers try to correct for this using a process called "risk adjustment" which takes patient mix into consideration when measuring hospital quality. Risk adjustment is discussed in greater detail in Chapter 12.

Randomized Experimental Evidence

In order to establish causality you need to make a strong case that one thing causing the next is the only explanation that fits the data. This is hard to do, but not impossible. Scientists have developed tools for this purpose, and gotten it down to, well, a science. The gold standard of these tools is a *randomized experiment.*

Here is how a randomized experiment works. First, you choose a population that you want to study, in the case of social science or medicine this is usually a population of people.[3] Then you get a large sample from this population and start tracking the outcomes of interest for the sample: perhaps blood pressure, or the amount of healthcare purchased. The sample is then randomized into at least two groups, a *treatment group* and a *control group.*[4] The treatment group is given an intervention that you wish to study, such as a medication or free health insurance. The control group is not given the intervention under study, but may be given a fake intervention, called a *placebo* (more on placebos in a moment) or a different intervention with already established properties (such as an older medication). Then, the researchers continue to track the outcomes of interest for both groups. The difference between the outcomes of the treatment group and the outcomes of the control group is the causal effect of the treatment on the outcomes.

Randomized experiments take advantage of a property of data called the *Central Limit Theorem* (CLT). The CLT shows that when you take a random sample from a population, then as the size of that sample grows, the mean value of a characteristic of that sample will converge to the true value for the population. So, if I take a random sample of people in the United States, then the average height of the people in that sample will get closer and closer to the average height of people in the United States as the sample gets bigger and bigger.[5]

Going back to thinking about treatment and control groups: they are both taken from the same population. As the size of the groups grow, the characteristics of the samples both approach the same population characteristics, except there is one key difference: the treatment group was given an intervention and the control group was not.

---

[3] You can run an experiment on anything: animals, plants, inanimate objects, etc.

[4] If you want to test more than one treatment at a time then you can randomize into more groups.

[5] Another cool feature is that the distribution of a random sample will be a normal (Gaussian) distribution, commonly referred to as a bell curve, regardless of the distribution of the underlying population. This greatly simplifies statistical calculations.

So, if we subtract the control result from the treatment result, we are left with the effect of the intervention of the outcome. Here is some simple math that shows this:

$$Outcome_{treatment} - Outcome_{control}$$
$$= (Outcome_{population} + Effect\ of\ treatment) - Outcome_{population}$$
$$= Effect\ of\ treatment$$

The outcome for the treatment group has two components, the population outcome and the treatment effect. The outcome for the control group is just the outcome for the population. Taking their difference cancels out the outcome for the population, leaving only the treatment effect. If the experiment is correctly executed, then you have established incredibly convincing evidence of a causal relationship.

Places Where Problems Arise in Experiments

The experimental approach is not foolproof. There are still many ways to mess up a randomized experiment such that the exact causal explanation remains murky.

Placebos

It is possible that the act of receiving an intervention itself might change the outcome for an individual. For example, getting a medication in pill form might change your health outcome in two distinct ways. The medicine in the pill might change your health, but so might the act of getting the pill itself. There might be some psychological change from receiving the pill that causes your health to improve.[6] Any change in an outcome caused by the mode in which the intervention is imparted, but not the intervention itself is called the *placebo effect*. Placebo effects are problematic because they muddy the waters with regards to a causal story. When placebo effects are present, it becomes unclear how much of an observed change in the outcome is due to the treatment itself and how much is due to the fact that a treatment was given at all.

Fortunately, we can net out the placebo effect by giving the control group a fake treatment or a *placebo*. A placebo is something that mimics the treatment itself but carries none of the actual intervention. For example,

---

[6] This is akin to kissing a toddler's scraped knee and the toddler feeling better. The kiss itself does not heal the knee, but changes the psychological state of the toddler causing them to feel better.

in the case of an experiment with a new drug, the treatment group would be given a pill containing the medicine and the control group would be given a pill that looks identical but contains an inert substance. This adds the placebo effect to the control group, allowing it to be canceled out when treatment and control group outcomes are compared:

$$\text{Outcome}_{\text{treatment}} - \text{Outcome}_{\text{control}}$$
$$= \left(\text{Outcome}_{\text{population}} + \text{Effect of treatment} + \text{Placebo effect}\right.$$
$$\left. - \left(\text{Outcome}_{\text{population}} + \text{Placebo effect}\right)\right.$$
$$= \text{Effect of treatment}$$

Placebos are recommended for experiments, but depending on the treatment being studied may not always be feasible. For medical interventions like major invasive surgery, a placebo invasive surgery would not be recommended due to the risks inherent in the intervention.[7] In other situations, it is simply impossible to give someone a fake intervention. If the treatment being studied is the effect of giving someone $1,000, then it is difficult to give the control group fake money and not have them know the difference.

Blinding

It is also possible that knowing whether or not you are treated in an experiment might change your outcomes. A researcher wants to guard as much as possible against situations where knowing something about the design of the study influences the behavior of the study subjects. Consider two people getting pills as part of a study. The pill might greatly improve their health, and it might be a placebo. If the people knew which was which, then the person getting treated might react differently than the control person due to this knowledge (perhaps they feel more optimistic and go for more walks). Creating a situation where the subjects of a study do not know who is in which group (treatment or control) is called *blinding* an experiment and removes this concern.

It is also possible that the researcher might have a behavioral response to knowing who is in which group. For example, a researcher who expects a patient to improve might shade toward being more generous in subjective assessments of a subject's health, and a researcher who expects a patient to not improve might shade toward being less generous in subjective assessments of a subject's health. Creating a situation where the researcher or

---

[7] There have been studies that have used placebos for minimally invasive, outpatient surgery. For example, Moseley et al. (2002) performed a randomized study of knee surgery which utilized fake surgeries as a placebo.

study administrator also does not know who is in the treatment or control groups is called *double blinding* an experiment and removes concerns of researcher bias influencing outcomes.

Sample Size

Randomized experiments lean heavily on the CLT. The argument for causality that is contained in a randomized experiment is based on the means of the sample (i.e. the average values for the measurements taken from the experiment's subjects) converging to the population means. This only happens if the sample size (i.e. the number of subjects in the experiment) becomes large.[8] If the sample size is too small, then this does not happen and it is possible that there are differences between treatment and control groups that are due to their composition and not the treatment.

Consider a study of 40,000 people, 20,000 men and 20,000 women. If they are randomly split into two groups, what is the chance that one group is almost completely men and the other almost completely women? The answer is: pretty small. Now consider a study of four people, two men and two women. Again, they are randomly split into two groups, however, now there is a much higher probability that the randomization yields a treatment group of one gender and a control group of the other. In this case, the sample means will not be the population means, they will be the population means plus any differences due to differences in the gender composition of the groups.

External Validity

Experiments provide the causal effect of treatment, but that effect is only valid for the sample that was studied. Results can only be extrapolated to other populations to the extent that those populations are similar to the one that was studied. The extent to which a result can be extrapolated onto other groups is referred to as *external validity*. A study's results may be externally valid for some, but not all other populations.

For example, I could take a large sample of students at the University of Colorado Denver, where I taught health economics for many years. I could randomize them into two groups and take some baseline biometrics

---

[8] How large is large enough? This actually depends on how big the true effect of treatment is, bigger effects are easier to detect (need smaller samples to pass the usual statistical scrutiny) and smaller effects are more difficult to detect (need larger samples to pass the usual statistical scrutiny). A researcher can perform a *power calculation*, which given an expected true effect size will yield the necessary sample size needed to detect it. How to do a power calculation is beyond the scope of this book, but can be found in most statistics textbooks.

for each group: resting heart rate, blood pressure, blood triglyceride levels – things like that. One group would get no intervention (i.e. be the control group), and the other would do an intense exercise program for 90 minutes every day for three months. At the end of the three months, I would again take the biometrics. My guess is that the experiment would show that exercise improves many of the biometrics, suggesting improvements in health.

Now, if I was to repeat this experiment with students at the University of Colorado Boulder, would I expect the same results? I think so. The populations are fairly similar (college-aged individuals living in Colorado), so it is reasonable to think that the results would be externally valid to this new population. What if I was to repeat this same experiment among a sample of individuals who are over age 80 and all have heart problems that leave them at high risk of heart attack? In this case, the results of the first experiment are not likely to be externally valid.

Examples of Randomized Experimental Evidence: The Effect of Health Insurance

Randomized experiments can be immensely informative and provide large contributions to knowledge in medicine and social science. To take a very prominent example, a big set of question when studying the healthcare sector fall under the umbrella of "What does health insurance do for people?" It includes questions like: "Does health insurance increase spending on care?" and "Does health insurance improve health outcomes?" These questions can be and have been addressed using randomized experiments.

The RAND Experiment

Between 1971 and 1986, the RAND Corporation (funded by the US government) conducted a randomized experiment where over 4,000 households were given health insurance with different levels of generosity. The study tracked, among other outcomes, household expenditures on medical care and various health outcomes.

The RAND study provided evidence in support of many of the theories presented in the previous chapter. For example, it demonstrated that more generous cost sharing (i.e. cost sharing more in the patient's favor) increased the amount of expenditures on medical care, and that more generous coinsurance rates made demand for care less price sensitive (more inelastic).

Interestingly, the RAND experiment found minimal evidence of health insurance actually improving health outcomes. Most of the measures of health used in the study did not show any change based on the generosity of insurance given to a household.[9] There were numerous studies published on the results of the RAND experiment, a good starting place is the study by Manning et al. (1987).

The Oregon Experiment

Another randomized study of health insurance was done in 2008 in Oregon. Oregon expanded its Medicaid program, but did so based on random draws from a list. This created a randomized experiment where around 6,000 individuals were given insurance and around 6,000 similar individuals were not.

Individuals who received insurance were more likely to use medical care. Also, while the researchers did not find any differences in biometric outcomes such as blood pressure or cholesterol levels for those who received insurance, those who received insurance were more likely to be diagnosed with and receive treatment for diabetes or depression – suggesting that health insurance made it more likely that people would catch and treat chronic illnesses. Much like the RAND experiment, numerous studies were published on the results of the Oregon experiment, a good starting place is the study by Baicker et al. (2013).

The IRS Experiment

In 2017, the Internal Revenue Service (IRS) was aware of 4.5 million households that had previously paid a tax penalty for not having health insurance.[10] Of these households, 3.9 million were randomly selected to receive a letter reminding them of this fact. This intervention (getting a letter) made individuals more likely to get health insurance in the next year.

The researchers (Goldin et al. 2021) were then able to match the IRS records to Social Security records on mortality. Those who received the letter and were between the ages 45 and 64 had a 0.06 percentage point lower mortality rate (i.e. one fewer death per every ~1,500 people).[11] There was no detectable mortality benefit for younger individuals.

---

[9] The study found stronger evidence of insurance improving health for lower-income portions of the sample.

[10] This was part of the Patient Protection and Affordable Care Act's "Individual Mandate" which stipulated that people needed to have insurance or pay a tax penalty.

[11] The oldest age included in the study was 64, as at age 65 people qualified for insurance under Medicare and would not be subject to a tax penalty for not having insurance.

More on Experimental Evidence: Medicine and Public Health

Experimental evidence is by no means limited to social science questions, in fact, a tremendous amount of experimental evidence is published every year in medical and public health journals. These journals make up the backbone of "evidence-based medicine" where medical and public health practices are informed by experimental studies recording the causal relationships between use of health interventions and health outcomes. One way to think about medical journals is as tracing out different parts of the health production function (in particular the relationship between m and H), one study at a time.

Quasi-experiments

There is a middle ground between associational evidence and experimental evidence: *quasi-experimental evidence*. This is where a large amount of the empirical evidence from social science and economics in particular comes from. Quasi-experiments can be broadly thought of as rigging up a situation that approximates an experiment under certain assumptions. The quality of quasi-experimental evidence thus depends on how well those assumptions are met.

For example, a common quasi-experimental approach is to look at a policy that impacts some, but not all of a population. A study that uses such a policy to try to approximate an experiment would want to argue that the populations that were affected and unaffected were otherwise similar (thus approximating a treatment and control group), and would attempt to rule out the influence of latent variables and reverse causality – usually by making arguments about how the policy was timed and by making compelling arguments that rule out likely alternative explanations.

Quasi-experiments have become increasingly common in empirical economics and other social sciences. In fact, the 2021 Nobel Memorial Prize in Economic Sciences was given to Joshua Angrist, David Card, and Guido Imbens in part for their work using and popularizing these techniques. There are also entire textbooks and courses dedicated to quasi-experimental approaches.[12]

---

[12] A classic book on this topic is *Mostly Harmless Econometrics* by Angrist and Pischke, but newer additions to the field such as *Causal Inference the Mixtape* by Cunningham, or *The Effect, An Introduction to Research Design and Causality* by Huntington-Klein have become increasingly popular.

When trying to assess the quality of a quasi-experimental study, and thus the believability of its causal claim, each study needs to be evaluated on its own merits. That said, there are a few common questions that you can ask (or at least that I ask) when trying to determine how good the evidence is.

1. Is there a treatment group and a control group? How comparable are they?
2. How forthcoming are the authors about the assumptions that need to be made in order for there to be a causal claim?
3. How well defended are these assumptions?
4. How forthcoming are the authors about the limitations of the method being used?

Assessing quasi-experimental study quality is an acquired skill, and does not necessarily come easily. However, quasi-experiments have opened up a new frontier of knowledge that would likely not have been knowable using only strict experimental methods.

Self-Assessment

1. You observe that people who wear pedometers (step counters) tend to be healthier based on various biometric measures than those who do not wear them. What is a latent variable that would cause this relationship to not necessarily be causal.
2. Describe a randomized experiment that you could run to demonstrate that having a pedometer improves health.
3. You observe that people who use illicit drugs tend to be less healthy based on various biometric measures. Make an argument that part of this relationship could be due to reverse causality – that being unhealthy may make you more likely to use illicit drugs.
4. Describe a randomized experiment that you could run to demonstrate that illicit drugs harm health.
5. Consider the statement "Randomized studies are always better than quasi-experimental studies, because they do not rely on many additional assumptions." What is correct about this statement? What is incorrect? Write a more accurate statement.
6. The authors of the RAND experiment noted that they did not find evidence of a relationship between insurance coverage and mortality. Based on the evidence from the IRS study, why do you think that is?

Supplement. Ethics in Human Subjects Research

After reading this chapter, you may have lots of great ideas for experiments that you could run to learn about human behavior – I know that I did after I learned about how to run randomized experiments. An important consideration that can be overlooked (sometimes to disastrous result) when doing research that involves other humans is that people have emotions, can feel pain, and need to be treated with dignity and respect. To protect the research subjects, any research that involves human subjects (or animal subjects for that matter) needs to adhere to ethical protocols and will not be allowed to go forward at an institution (such as a university or a hospital) without approval from their Institutional Review Board (IRB).

An IRB reviews proposals for research to make sure that they follow accepted ethical standards for the treatment of subjects as well as standards for the protection of confidential (and sometimes deeply personal) data. Anyone who serves on an IRB, or who is involved in research involving human subjects (i.e. is part of a study that will be submitted to an IRB for approval) needs to be appropriately trained in correct practices for their role in the project. Training is commonly provided by a third party such as The Collaborative Institutional Training Initiative (the CITI Program; www.citiprogram.org).

PART II
Providers

6

Provider-Firms and the Market

We now have an understanding of how buyers (patients) operate within the healthcare sector. The next step is to think about how sellers (providers) behave. When thinking about sellers, economists like to use the concept of a *firm*, or a business entity that produces and sells goods or services. To think about the production of medical care, we can begin by establishing how a typical firm operates and then look at how a producer of medical care fits into, or does not fit into this framework.

A Typical Firm

A firm is not a human. That said, there are some similarities between the behavior of firms and humans. Much like a human, a firm has a goal, and will try to achieve this goal in a rational way. In the case of a human, the goal is trying to get the most utility possible. In the case of a firm, the goal is to make as much *profit* as possible. Profit, to an economist, is revenue minus costs, or the money that a firm makes by selling its products minus the amount of money that was spent to make said products.

Profit is straightforward to calculate.

$$\text{Profit} = \left(p_{\text{product}} \times q_{\text{product}} \right) - c(q)$$

where

$$c(q) = \Sigma(p_{\text{input}} \times q_{\text{input}})$$

The profit equation may look complex, but all that it is saying is profit is equal to *revenue* minus *costs*. Let's break it apart piece by piece. $\left(p_{\text{product}} \times q_{\text{product}} \right)$ is the amount of the product sold (q_{product}) multiplied by the price of the product (p_{product}). Together this is *revenue*, the amount of money made from sales. *Cost* is represented by $c(q)$, some function c of the amount of the product made. In this case, the function is known, and simple, it is $\Sigma(p_{\text{input}} \times q_{\text{input}})$ the sum of the amount of money spent on each input used to make the product.[1]

---

[1] Σ is math notation for "add up all the stuff that comes after me." So the statement $\Sigma(p_{\text{input}} \times q_{\text{input}})$ translates to "multiply the price of each input by the quantity of each input that you use, and then add them all together.

The inputs used to make a product are sometimes referred to by economists as the *factors of production*. A good or service may need few inputs. A peanut butter and jelly sandwich needs bread, peanut butter, jelly, and some labor to assemble the sandwich. On the other hand, a car requires a much larger number of inputs. For example, building a car requires the different components of the car (of which there are many), the labor used to assemble the car, and the energy used to power the various tools and machines used in assembly.

A firm will try to get as much profit as possible given that:

- inputs are not free, the firm has to pay for them, and
- inputs can only be made into output (the product) based on the technology that is available.

This is an optimization problem, just like when a human tries to get the most utility possible given their resources and preferences.[2] In this case, instead of worrying about where options land on a utility function and how much those choices cost, the firm instead worries about what amounts of production are feasible given the technology available and how much the inputs needed to produce those amounts cost.

To figure everything out, a firm will look at the prices of inputs used to make their product as well as their available technology, represented by a *production function*:

$$q = f(\text{input}_1, \text{input}_2, \ldots)$$

The production function works the same way as the health production function from Chapter 2. This production function says that the amount produced (q), is some function (f) of a bunch of inputs ($\text{input}_1, \text{input}_2$, etc.), the "..." is just there to show that we can add as many inputs into the function as we like. The peanut butter and jelly sandwich would only require a few inputs, whereas other goods and services (such as the car mentioned previously) would require a lot more. You plug the input amounts into a production function and it tells you how much of your output you can make.

Production functions are a bit different than utility functions. Utility functions give a ranking as to which options are better than others, whereas production functions give actual amounts that are produced. A second difference is that when humans make choices, they only care about getting the

---

[2] Mathematically, both utility and profit maximization are what are called "constrained optimization problems" and can be solved using calculus techniques when certain pieces of information (such as the utility function) are known.

greatest utility possible, whereas for firms, choosing the most production possible is not necessarily the most profitable choice. The production function is a very important part of firm optimization, but the final goal of the firm is to get the largest amount of profit possible, not the largest amount of production possible.

Provider-Firms

Can we put a provider of healthcare into the framework of a firm? I think that the answer is yes. In order to do this, the first thing I need to convince you of is that providers are trying to maximize profits. This may seem incorrect to some. For instance, you might argue that a healthcare provider isn't motivated by money, but by more abstract and altruistic motives such as "duty and humanity." This does not necessarily run counter to profit maximization. If I rephrase the objective of a firm from "maximize profits" to "given that you are helping people, also maximize profits" then we functionally have the same thing: an actor trying to maximize profits. Our provider is now a firm that operates with one additional constraint: so long as they are meeting some desired level of "helping," they will try to make as much money as possible.[3]

The next step is to fill in the rest of the features of typical such that it is also a healthcare provider, or provider-firm.

What Is Being Produced?

What is it that a provider-firm produces and sells? This depends on the type of provider that you are seeing, but also can vary quite a bit from visit to visit with the same provider. If you think about all of the different times that you have gone to your provider to get medical care, you likely had different things that you wanted different times that you went. The service being produced by the provider, which we can call a *provider visit* is a somewhat amorphous amalgam of different services. You may want some combination of the following services in a provider visit:

- An examination: you may want the provider to examine you, and/or take biometrics.
- A diagnosis: you may want the provider to make a determination as to what a specific ailment is.

---

[3] To put this a different way, if given option A: "save someone's life," and option B: "save someone's life and then get paid $100," I would pick option B.

- A prescription: you may want the provider to give you permission to purchase a controlled substance to treat an ailment.
- Medical advice: you may want advice as to how to deal with a condition or prevent developing one in the future.
- A referral: you may want your provider to suggest a different provider to you – often with a different specialty.[4]
- Treatment: you may want your provider to perform a medical procedure on you.

For the moment, let's just treat all provider visits as the same thing: some mix of the above. We can think of a provider visit as the output of the provider-firm's production function, and a provider visit will have some associated price. In reality there may be different prices for different services rendered, but there is still a baseline "office visit" which is the most commonly billed service upon which most bills are built upon.[5]

What Are a Provider-Firm's Inputs?

There are many inputs used to make provider visits. Let's lump them into two categories: *non-labor inputs* (K) or inputs that do not come from a person doing a job and *labor inputs* (L) or inputs that come from a person doing a job. So, we can write the production function as:

$$q = f(K, L)$$

This simply says that our provider visits are produced via some combination of non-labor and labor inputs.

Non-labor inputs will include things like office space and medical equipment, but also inputs like a computer system for keeping records, magazines for the waiting room, electricity and water for the building, toilet paper and soap for the bathroom, and so on. Anything that the firm needs to spend money on to keep the office up and running that is not a person working is a non-labor input.

Labor inputs will include at least one physician, as in order to run a medical practice at least one person needs to have a medical license. But there may also be non-physician labor inputs providing care such as nurses or technicians. Additionally, there may be other forms of labor such as someone who is in charge of scheduling or billing. The firm may also use some labor on an as-needed contract basis, such as accounting, tech support, or legal counsel.

---

[4] Sometimes, you might ask for a referral for the same specialty to have another doctor verify a diagnosis, this is called a *second opinion*.

[5] We'll talk more about medical bills in Chapter 12.

Every input will have an associated cost. Some of the costs will be *fixed costs* which are paid once and stay the same (or fixed) regardless of how many provider visits are produced. This is something like renting the office space. The office space will cost the same per month regardless of the number of provider visits performed. Likewise, a computer system will cost the same to purchase whether it keeps 10,000 records, or only 100 records and a lot of cat videos. Some of the costs for an input will be *variable costs*, which scale based on the amount produced. If you are going to produce more provider visits you may need additional hours of nursing, meaning that the cost of the input will grow as the amount produced grows. You would also likely use more medical equipment as you produce more provider visits: if every office visit uses one tongue depressor, then the cost of tongue depressors scales up as the number of visits increases.[6]

Given the production function for making provider visits and the prices in the market for inputs and provider visits, the provider-firm can now attempt to optimize their production and maximize profit, just like any typical firm.

Physician Labor and Production Efficiency

By law, a provider-firm needs to have at least one physician. This is because a physician holds a medical license, which is required to operate a medical practice. That said, physicians are a somewhat expensive labor input, so there may be ways to produce provider visits in a more cost-efficient way by using fewer hours or physician labor, and more of other types of inputs.

In general, a firm will always try to find the most efficient way to combine inputs to make its product. That means that as the prices of different inputs change over time, a firm may try to switch from a more expensive to a less expensive input to make the same product. Switching between different mixes of inputs is referred to by economists as *factor substitution*, which is a fancy way of saying that I switch in one input for another, typically cheaper, one.

For the physician firm, due to the multifaceted nature of a provider visit there are several different inputs that can substitute for physician labor, such as nurses or equipment technicians. By separating out individual tasks that make up the service, it is sometimes possible to produce more efficiently. There are a few reasons for this.

---

[6] Unless you reuse the tongue depressors, which is incredibly gross.

Table 6.1 Doctor productivity in one hour		
	Dr. Acula	Dr. Watson
Number of blood draws	8	4
Number of patients diagnosed	4	4

Gains from Specialization

First is that overall production can be increased when different parts of the production process specialize. If everyone does the task that they are the best at comparatively, then more is produced in total. To illustrate, we can look at a simple medical practice. There will be two tasks, taking blood and diagnosing illnesses. There are two doctors working in this practice Dr. Acula and Dr. Watson. Table 6.1 shows what each doctor can do given one hour.

Notice that Dr. Acula better at drawing blood. He can draw blood twice as fast as he can diagnose patients, his tradeoff in an hour is 2 to 1. Dr. Watson is equally good at both activities and thus has a tradeoff of 1 to 1, so in this case Dr. Acula has a *comparative advantage* in drawing blood. The comparative advantage goes the other way for Dr. Watson, while he is the same in an overall sense as Dr. Acula at diagnosing, he is better comparatively: he gives up one blood draw to do one diagnosis, whereas Dr. Acula has to give up two.

So let's consider a strenuous two-hour workday for our doctors. In the first situation, each doctor will do both tasks, each for one hour. Dr. Acula will draw blood eight times, and make four diagnoses, and Dr. Watson will draw blood four times and make four diagnoses. So, in the two-hour workday the practice will take blood 12 times and make 8 diagnoses.

But what if the doctors specialize based on their comparative advantages? Dr. Acula does nothing but draw blood for two hours and Dr. Watson does nothing but diagnose? Then in the tiring two-hour workday, the practice will take blood 16 times and make 8 diagnoses. By rearranging who does what to specialize, the firm has become more efficient, producing more with the same labor inputs.

Learning by Doing

Gains from specialization can be reinforced by improving skills through experience. This is sometimes referred to as *learning by doing*. If labor specializes into different tasks, then over time their comparative advantages may increase as their skills relevant to their specialized task are improved. Think about the first time you tied your shoes. It likely took a long time.

With practice and experience you likely improved dramatically, and can now tie your shoes very quickly. The same principle applies to a wide array of tasks including those in the production of medical care, with practice workers get faster and better at their tasks.

Reducing Task Switching

Another place where specializing helps productivity is by reducing time and mental energy spent switching between tasks. Every time a worker switches to something different, time is lost in the transition. By keeping focused on fewer tasks, or even a single task, workers can become more efficient.

Substitutes for Physician Labor: "Practice at the Top of Your License"

Since specialization has so many potential benefits in terms of productivity, it is no surprise that provider-firms have sought out ways to specialize their labor force. One way this is done is by using several different care providers with different levels of training. For instance, a provider-firm may employ physicians, nurse practitioners, physician's assistants, nurses, equipment technicians, and other types of caregivers. Each of these forms of labor has its own skillset and scope of practice, which may overlap with the skillset and scope of practice of other workers within the firm.

To help specialize, many provider-firms have adopted the strategy that workers should strive to "practice at the top of your license," or in other words, always try to be performing tasks that require the most skill intensive portion of your particular skillset. If every worker does this, it creates a natural specialization: in any instance, each worker is trying to do the most skill intensive task that they can do, which presumably means that few workers with different (but potentially overlapping) skillsets are doing the same thing.

Factor Substitution for Physician Labor: Evidence from a Randomized Study

To give an example of gains from specialization with regards to splitting tasks, let's turn to an example of a task that can be done by different labor inputs: recording information. When a patient comes into a medical practice for a provider visit, someone working in the practice will keep a *chart*, or record of all of the ailments presented and procedures performed. Typically, this is entered into a computer and kept as an electronic medical record, although in some cases paper records are still used. Keeping a chart is time consuming, and requires the time and energy of a labor input.

A form of labor that can be used instead of a physician to write things down is a medical scribe, who is a designated chart keeper. Their job is to follow around the provider from visit to visit and record everything in the provider's stead in the chart. In this case, the provider-firm is breaking off the task of writing things down (or typing things up), taking it away from the caregiver (for whom this task is unlikely to be at the "top of her license"), and giving it to a chart keeping specialist.

Scribes have become incredibly popular in care settings such as emergency rooms, where providers may need to see many patients in rapid succession, and charting may need to be done after the shift – for which the provider can charge overtime. This creates a situation where you are paying a provider extra to perform a task that is not even close to the "top of their license."

I ran a randomized experiment on medical scribes in several emergency departments at hospitals in the Denver suburbs (Friedson 2018). For several months, I took the shifts that were scheduled in the emergency departments and randomly assigned some of the shifts to have a scribe and some of them not to. When an emergency department doctor showed up for work, they either had a scribe or did not. Shifts with scribes ended up using less overtime: about 13.5 fewer minutes of overtime per shift, which adds up to a lot of money over months of shifts at physician pay rates. When scribes were present, the emergency departments also moved more quickly: patients spent on average about 12.5 fewer minutes waiting during shifts that had scribes.

Supply

Once you have all of a producer's relevant production information: their production function and relevant costs and prices in the sector, you can solve mathematically for how much they will want to produce given any prevailing price of their output.[7] The final result of this exercise is a supply curve, as shown in Figure 6.1.

A supply curve works much like a demand curve, you look at a given price and the supply curve tells you the quantity that a firm will produce. For Figure 6.1, if the price of the good or service is P_1 then the quantity supplied is q_1. In most cases a supply curve will slope upward, which means that when the price is higher a firm will produce more, and when the price is lower the firm will produce less.

---

[7] This exercise is covered in most intermediate microeconomics textbooks, but the calculation itself is not central to understanding the behavior of the firm.

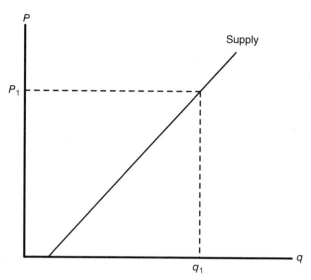

Figure 6.1 Supply

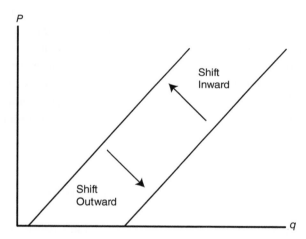

Figure 6.2 Shifts in supply

You can do many of the same things with a supply curve that you can do with a demand curve. For example, supply curves have shifters as well: anything other than the price of the product that influences the production process will shift supply. Price of an input increases? Supply shifts inwards as it is less profitable to produce at any given price. Price of an input decreases? Supply shifts outward as it is more profitable to produce at any given price. Changes in technology can shift supply as well. More efficient production method? Supply shifts outward. Shifts in supply are shown in Figure 6.2.

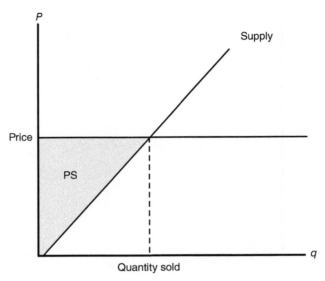

Figure 6.3 Producer surplus

Likewise, you can calculate surplus for producers much like was done for consumers with consumer surplus. *Producer surplus* is what you are paid for a good or service minus what you would have needed to have been paid to be willing to sell it. If I would have sold a service for $5 and was paid $15, then I made $10 in producer surplus. So, given a supply curve, producer surplus is the area below the price (what you were paid) but above the supply curve (what you needed to be paid in order to sell) – this is labeled "PS" in Figure 6.3.

Market Equilibrium and Perfect Competition

This brings us to the workhorse model that economists use to analyze a wide variety of markets. Plot both supply and demand in the same picture, and you have a picture of a market under perfect competition as shown in Figure 6.4.

The point where supply intersects demand is called *equilibrium*, and has an associated *equilibrium price* and *equilibrium quantity*. If we assume a few things about markets, then we will always end up at this nice, easy to spot equilibrium point. If for some reason the market has too low a price, then buyers will compete and bid up the price until we are back to equilibrium. If for some reason the market has too high a price, then sellers will compete and undercut each other until we are back to equilibrium. If supply or demand shifts, then we settle into a new equilibrium – the new intersection point.

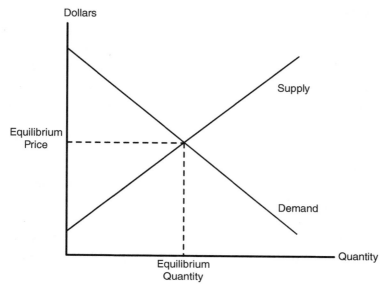

Figure 6.4 Market equilibrium

Markets under perfect competition do a lot of things that we as a society like. For example, they produce the maximum possible amount of surplus. That is to say, if you take consumer surplus and producer surplus and add them up, you'll get the largest possible number if you let a free market under perfect competition run its course unimpeded.

Breaking Perfect Competition

While the perfect competition model is useful and easy to work with, it requires a few things to get all of the nice outcomes. There need to be a lot of buyers and sellers, prices and other information need to be clearly visible to all, and the product in question can't have certain properties such as carrying additional costs or benefits to those not involved in the transaction. Each of these things, and a few others, which I will list next, will cause markets to have different, and in some cases very undesirable properties.

Price Distortion

The ability of a market to reach equilibrium depends on buyers and sellers being able to coordinate. The piece of information that they coordinate on is the price. If the price is in some way garbled, then the market will not necessarily reach the correct equilibrium.

Prices in the healthcare sector are not always determined by the direct interaction of buyers and sellers. In fact, in most cases in the US there is an intermediary: the insurance company through which the price felt by buyers and the price felt by sellers is transmitted. Health insurance can lead to a situation where the buyer and the seller experience different prices for the same good or service being transacted. This feature of the market, and its implications are the focus of Chapter 12.

Uncertainty

When actors in a market are uncertain as to what the outcome is going to be, then they have to make decisions based on their best guesses. These best guesses may be correct on average, but that does not mean that they are correct every single time. So, once uncertainty is involved, many actors will make "correct" decisions, but still end up with "bad" outcomes.

Think about a decision whether or not to get major surgery. The surgery will have some risks and will also have some benefits, and many of each will be uncertain. You might make the best guess that you can, and thus the best decision that you can make under the circumstances, but still, through luck of the draw, end up with a bad outcome. The same can be true for actors in many markets, they do the best they can but may still end up in bad scenarios regardless.

Uncertainty is prevalent in the healthcare sector. Many diagnoses and treatments have a degree of uncertainty baked into them. There is also uncertainty as to when and if an individual will develop an illness, uncertainty in research and development of new pharmaceuticals, and uncertainty about the degree to which a lifestyle choice will help or hurt you (some of these are called "risky behaviors," risk is part of the name).

Market Power

Competitive markets depend on *competition*, the idea that players in a market have others that they are trying to beat to the punch. A buyer has other buyers to outbid in order to get a desired product, and a seller has other sellers to undercut if they want to move their product. When there are few buyers or few sellers, then the party for which there is few of has *market power*, additional leverage when buying or selling. In a market with a single seller, the seller has complete market power and is a *monopoly*, and in a market with single buyer, the buyer likewise has complete market power and is a *monopsony*. The more monopolistic (or monopsonistic) a market is, the more the group with market power can leverage that power for greater profits or greater consumer surplus. This comes at the cost of the well-being of the other parties in the market.[8]

There is a large degree of consolidation in the healthcare sector. How many choices do you have for health insurance companies in your local area? How many choices for hospitals? How many options do you have for a prescription medication? The fewer choices you have, the less competition and the more market power.

Externalities

An *externality* is a situation where a good or service carries an extra benefit or extra cost that impacts someone who is not part of the transaction for the good or service. *Positive externalities* are additional benefits, and *negative externalities* are additional costs. When an externality is present, even a perfectly competitive market will produce too much of a good with a negative externality, and too little of one with a positive externality. This is because the actors in the market will appropriately weigh their own costs and benefits when making a decision, but will not usually fully consider the benefits or costs to others.

Smokers will decide how much they want to smoke based on their desire to smoke, the cost of the cigarettes and the cost of the harms to themselves. They will not appropriately consider the costs to others that come from exposure to secondhand smoke. Similarly, when choosing how much to exercise, I weigh the benefits of exercise with the time and discomfort costs of doing so. I do not appropriately weigh the benefits to others of seeing me looking FABULOUS.

Externalities are present in many decisions that have profound implications for the healthcare sector as well as for public health. For example, one incredibly important externality is the risk of contagion for communicable diseases. Many behaviors such as travel, wearing masks, and vaccination carry externalities that influence this contagion externality and can literally save or cost lives. Externalities are the sole focus of Chapter 16.

Asymmetric Information

A competitive market also requires a free flow of information. However, situations can arise where one party in a market knows something that the other does not and can use this to their advantage. This one-sided information can be having hidden knowledge or having an ability to take a hidden action. Each of these information imbalances and their specific relevance to

---

[8] In some (but not all) cases this can makes the market produce less than it would under perfect competition.

the healthcare sector will be discussed as they arise in turn in later chapters. In general, asymmetric information can lead to some very bad outcomes, from buying things that you don't necessarily want to markets completely unraveling in spectacular fashion.

Government Intervention

Government intervention is another place where markets can perform badly. The answer to why government intervention is bad for markets will depend on which economist you ask. Some economists believe that markets inherently perform nicely, so when the government gets involved, the market is bound to be in trouble. From that perspective, the government is what breaks the market. Other economists believe that there are lots of problems with markets and the government is needed to intervene and get a better outcome. From that perspective, the government being involved is a symptom that something is wrong with the market in the first place. What all of these types of economists will agree on is that if the government is present in a market, then something is likely wrong with that market.

The government is all over the healthcare sector. It is the largest health insurance provider in the United States, it decides what can and cannot be sold as medicine, who can and cannot serve as a practitioner as well as their scope of practice. There are thousands of laws that impact the healthcare sector in important and sometimes subtle ways.

Imperfect Markets and the Healthcare Sector

The big picture is that up until now, we have been developing fundamentals to make a well-functioning, perfectly competitive market – the base standard for economics. We have buyers (patients) and sellers (provider-firms), and more or less understand how they behave. As we move forward through the rest of the book, we are going to start exploring the wrinkles that make the healthcare sector non-standard in greater depth.

This is not to say that these issues with markets do not show up in other places in the world – they certainly do. It is just that the healthcare sector in particular has all of these problems all over the place, and in spades. If you want to understand the healthcare sector then you need to understand complicated markets that do not fit the "perfect competition" ideal.

Self-Assessment

1. As technology improves, we can often produce services using fewer inputs – making production less expensive. However, some technological

changes allow us to treat ailments in a higher quality manner that is also more expensive to produce. Could switching to this type of production technology be more profitable? Why or why not?

2. Can a provider-firm that gives out charity care still be a profit maximizer? Why or why not?

3. Consider the following pieces of information:

    (a) Provider visits contain many different possible services.

    (b) There are benefits to specialization between different labor inputs in a provider-firm.

    What is an example of gains from specialization across services within a single provider visit?

    What types of services do not get specialized within a single provider visit? Why do you think that is?

4. If a provider-firm switched from a culture of "everybody does everything they are allowed to do" to a culture of "practice at the top of your license," we might expect that firm to become more efficient. Would you expect the efficiency gains to all happen immediately, or grow over time? Why?

5. In 2018, Hurricane Maria knocked out a portion of the world's production for IV saline (the filling for IV bags for rehydration, and the base used for many types of IV drugs). What do you think happened to the supply curve for IV medications? What do you think happened to the price of those IV medications?

6. Consider the statement "Much of the healthcare sector is not a perfectly competitive market, so there is no need to use economics." What is correct about this statement? What is incorrect? Write a more accurate statement.

Supplement. A Brief Rant on "Broken" Healthcare Markets and Economics

Many people talk about the healthcare sector and assume everything is the perfectly competitive market that they learned in their first ever economics class. This is wrong. The healthcare sector is highly irregular, and trying to use perfect competition to understand it can lead to some very bad policy.

A second mistake that people make is to notice that the healthcare sector contains many markets that are non-standard and think that means that you throw economics out the window and find a different way to think about it. I don't call a lot of things dumb, but this is incredibly dumb. The non-standard nature of healthcare is precisely why economics is so valuable. The fundamentals of human and firm behavior have not changed, it's just a question of carefully unpacking all of the incentives present and how they impact the parties involved. This is exactly what economics is good at doing.

What I hope the rest of this book will show you is that not only is the economic toolset still relevant in these "broken" cases, but that it is essential to obtaining quality policy, business practice, and citizenship.

7 The Healthcare Labor Force

Medical care cannot be provided without using labor inputs.[1] Many of the people providing labor used in the production of medical care have specialized training that is specific to medical care. We will refer to these people as the healthcare labor force. This is to differentiate the healthcare labor force from other labor inputs used to create medical care that are not directly involved in caring for patients (such as legal, information technology, or custodial services professionals).

As the healthcare labor force is essential to being able to have a market for medical care, it is important to understand (a) what causes the healthcare labor force to grow or shrink, and (b) what causes the healthcare labor force to move around between locations. These two features of the healthcare labor force as well as policies that influence them will be the focus of this chapter.

How Much Labor Is Available?

When producing medical care (i.e. the provider visits discussed in the previous chapter) firms need to use labor inputs. The relevant unit for how much of a given labor input is used is time. A provider-firm uses *hours* of labor. So, when considering how much labor is available at a given moment, we care not only about how many people are around to work, but also how many hours each person is willing to work.

If we want to know how to get more labor – which is a common question asked by policymakers or by those who are running healthcare firms – what is being asked is how to get more hours staffed. This can be done by adjusting along either the *extensive margin*, or the *intensive margin*, to bring back some terminology from Chapter 2. You can hire more workers (if you are a firm) or add more workers to the labor force (if you are considering the overall stock of labor in a given market) and that would be increasing the amount of labor along the extensive margin. The relevant change in circumstances is workers going from "No, I am not working" or "No, I am not

---

[1] Yet.

working for you" to "Yes, I am working" or "Yes, I am working for you," this is the "yes/no" change that is the hallmark of the extensive margin.

The amount of labor available can also change along the intensive margin: workers can change the number of hours that they work. Workers increasing (or decreasing) their hours are changes in labor along the intensive margin. This is a change in amount given that some exists, which is the hallmark of the intensive margin.

Both types of changes (extensive or intensive) impact the same end measure of labor: the number of hours available, they just come from different sources. Hours of labor can change from bringing workers in or taking them out of the labor force but can also change from workers who are in the labor force changing the number of hours that they are working.

Intensive Margin Changes

Changes in the amount of labor an individual is willing to provide usually depend on the compensation for their time. When individuals are compensated more per hour of labor, they are usually willing to provide more hours, and when they are compensated less per hour of labor, they are usually willing to provide fewer hours.[2] Notice, that we are talking about compensation as a whole and not just wages. Individuals are willing to accept less in the way of wages when they are compensated with other valuable things (such as employer-provided health insurance or a free parking spot). That said, the items being used instead of wages will only be effective at generating hours of labor if they are valuable to the worker. The amount of wages that a person is willing to give up for an amount of non-wage compensation while keeping the number of hours the same is referred to by economists as a *compensating wage differential*. The value of the compensating wage differential (the amount of wages given up) for a given non-wage form of compensation (i.e. benefit) can be seen as the worker's implicit valuation of that benefit.[3]

In general, individual labor supply looks like most other supply curves as shown in Figure 7.1.

---

[2] At some point, compensating workers more can *decrease* the hours of labor provided on the intensive margin. This is due to something called the *labor/leisure tradeoff*, where workers can decide that additional resources are better used to free up time for leisure activities.

[3] Compensating wage differentials can run the other way too. If a job has an undesirable feature, then a worker will need to be paid more to supply the same number of hours than if that job did not have that undesirable feature. The increase in wages needed is how much the person values not having the given undesirable feature. This is why "hazard pay" exists: you have to pay people additional amounts to take jobs with the undesirable feature of additional risk to life and limb.

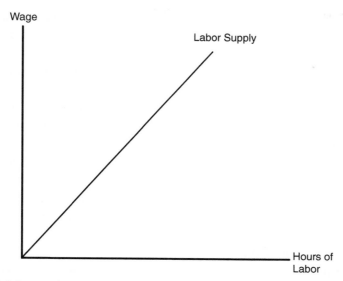

Figure 7.1 Labor supply

Given a level of compensation (which is usually represented by the wage) you can simply read off the number of hours that a person (or group of people) is willing to supply. The elasticity of supply (which is related to the steepness of the supply curve) shows how responsive a person (or group of people) is to changes in the wage with regards to hours worked. Steep (inelastic) supply means that changing wages will do little to change hours, whereas flat (elastic) supply means that changing wages will do much more to change hours. Understanding what the elasticity of labor supply with respect to wages is in a given labor market is central to understanding how many hours of labor are potentially available.

Extensive Margin Changes: Inflows

The other way that the amount of available hours of healthcare labor can change is via changes along the extensive margin. New workers can start working, or existing workers can stop working. First, let's consider new workers starting to work.

One way to get additional workers is to train them. You can get more physicians from medical schools, more nurses from nursing schools, and more of various types of specialized labor from their specific training programs. Training comes with a time lag: students need to enter into training programs, complete the programs, and then pass any relevant certification exams.[4]

---

[4] For example, new nurses in the United States cannot get a nursing license without first passing the NCLEX exam.

There is also some leakage of students along the way, some students do not pass the necessary certification exams, and some students do not complete their programs.[5]

Another way to get additional workers is to bring in existing workers from a different location. This is *in-migration* of workers, as more workers are coming "in" to a given market. In-migration does not change the overall number of workers in the larger healthcare system but can create meaningful changes in the number of workers in a single location. If 5,000 nurses move from California to Colorado then this grows the nurse labor force in Colorado (and shrinks the nurse labor force in California), potentially a large change for each state. That said, the nursing labor force for the United States as a whole would be unchanged by these moves.

Extensive Margin Changes: Outflows

Just as you can gain workers from in-migration, you can lose workers due to *out-migration*. Again, this is a location specific change and does not impact the number of workers in the larger healthcare system. Workers moving between states change state-level labor availability but not national labor availability and workers moving between nations change national level labor availability but not world labor availability. The overall effect from labor migration is zero-sum: if one location gains workers due to migration then another has lost workers from that migration.

There can also be outflows along the extensive margin due to workers exiting the labor force. Workers can choose to change careers and join a different labor force, such as the physician who discovers a deep love for making pizza and leaves their medical practice to open up a restaurant, or workers can simply retire. There are also other involuntary exits from the labor force: workers who lose their license, perhaps due to disciplinary action or workers who die while still part of the labor force have involuntarily exited the labor force.

Stocks, Flows, and Orders of Magnitude

When thinking about available labor, it is important to distinguish between how much labor is presently available (the *stock of labor*) and how much labor is coming in to or going out of the pool of available labor (the *flow of labor*). Policies which attempt to recruit more healthcare labor, such

---

[5] This can be for a number of reasons. Some students may not be able to pass the coursework, whereas other students might see something really gross and say "You know what? Nope. That belongs inside of a person, and I do not like how it smells. No thank you. I'm going to become an actuary or something." Just for example.

as incentives to relocate or incentives to obtain relevant training make changes to the flow of labor, but may be small relative to the size of the stock and thus take considerable time to make a large difference in the overall healthcare system.

To illustrate, in 2018 there were approximately 985,000 physicians in the United States (Young et al. 2019). In the 2017–2018 academic year, US medical schools graduated approximately 19,500 new MDs (Association of American Medical Colleges 2022). This means that this flow of 19,500 new physicians represented 1.9 percent of the total stock. So, if we wanted to grow the labor supply of physicians, then a policy which doubled the number of new graduates from MD-granting programs each year (a rather large change to the education system) would double the flow of new workers but would add less than 2 percent to the total stock each year (and that is not even counting any flows of workers out of the profession). Changing a smaller flow can make meaningful changes to a larger stock, but it takes time for it to add up.[6]

The Decision to Become Part of the Healthcare Labor Force

If we care about training workers for the healthcare workforce, then a foundational question to ask is: "What determines whether an individual becomes a certain type of worker?" This decision presents a chance to apply the tools for thinking about individual decision-making developed in the first part of the book: workers are humans and as such try to make the best decision possible given the resources that they have available. The only difference here is that the decision is about what to do with your time: should you get additional education, or should you do something else?

The decision to become a physician, or a nurse, or a public health practitioner (or a lawyer or an economist for that matter) comes down to comparing possible futures and picking the one that you think will make you the best off. Economists like to think about this in terms of evaluating different streams of utility that you might get, or to keep things simple for a moment, the different streams of income that you might get. In one world, you skip the additional schooling and go into the workforce, earning a steady wage immediately – this is shown in Figure 7.2 as the dark line. In another world, you go to school, where you make considerably less money

---

[6] When thinking about stocks and flows, relative size of the flow to the stock is enormously important. Dropping a bucket of water (a flow) onto a campfire has a very different effect than dropping the same bucket of water onto a 100-acre wildfire.

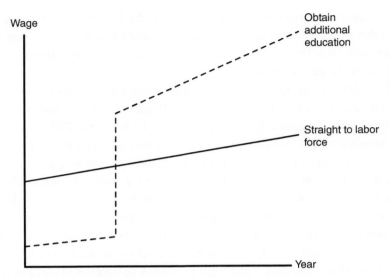

Figure 7.2 Possible streams of income

(and perhaps even go into debt), but then make a higher wage in the future when you have your additional credentials (such as a medical or nursing degree) – this is shown in Figure 7.2 as the dashed line.

When making a decision between these two options you evaluate the two different streams of value – taking into consideration the fact that you have to wait to get the stuff that comes later. An individual's rate at which something loses value the longer you have to wait for it, their *discount rate*, as discussed in Chapter 1, becomes very important in this decision. A more patient individual (i.e. someone with a lower discount rate) will place higher weight on the value gained later in life than a less patient individual (i.e. someone with a higher discount rate). This could lead them to make different decisions. Given this representation of the choice, it becomes a little easier to see which sorts of changes in circumstance should have an impact on the flow of new healthcare labor: anything that changes how much value you get from the different options at different times will impact your decision.

The Economic Environment

The current and forecasted future economic environment is extremely important to this choice. If your choice is between medical school and a general job market where wages are low then medical school becomes comparatively more attractive. However, if the general job market favors workers, and you could earn a high salary with no additional school, then medical school becomes comparatively less attractive.

To make this point in a different way, I will assume (possibly correctly) that you are currently in school. If you are not currently in school, just pretend. Now imagine that I came up and offered you a job if you quit school, you'll earn $50,000 a year to be a full-time professional cake taster. Would you quit school to take this job? What about if the salary was increased substantially due to a change in the market for cake tasters, it is a dangerous job after all. The salary is now $250,000 per year. Would you quit school? The job as a cake taster is the *opportunity cost* of additional schooling. As the best alternative outcome (sometimes called the *outside option*) to schooling becomes more attractive, school becomes more costly and thus less attractive.

Income Isn't Everything

The decision is not solely about comparing possible future streams of income, it is about comparing future streams of utility, part of which is determined by income. The other part of the choice will revolve around how much you like the different job possibilities and educational options on their own merits. If you strongly dislike interacting with people, then nursing school is unlikely to be a good choice, regardless of salary. Likewise, if you strongly dislike cake, then the option of becoming a professional cake taster is unlikely to be appealing.

These considerations can be extremely relevant when the values of income streams are similar. If you are trying to decide between becoming a neonatal intensive care nurse or a pediatric intensive care nurse a big part of the decision is "do you prefer working with premature babies or do you prefer working with children?"

Uncertainty

The future is also uncertain. Any decision made about the future is thus made based on a person's best guess as to what the outcome will be. People will also take into consideration how risky a given choice is. Given the same average outcome, an option will become less attractive as it becomes more risky (more uncertain) and will become more attractive as it becomes less risky (less uncertain).

Where Does Labor Locate?

The decision over where to locate is remarkably similar to the decision over whether or not to get additional education: individuals evaluate competing future streams of utility and pick the one that they think is best. Instead of picking between states of the world where they have made different educational decisions, they are picking between different possible locations. These locations will have some characteristics that will help determine their values.

Amenities

Whereas different jobs have different job characteristics that people will place a value on, different locations have different locational characteristics that people will place a value on. A locational characteristic that people value is called an *amenity*. If the characteristic is bad, it is sometimes referred to as a *disamenity*.

When comparing potential locational decisions, amenities can carry a lot of weight in terms of giving utility. Consider two otherwise identical jobs that are in two different locations, these jobs are both searching nationally for a new employee. The first job is in a really awesome location that we'll call Denver. Denver has numerous available outdoor activities, vibrant culture, and an active social scene for many types of interests. It has many amenities. The second job is in a place called Stinkville. Stinkville has none of Denver's amenities, although it does smell very bad. Given the two otherwise identical jobs, which one would you choose? In order to get people to move to take the job in Stinkville, there would need to be a sizable difference in the wage – a compensating wage differential.[7]

Local Labor Shortfalls

One consequence of workers being able to move to different places is that some locations may find it difficult to get sufficient workers to provide their population with medical care. If a location is not attractive enough (relative to other options) in terms of its wage and amenity package, then it may be perpetually understaffed. For example, according to the National Advisory Committee on Rural Health and Human Services (2011) there were roughly half as many primary care physicians per person in rural areas than in urban areas in 2010. In 2019, a survey of rural Americans found that just over 25 percent of them had needed healthcare in the past few years but did not get it (NPR/Robert Wood Johnson Foundation/Harvard T.H. Chan School of Public Health 2019).

---

[7] When dealing with locational choice, property values also capture some of the value of amenities along with wages, making things a bit more nuanced. In the above example, Stinkville would also likely have much more affordable property than Denver. The interplay of amenities, wages and property values is a classic topic in a different field of economics, urban economics, and is discussed by Roback (1982).

This is in spite of programs specifically designed to attract providers to underserved areas. The National Health Services Corps (NHSC) is a program that has been active since the 1970s. In exchange for working in a health professional shortage area, the NHSC pays the student loans of the participants. For example, via one of the NHSC programs "Students to Service," up to $120,000 in loans can be paid off over 4 years. Even with large financial incentives like the NHSC it is difficult to get adequate staffing in some locations.

Brain Drain

Another consequence of mobile labor is that large differentials in the wage and amenity packages between locations can cause a large portion of a local labor force to out-migrate continuously. This can happen to such an extent that the location subject to out-migration is left with little to no labor force while continuously supplying new labor elsewhere, a phenomenon sometimes referred to as "brain drain." An example of this is nurses trained in the Philippines. As of 2004, 85 percent of purses trained in the Philippines were working internationally (i.e. somewhere that was not the Philippines), and in 2001, roughly a quarter of the active nurses in Philippine hospitals left for employment elsewhere.[8]

Licenses

Another feature of the healthcare labor force is that most of the jobs performed by this labor force require some form of license to be able to be employed. Licenses do two important things, which trade off against each other. On one hand, licenses provide a minimum quality level. In order to participate in healthcare provision, you need to be able to meet the minimum qualifications to obtain a license.[9] At the same time, licenses also serve as a barrier to entry into a labor market, only those with licenses are allowed in.

So, when licensing requirements are more stringent, the baseline (and also average) level of quality in the labor force is higher, but this comes at the cost of having less labor available. Likewise, licensing requirements can be made less stringent, which expands the pool of available labor at the cost of the baseline (and also average) level of quality being lower.

---

[8] These numbers come from Aiken et al. (2004), who also provide a deeper discussion of international nursing flows.

[9] A famous joke that illustrates licenses operating as a floor on quality: "What do you call someone who almost failed their medical school exams but didn't? Doctor."

The Labor Market

The labor market is typically thought to be determined by interaction between buyers and sellers. The workers (who are the sellers) have a supply of labor, and the employers (who are the buyers) have a demand for labor. The intersection of supply and demand is the equilibrium.

The equilibrium determines the amount of labor provided (in hours) and the price of labor (the wage). In the discussion to follow, consider the wage as a stand-in for the full compensation package (i.e. the wage as well as the value of any benefits). An example of a labor market is shown in Figure 7.3.

When firms want to hire more labor, the elasticity of labor supply (i.e. the steepness of the supply curve) will be very important. Increasing demand for labor (i.e. shifting out the demand curve) will make labor much more expensive when supply is inelastic (steep, shown in Figure 7.4A) as compared to when it is elastic (flat, shown in Figure 7.4B).

The elasticity of labor supply will depend in part on how easy it is to find that type of labor. For some workers, it is easy to find lots of hours at a single prevalent wage. These are most commonly the types of workers that can work across sectors. For production of medical care, this includes the non-healthcare labor force. As the type of labor becomes harder to come by, we would expect the labor supply to become more inelastic: in order to attract more hours of labor an employer will need to ramp up compensation to a greater degree. The rarer the worker, the more leverage the worker has with regards to bargaining for higher compensation.

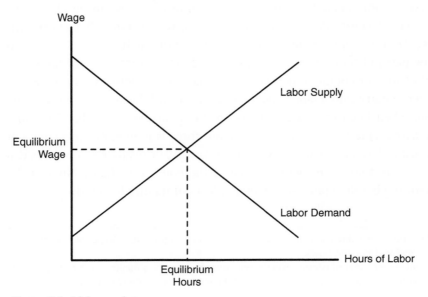

Figure 7.3 A labor market

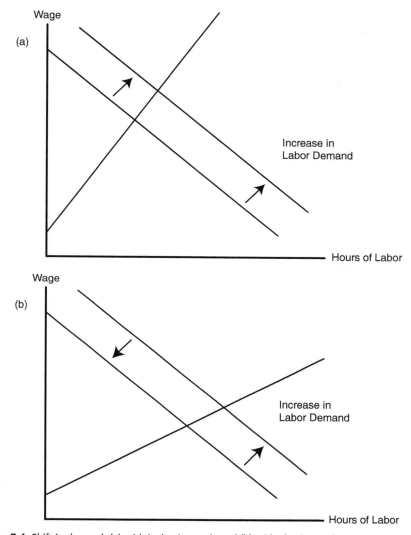

Figure 7.4 Shift in demand. (a) with inelastic supply and (b) with elastic supply

Market Concentration

Rarity of labor creates bargaining power, but so does rarity of employers. If an information technology specialist or a custodian is given a job offer from a physician firm (such as a medical practice or a hospital) that is below what is being offered in the wider market, then it is very easy for them to find employment elsewhere. There will be many employers across many sectors that want their labor.

As the number of employers for a given type of labor shrinks and, importantly, as it shrinks relative to the number of potential workers, the workers have fewer options to turn to if they do not like a job offer. Market concentration of employers (fewer employers controlling more of a market) increases the bargaining power of employers and pushes down worker compensation.

Monopsony

The most extreme case is a *monoposony* or a single employer in a market for a given type of labor. This exists (or comes close to existing) for certain types of specialized labor. For example, nurses with training to work in pediatric hospitals are specialized and there may be only one pediatric hospital in a given city. Unless these nurses are willing to relocate, the job offer that they get from a pediatric hospital might be the only possibility for employment for their specific skillset.

Self-Assessment

1. Why are hours used as the relevant measure of labor as an input in production as opposed to the number of people?
2. Physicians exit the labor force by dying, as dead people no longer work. But what if dead physicians could come back as ghosts and continue practicing medicine? How would this impact the number of hours of physician labor available? What if the ghost physicians could only speak to existing doctors and make recommendations?
3. Explain how it is possible for two people with the exact same capabilities and educational opportunities to make different choices with regards to how much education to obtain.
4. Explain how it is possible for two workers with the exact same skills and the exact same job offers (two different jobs in two different cities) to choose to work in different cities.
5. If you ran a hospital and needed to quickly expand the number of nurses in your hospital, what types of policies could you enact to do so? How would these policies differ if you ran a city and needed to quickly expand the number of nurses in your city?
6. Imagine that anyone who worked in a hospital required additional specialized training just to be able to walk into the building. This training would require a two-month course of study, a qualifying exam, and would apply to everyone, including those who are not part of the healthcare labor force. How would this impact the compensation for the non-healthcare labor force workers employed by hospitals?

Supplement. Practical Economist Skills: Calculating Market Concentration

In this chapter, we discussed the idea of market concentration: that a more concentrated market (i.e. fewer buyers or sellers) gives more bargaining power to the side that has the concentration. But how do you tell when a market is concentrated? There are obvious cases such as a *monopoly* (one seller) or a *monopsony* (one buyer), but how do you tell the difference between all of the different degrees of concentration?

To help with this, economists have developed various measures of market concentration. One of the most commonly used is the Herfindahl–Hirschman Index (HHI). To calculate the HHI you need the percentage of the market that operates through each firm in that market, which is known as the market share. You then take the square of the market shares and add them all together. So the formula is:

$$HHI = \sum_i s_i^2$$

The HHI runs from 0 to 1, with 1 being a monopoly and 0 being perfect competition. Bigger numbers are more concentrated. To illustrate, a single firm with all the market would be:

$$HHI = 1^2 = 1$$

And two firms with equal half market share would be:

$$HHI = (0.5)^2 + (0.5)^2 = 0.25 + 0.25 = 0.5$$

Sometimes the HHI is calculated using the market share as percentage written as a number between 0 and 100 as opposed to a number between 0 and 1. This just changes the scaling on the HHI to running between 0 and 10,000 as opposed to between 0 and 1. A HHI of 0.5032 would be changed to a HHI of 5,032. The information would be the same, bigger is more concentrated.

The Kaiser Family Foundation reports HHIs for large group health insurance markets (you can see the data for yourself here: www.kff.org/other/state-indicator/large-group-insurance-market-competition). For 2019, the most concentrated state was Alabama with a HHI of 8,950 (this is one insurer with almost 95 percent market share). On the other end of the spectrum is New York with the lowest state HHI in this market of 1,176. The largest insurer in New York in 2019 had around 16 percent market share, and New York has seven insurers with over 5 percent market share.

Providers and Incentives

As discussed in Chapter 1, in general humans will try to make choices that make them as happy as possible given their constraints. The choices available, and the costs associated with the choices can change, which will in turn influence human decision-making. Changes in circumstances which change the perceived costs or benefits of different choices can be referred to as *incentives*. If something changes that makes a choice more attractive, then that choice has been *incentivized*, and, if something changes that makes a choice less attractive, then that choice has been *disincentivized*.

In this section of the book, we are discussing providers of medical care, and importantly, these providers are humans. When you give a provider an incentive, that incentive has the potential to change the provider's behavior. This chapter will explore some of the big incentives at play and how they potentially influence provider behavior, sometimes in undesirable ways.

How You Pay People Matters

One of the most common ways to incentivize someone to do something is to pay them to do it. Payment is an excellent incentive. Telling my kids to clean their rooms "because I said so" is not nearly as effective as offering them money in exchange for cleaning their rooms.[1] That said, how the money is paid out can also be an incentive itself. Consider these alternative payment schemes:

1. When your room is clean, you can get a dollar.
2. You get a dollar for cleaning your room for 5 minutes.
3. You get a dollar for each 20 things that you put away.

Each of these schemes creates a slightly different incentive.[2] Scheme 1 creates an incentive to clean the room as quickly as possible, and to do

---

[1] I am not claiming that this is good or bad parenting practice, just that it is effective. This isn't a book on parenting, stop judging me.

[2] It is not guaranteed that any of these incentives will be sufficient to change behavior, it is possible that the payment will not be enough to convince my kids to clean at all.

the minimum quality job that will qualify for payment. Using scheme 1 increases the likelihood that my kids will shove all of their toys into the closet and hope that I do not look there. Scheme 2 creates an incentive to clean the room as slowly as possible, and, scheme 3, if known about in advance, creates an incentive to make the biggest mess with as many small things to put away as possible.

Similar incentives can exist with regards to how you pay healthcare providers. Having payment set up under different schemes can create powerful incentives to practice in different ways.

Fee for Service vs. Salary

Let's consider two alternative ways of paying providers. The first is "fee-for-service" where the provider will collect a payment for each thing that they do. A fee-for-service payment scheme can be quite complex, with different payment amounts for each different type of procedure performed. For simplicity, we can for the moment think about fee-for-service as the provider being paid a flat amount for each provider visit that they produce. The second payment scheme is "salary." Under this scheme the provider is paid a flat amount for working a fixed amount of time. Salaries are commonly paid per year but could be paid over other timeframes such as a daily or weekly salary.

These two pay schemes present very different incentives for how to behave. Under fee-for-service, a provider is paid more when they do more, so their incentive is to do as much as possible as quickly as possible. Producing five provider visits in an hour will pay more than producing four provider visits in an hour and producing six in an hour will pay even more. There is likewise an incentive to work more hours, an additional hour of work will yield more provider visits and more pay.

On the other hand, salary provides no such incentive. A provider paid via salary has an incentive to do the least amount of work that will allow them to collect their salary. Caring for an additional patient will not increase compensation. There is also no incentive to work any additional hours. On an annual salary, an 8-hour workday pays the same as a 10-hour workday which pays the same as a 5-hour workday where you watch cat videos for two of them (if you can get away with it).

Suppose that we observed some physicians paid via fee-for-service, and some paid via salary. We also observed that the fee-for-service physicians saw more patents in a day, that the visits were shorter, and that they worked more hours. Likewise, the salaried physicians saw fewer patients in a day, that the visits were longer, and that they worked fewer hours. Can we say that this is all due to the payment schemes?

Selection into Jobs

The answer is "no." While payment schemes causing behavior would be a theory that fits the facts presented, there are other theories that could also explain some, if not all of the pattern. The leading alternative theory would be one where there are different types of providers, those who like to work quickly and those who like to work slowly. The quick workers have a keen eye for diagnosis and can move through patients very fast. The slow workers on the other hand like to think deeply and get to know patients and prefer to work at a more leisurely pace. If you were a quick worker looking for a job, would you prefer a fee-for-service or a salary contract? If you were a slow worker looking for a job, would you prefer a fee-for-service or a salary contract?

In this situation, the quick workers would select jobs that pay fee-for-service and the slow workers would select jobs that pay salaries. It would not be that the incentives change the behavior of the providers, but that the incentives attract providers with different working styles and skillsets. In this case, paying everyone with the same pay scheme would not change the number of patients seen, as the differences in outcomes across the pay schemes would be due to bunching of different worker types into different contracts, not any effect of the contracts themselves. We now have two theories that would fit the facts, and the truth could be one, the other, or a little bit of both.

Evidence on Provider Pay Schemes

In order to figure out how exactly pay schemes influence provider behavior, one would need to run a study. Fortunately, some have already been done, so we can skip designing one and jump straight to the results. Hickson, Altemeier, and Perrin (1987) took 18 pediatric residents working 2.5 hour shifts at a pediatrics clinic and broke them into pairs. Then one person in each pair was (based on a coin flip) paid $2 per patient visit, and the other was paid $20 per month. The fee-for-service group averaged 3.69 visits per patient and the salaried group averaged 2.83 visits per patient.[3] This shows that pay schemes do matter (at least to pediatric residents) for determining practice behavior.

A more recent quasi-experiment by Cadena and Smith (2022) looked at a community health center that switched from salary to fee-for-service compensation. This allowed them to observe what happens when individual workers switched from one pay scheme to another. When the authors compared all provider-months (one provider working for one month),

---

[3] The average number of visits per patient were statistically different from each other.

the provider-months which were fee-for-service had 18 percent more patient encounters than those which were salary. However, the authors also showed that a substantial portion of this difference was due to more productive providers switching to fee-for-service as soon as possible, and less productive providers finding ways to delay and stay on salary as long as possible (meaning that the 18 percent difference was partially due to the fee-for-service group containing more provider-months from high productivity providers). When they looked at the same providers before and then after the change from salary to fee-for-service, the providers had around 5 percent more patient encounters when they were paid via fee-for-service as opposed to paid via salary. This study showed that while payment scheme is important for determining practice behavior, selection of workers is substantial and can throw off estimates based on comparisons of raw averages.

Other Payment Schemes

Fee-for-service and salary are by no means the only payment schemes that exist. You can pay people with a wide array of payment schemes with a great deal of complexity. We'll return to this idea again in Chapter 13 when we discuss *managed care*, a type of health insurance that tries to influence provider behavior in many ways, including via how providers are paid.

Before moving on, let's discuss one more payment scheme, because it's a popular one: profit sharing. If you give workers a share of profits, then theoretically, this gives them an incentive to behave in such a way that will maximize firm profits. Workers won't want to do too little (as they might under salary) and they won't want to do too much (as they might under fee-for-service), putting them into a sweet spot where they want to do just the right amount to maximize profits. These sorts of incentives work well only to the extent that a single worker's behavior actually influences profits. The more that workers feel like their work actually matters for profits, the more profit sharing will improve firm profits, and the less workers feel like their work actually matters for profits, the less profit sharing will make a difference.

Size of the Firm

Another source of incentives can be the size of the firm that you are working for. Put the same worker into a larger or smaller firm and you might get different behavior from them. This has to do with workers' tendency to *shirk* or goof off. When given an opportunity to spend some work time on non-work activities without penalty, people will tend to take it. If I gave you an hour to work on an assignment, would you spend some of the time goofing off on your phone? Would how much time you spend goofing off change if I left you alone in a room by yourself?[4] Would your answer change if I left someone in the room to watch you work?

The same can be true of healthcare providers. If you give a provider 20 minutes alone to think about a case, how much of that time will be spent thinking about the case and how much will be spent thinking about their grocery shopping for the week? The answer might depend on a number of things, including if the time is monitored.

Where the size of a firm comes into play has to do with this idea of monitoring. How easy it is to tell if a worker is not pulling their weight is in part determined by how large the firm is. If there is a two-person medical practice and the practice isn't seeing enough patients to break even, and one of the physicians is spending a lot of time in each visit talking about baseball, then it is pretty easy to tell what is happening. As firms get larger and larger, it becomes more and more difficult (and costly) to tell where shirking is occurring (if it is occurring at all).

This is for a few reasons. The first is that it is harder to detect shirking in a larger firm. In the firm of two mentioned above, one person might be responsible for one half of all of the work, making it obvious when the work isn't getting done. In a firm of 500, that same worker might be responsible for 1/500 of the work, making it far more difficult to detect if there is a slowdown from a single shirker. This is similar to why it much easier to do an online quiz for "which Harry Potter house do you belong in?" without the professor noticing when you are sitting in a packed 500-person lecture hall than if you are in a ten person discussion group. In the first situation, you are responsible for a scant 1/500 of the class participation, whereas in the other situation you are responsible for 1/10.[5]

A second reason is that the more workers you have to monitor, the more costly it becomes to monitor them. Keeping track of two workers is simpler than keeping track of 10, which is simpler than keeping track of 500. Also, at some point, you need to monitor the workers you have monitoring your other workers, because they might themselves shirk, and so on, which increases the cost of monitoring as the size of the firm increases.[6]

---

[4] While reading this chapter, how many times have you checked your phone?

[5] I got Hufflepuff. I'm writing this in an office by myself, it's very easy to shirk.

[6] A great example of this phenomenon of monitors monitoring monitors can be found in Seuss (1973).

Induced Demand

There are also situations where providers have an incentive to convince patients to purchase care that is not in the patient's best interest. This does not mean that the care is necessarily bad from a health perspective, but that the care is not in the patient's best financial interest. If we go back to the profit maximization for a provider-firm from Chapter 6, we can see that this type of behavior would be consistent with how we would expect a provider-firm to act. The firm will maximize profits so long as they are helping people. If the definition of "helping" is limited to help with regards to health and not with regards to finances, then we have a situation where provider firms will attempt to sell patients care that is not in their financial best interest, to *induce demand*.

The Principal–Agent Problem

Induced demand falls under a category of misaligned incentives known as the "principal–agent problem." The "principal" hires an "agent" to act on their behalf. There is usually some skill or expertise that the agent has that the principal does not, which is why they have been hired. Issues arise when the agent has a different set of incentives than the principal, which can lead to the agent acting in a way that the principal would not have acted had they been their own agent.

A classic example of a principal–agent problem is hiring a real estate agent. You hire a real estate agent to sell your house. Your objective is to get the highest price possible for your house. The real estate agent is paid a percentage of the sale, which creates an alignment of incentives: the real estate agent makes more money when the sale is for a higher price. The problem arises when the real estate agent is selling more than one house (which they usually are). The agent also has an incentive to sell quickly and move on to selling the next house. Not putting in the effort for a slightly higher price in order to sell additional houses may make the real estate agent more money than getting the absolute highest price for each house. There is now a situation where the agent is incentivized to act contrary to the principal's best interest.

Induced Demand as a Principal–Agent Problem

Demand inducement fits the framework of a principal–agent problem and is not unique to healthcare settings. Automobile mechanics are also in situations where demand inducement could arise. Suppose that I go into a mechanic to have my car tuned up: I want an oil change, a tire rotation, and the car checked out. I do not know very much about cars, so I hire the mechanic to act on my behalf and keep my care running nicely.

The mechanic can recommend additional work to be done on the car. She could say to me "your thingamajig is showing some signs of wear and should probably be replaced," even if the car component in question is most likely good for another 10,000 miles. The point is that I don't know, and I rely on the mechanic's expertise to make decisions. Replacing the thingamajig might be the right call, but it might also be overly cautious and overly expensive. My incentive is to keep my car running as cost-effectively as possible, and the mechanic's incentive is to keep my car running while making as much money as possible. Her incentive might get her to convince me to purchase additional parts and services that are not in my financial best interest.

This example carries over to healthcare providers. If a provider is paid via fee-for-service, then they may recommend additional care that is not necessarily in my financial best interest. If my surgeon says that she wants to see me for repeated follow-up appointments every 2 weeks, I will most likely come as recommended, even if this is actually overly cautious, and once every 4 weeks would be sufficient. I rely on the surgeon's expertise to make my decision, and she might have a financial incentive to get me to purchase more care than is truly necessary.

One trouble with demand inducement is that it is very difficult to detect with certainty. If you were to ask a provider if additional care is necessary or if it is just lining their pockets, it is extremely unlikely that the provider would say "oh boy, you got me, you don't really need that, good job." It is much more likely that they would tell you something about how "in their professional opinion, yes, the care is needed."

Evidence on Induced Demand

Do providers engage in demand inducement? One of the best pieces of evidence on this question is an *audit study* by Currie, Lin, and Meng (2014). An audit study has many similarities to a randomized experiment but is not exactly the same. In an audit, teams of actors (the auditors) are sent to interact with real people who do not know that it is an audit and not a "real" transaction. The auditors are trained to behave identically except for one thing that they do differently, which is the behavior being studied. They go in random order and how the real people respond is tracked. The difference in the responses of the real people is then attributed to the one thing that the auditors did differently.[7]

---

[7] The quality of an audit is thus dependent on how good a job the auditors do at being identical other than the behavior being studied, as well as dependent on the real people

In Currie, Lin, and Meng's study, actors were sent to see physicians in Chinese hospitals with pretend symptoms. The pretend symptoms were mild and did not indicate whether the ailment was bacterial or viral in nature, meaning that antibiotics, which only treat bacterial infections were not necessarily correct (the authors argued that prescribing antibiotics in this case was inappropriate).

The key thing to understand about Chinese hospitals at the time is that though physicians were paid via salary, they also received additional payments based on the value of drugs sold from the hospital that they had prescribed, creating an incentive to induce demand. Here's how the audit study got at this behavior: while one set of auditors presented the set of vague symptoms, a second set of auditors presented the same symptoms but at some point during the visit also said that they planned to purchase any prescriptions at a drug store, which indicated that their purchase would not go through the hospital and would not make the physician any additional money.

When the auditor provided the vague symptoms but did not indicate where they would buy any drugs, the physicians prescribed antibiotics 55 percent of the time. When the auditor provided the vague symptoms but indicated that they would buy the drugs elsewhere, the physicians prescribed antibiotics 10 percent of the time. The financial incentive accounted for a 45 percentage point change in the rate of prescribing antibiotics.

Fee Splitting

Another form of demand inducement is *fee splitting*, where a provider sends a patient to another actor in the market such as a different provider, or to a specific drug company (by prescribing their drug), and the other actor in the market sends back money. This is also known as a *kickback*. In this situation, the provider has a financial incentive to induce demand for someone else (i.e. the actor sending the kickback).

Fee splitting arrangements are deemed unethical by the American Medical Association (American Medical Association Code of Medical Ethics Opinion 11.3.4) and are prohibited by their ethical code. However, this does not prevent organizations from engaging in activities that are not fee splitting, but that generate similar incentives. If I am a pharmaceutical company, I

---

not knowing that it's an audit. Audits have been famously used to detect discrimination in places such as the housing and lending markets (see e.g. Yinger 1986 or Ross and Yinger 2002).

am not allowed to pay physicians who prescribe my drugs. What I can do is take my top 10,000 prescribing physicians and invite them to a conference that I sponsor in a tropical location and pay them speaking fees for doing so. This would not technically be fee splitting but creates many of the same incentives.

There is associational evidence that providers that receive these types of benefits from pharmaceutical companies prescribe more of the drugs made by those companies. For example, Nguyen, Bradford, and Simon (2019) showed that physicians receiving payments (or other transfers of value) that were intended to help promote the pharmaceuticals tended to prescribe more of those drugs. This study focused on opioids, with the strongest associations existing for hydrocodone and oxycodone, but there are numerous other studies that look at payments for other types of pharmaceuticals.[8]

Self-Referral

A third form of demand inducement is referring patients to a business that you have a financial stake in, known as *self-referral*. Self-referral largely deals with ownership and investments. If a physician is a part owner of an imaging center (a facility that does various types of medical scans such as X-rays, MRIs and CT scans) and sends all of their patients to that facility, then they are creating demand for themselves. Self-referral is not allowed in the United States for a wide array of service types when the patient is paid for by Medicare or Medicaid. These provisions are known as the Stark Law, which prohibits these types of arrangements from being eligible for payment (see Section 1877 of the Social Security Act).

These arrangements can still exist under other circumstances and create a powerful financial incentive to change practice behaviors. For example, Mitchell (2008) documented a case where a new physician-owned specialty hospital opened in a city. She compared eventual physician-owners' to eventual physician-non-owners' practice patterns before and after the opening of the hospital. Compared to the non-owners, the owners of the hospital increased their utilization rate of more complicated (and expensive) surgery as well as their utilization rate of more complicated (and expensive) scans, while decreasing their utilization rate of less expensive substitutes.

---

[8] See for example Datta and Dave (2017), DeJong et al. (2016), Perlis and Perlis (2016), and Rhee and Ross (2019).

Self-Assessment

....

1. Fee-for-service and salary compensation schemes create incentives to provide different quantities of care. Would they create an incentive for quality differences? Why or why not?

2. Consider the following strategy: "If you want to find out if your workers are goofing off, just give them profit sharing and see if profits go up." Under what circumstances would this work well? Under what circumstances would this not work well?

3. Consider the following statement: "The more you trust your agent, the more susceptible you are to a principal–agent problem." Do you agree? Why or why not?

4. If you wanted to run an audit study in the United States to detect demand inducement, what would your study look like? Bonus throwback to the Chapter 5 supplement: who would need to approve your study before it could go forward?

5. Come up with an arrangement that is not fee splitting, but that still generates similar incentives for a provider.

6. Would switching all providers from fee-for-service to salary eliminate all forms of demand inducement? Why or why not?

Supplement. Cognitive Biases and Behavioral Economics

This chapter has focused on how incentives can influence provider behavior. The study of behavioral changes based on incentives is a classic topic in economics. A related, and more recent area of study recognizes that the human brain has certain baked in cognitive biases that can be taken advantage of in order to influence behavior. This area of economics is known as *behavioral economics* and has connections to psychology and neuroscience. For a nice introduction to many (but certainly not all) of the ideas from behavioral economics, I would recommend the 2008 book *Nudge: Improving Decisions about Health, Wealth and Happiness* by Richard H. Thaler and Cass R. Sunstein.

One such cognitive bias is that individuals tend to place additional weight on options that are viewed as the "social norm." The desire to be like one's peers can be used to influence individual behavior. The Denver Water Department uses this strategy. During the summer they send letters comparing your water usage to that of your peers, presumably in order to get you to use less water. I infer this from the letters I got having a smiley face when I was using below the neighborhood water average the month before and a frowny face when I was using above the neighborhood water average the month before.

These types of behavioral economic interventions can be used to influence healthcare providers as well. Meeker et al. (2016) conduced a randomized trial where they sent some but not all primary care physicians in several medical practices e-mails that compared their antibiotic prescribing rates to "top-performing peers" with the lowest antibiotic prescribing rates. This e-mail intervention decreased antibiotic utilization by slightly over 5 percent.

9 | Hospitals

The United States had approximately 4.1 trillion dollars in health expenditures in 2020 (that's a little over 19.5 percent of the 2020 US GDP). Of those 4.1 trillion dollars, 31 percent, or almost 1.3 trillion dollars were spent in hospitals.[1] That is a tremendous amount of resources. In this chapter, we will explore how those resources are allocated. This will be determined by how hospitals operate, which is far more complicated than the operation of a smaller provider-firm. A hospital's operations will be steered by a number of actors, each with their own set of objectives and their own ways of exerting influence.

For-Profit and Not-for-Profit Hospitals

To start, we can think about two different classifications of hospitals, *for-profit* hospitals and *not-for-profit* hospitals. While the difference between these classifications may seem like for-profit hospitals make profits and not-for-profit hospitals do not, it is a bit more subtle. Both types of hospitals are able to make profits from an economist's point of view: they both can bring in revenues over and above their costs. The difference has to do with what they can do with those profits. For-profit hospitals can pay those profits out directly to investors or ownership of the hospital. Not-for-profit hospitals cannot pay out profits and need to find something else to do with them. In exchange for this restriction, not-for-profit hospitals enjoy certain tax advantages.[2]

The distinction between for-profit and not-for-profit also makes changes in the composition of stakeholders interested in how the hospital operates. This comes from the presence or absence of certain types stakeholders such as investors or charitable donors, but also in the composition of people within each stakeholder type that is present in both for-profit and not-for-profit

---

[1] These numbers are from Kurani et al. (2022), who provide various descriptive statistics based on the National Health Expenditure data from the Centers for Medicare and Medicaid Services.

[2] The main tax advantage is being exempt from the majority of federal, state, and local taxes. These benefits are usually tied to some additional requirements for the hospital, such as using some hospital resources for public services.

settings. For example, the senior leadership of a for-profit hospital is commonly selected by the shareholders, this is different than in a not-for-profit hospital where the senior leadership is chosen through different means such as by the board of a charitable organization, or by a board of trustees. The types of leaders preferred by and chosen by these different entities may exert influence on a hospital's operations in systematically different ways.

Day-to-Day Operation of a Hospital

To understand hospital behavior, we need to understand who exerts influence over the hospital's decision-making process. Typically, when we think of a person, they will make decisions based on their individual preferences and constraints, and when we think of a firm they will make decisions based on their individual technology and input prices. Hospitals present a somewhat unique blend of individual and firm decision-making processes. This has to do with who is in charge, because the answer is different depending on the decision that is being made.

Hospitals typically have two separate authority structures. The first looks a lot like a typical firm's authority structure: there are workers who report to their supervisors and managers, who report to their supervisors and managers up the chain to senior leadership, where the ultimate decision-making power will rest with an executive (either an individual or a board). The workers will be broken into different departments (and possibly sub-departments) each with their own operational responsibilities. We will refer to these workers as the *line staff*. Line staff will handle all operations within the hospital, such as delivering treatments and medicines, keeping technology running, keeping track of medical bills, and so forth.

Though the line staff will be responsible for carrying out the actions that make up patient care, any decisions related to how to care for a patient such as which treatments to give to a patient and when, are handled through a siloed and separate authority structure. This structure includes any practicing physicians and can also include other providers with the authority to direct care such as nurse practitioners, and is referred to as the *medical staff*. The medical staff has their own hierarchy, and while employed by the hospital (or employed by a separate firm that contracts with the hospital) the hospital cannot tell them how to practice medicine. The medical staff have medical licenses and the hospital does not.[3]

---

[3] It is illegal for an individual or a corporation to hire a physician to practice medicine "on their behalf," this is referred to as "corporate practice of medicine." What this means is

These two authority structures thus influence the daily operations of the hospital in different ways. The hospital leadership will decide things like how many X-ray machines to have in operation, how many nurses and technicians to have on duty, and what will be served in the cafeteria. However, the medical staff will make all of the decisions as to how those resources are to be used for patient care: if a patient needs to have an X-ray, which medicines the nurses should administer, and which (if any) restrictions on foods that a patient is permitted to be served should be applied.

Who Has Influence over Resource Allocation?

A hospital is thus a very large firm that will make considerable profits (in the economic sense of revenues greater than costs). The question will then be, how should these profits be spent? Should some of them be paid out to shareholders? If so, how much? And for the profits not paid out (which is all the profits in a not-for-profit hospital), how should they be spent?

For each hospital, there are going to be different parties who have different opinions as to how these questions should be answered. Each party is going to want something (or several things), and each party is going to have different ways of exerting influence to try to get what they want. There is obviously a lot of variability in the exact circumstances and power dynamics from hospital to hospital, so what follows is meant to be a general overview of broad categories of players.

Hospital Leadership

In terms of who has the authority to direct resources that are not a direct decision about the care of a patient, the leadership of the hospital usually is the ultimate decision-maker. If a hospital has profit to spend, the leadership can decide whether to spend it on new diagnostic equipment, upgrades to the hospital computer systems, additional staff, or any number of possibilities. This decision will be made in part on the basis of what leadership thinks the hospital's needs are, but also in part on the basis of what leadership thinks the hospital's goals are. This gives the leadership considerable discretion and brings a very human element into the resource allocation decision process.

To illustrate a bit more concretely, consider a 20 million dollar chunk of a hospital's discretionary budget. Should this money be spent on technology

---

that for practice of medicine to be legal, a physician must be allowed to follow their own best medical judgement and not be directed by a non-licensed entity.

upgrades, which would improve the quality of care that can be provided by the hospital, or should it be spent on capacity upgrades, which would improve the quantity of care that can be provided by the hospital? The decision will be made by hospital leadership, and the "correct" answer will be specific to the individual preferences of those in charge. So, in the discussions to follow, many of the methods for steering hospital resources will center around convincing (or compelling) hospital leadership to spend resources in the way that your party would like them to be spent.

The Medical Staff

The medical staff is part of the hospital's workforce. As with any workforce they will want hospital resources to be spent on two different things: better pay for them and better features of their job. Pay is easy to understand: all else equal, a worker will want to be paid more to do the same job. I would rather be paid $5 to make a hamburger than be paid $2 to make a hamburger.

The concept of better features of a job is a little less singular. While some job features, such as health insurance and retirement contributions, are commonly part of a "compensation package," and can be easily thought of in terms of their cash value, the medical staff will want hospital resources to be spent on anything that brings them satisfaction on the job. So along with traditional benefits, this can include job "perks."[4] This might include things that improve day-to-day quality of life such as better parking spaces or better food in the cafeteria. It can also include things that enable the medical staff to provide higher quality care, such as newer and better medical equipment.[5]

In order to get the hospital leadership to direct resources in their desired way, the medical staff has considerable leverage. Patient care within a hospital is directed by the medical staff, so if they tell the hospital leadership that certain equipment or other resources are needed for said care, it may be less effort to just get the equipment than to pay to evaluate whether or not the claim that the equipment is needed is warranted. Also, as the medical staff operates under their own authority, and often under a contract

---

[4] You can think of perks in terms of compensating wage differentials (from Chapter 7). If the item or service in question is something that a worker would be willing to accept less pay to get, then it is something that the medical staff would want to have the hospital spend resources on.

[5] We don't need to know exactly why medical staff want better technology, just that this is something that they want the hospital to spend resources on. Whether they want a surgical laser because of its increased precision, or they want a surgical laser because it's fun to shoot lasers (or both) is irrelevant.

between the hospital and a physician group, the physicians create a more concentrated supply of physician labor, increasing their bargaining power when negotiating compensation.

This is not to claim that the medical staff is always a unified front. Different departments may want different hospital investments: the heart surgeons may want updated electrocardiograms (heart monitors), whereas the radiologists may want new X-ray machines. Larger departments that account for a larger portion of hospital operations will likely have more clout with leadership and will be better at steering resources as they see fit, whereas smaller departments that make up a smaller portion of hospital operations will likely have less clout.

The Line Staff

The line staff will have many of the same wants as the medical staff: pay and desirable job characteristics. Most of the differences between what the medical and line staff push for will be with regards to job characteristics. While many characteristics such as health insurance, parking and coffee availability are common across groups the quality of things like equipment will depend on which equipment the specific types of staff uses. The information technology department is unlikely to care about easier to use medical equipment and the nursing staff is unlikely to care about better tools for facility maintenance.

The line staff also has a different relationship with hospital leadership than the medical staff. The line staff is employed as part of the authority structure that reports up to hospital leadership which changes the power dynamic. There is also a greater diversity of job type with regards to the line staff: while the medical staff is almost singularly concerned with directing patient care, the line staff covers a wide swath of different services, not all of which are directly involved in caregiving. This makes it less common (but not impossible) that the line staff uniformly tries to get resources directed to the same thing. Lastly, the medical staff has a form of collective bargaining with the hospital baked in as they often contract with the hospital as a single unit and handle their individual employment internally. On the other hand, the line staff is hired directly by the hospital and can only collectively bargain to the extent that they are able to form or join unions.

Patients

Patients are consumers of medical care from the hospital. They want two things: less expensive care, and higher quality care. We need to be a bit careful when defining the wants of patients. When I say "patients want less expensive care" I am not saying patients want care that is less expensive due to sacrificing quality.[6] What I mean is that for the exact same care, patients would prefer to spend less money than to spend more money. Likewise, when I say "patients want higher quality care" I am not saying patients want to pay more to get that quality.[7] What I mean is that for the same price, patients would prefer to get higher quality care.

Patients' desire for a lower price refers to the price that they pay out-of-pocket, not the "sticker price" of the care.[8] This means that patients will look for less expensive care only to the extent that they bear responsibility for paying. Therefore, the details of a patient's health insurance plan with regards to hospital care will be one of the largest determinants of the price that they face, and of primary concern when patients look to get the best price by shopping around between hospitals. For example, if I have an insurance plan for which every hospital visit has the exact same flat copay, then I have no incentive to shop around based on price whatsoever, the price will be the exact same everywhere and I will only care about getting the best quality possible.[9]

With regards to hospital quality, patients will shop based on quality to the extent that they are capable of perceiving quality. This is somewhat difficult, because the average patient does not have a sophisticated understanding of what factors truly matter for patient outcomes. As such, they often have to rely on intermediaries who provide summary quality information. For example, using a quasi-experiment that compared nursing homes just under and just over a given star rating (on a five-star scale), Perraillon et al. (2019) showed that facilities with higher star ratings from a comparison website attracted more patients.[10] Patients may also shop based on non-care related quality such as creature comforts offered at the hospital, this is discussed more in Chapter 12.

---

[6] That is not to say that people will never sacrifice quality for a lower price, people do this all the time, even for medical care. It is just that sacrificing one for the other is a tradeoff, whereas same quality with a lower price is just plain desirable.

[7] Again, this is not to say that people will never spend more for quality, people do this all the time for medical care. Again, sacrificing one for the other is a tradeoff, whereas paying the same price for a higher quality is just plain desirable.

[8] Chapter 12 provides a deeper discussion on the different prices experienced by different parties within the healthcare sector.

[9] Health insurance can also be a powerful price factor for patients by covering care in some but not in other hospitals. The hospitals that are covered (referred to as being "in-network") will have much less expensive care from the patient's perspective than the hospitals that are not covered (referred to as being "out-of-network"). This concept is explored more in Chapter 13.

[10] This is not unique to nursing homes, there is work showing similar behavior for hospitals. For example, Varkevisser et al. (2012) found increased demand for hospitals with higher quality metrics. The design of the nursing home study is just a nice and simple example of summary quality signals steering patient behavior.

What patients want is for a hospital to spend its resources lowering prices (while maintaining quality) or increasing quality (while maintaining prices – or at least the prices that the patients pay out of their own pockets). How do patients influence hospital leadership to do this? The answer is by showing up. If one hospital is doing a better job than another in a way that is palpable to the patient population, then patients will try to go to the "better" hospital. This is sometimes referred to as "voting with your wallet" or "voting with your feet." Patients spend money (theirs and the insurance company's) in hospitals, and that signals to the hospital that patients like what that hospital is selling better than what other hospitals are selling.

Investors

Investors in a for-profit hospital want a return on their investment. They are periodically paid out *dividends*, or shares of the profits made by the hospital, and can sell their stake in the hospital for a personal profit if the hospital has become more valuable. As such, investors want a hospital that makes as much profit as possible, and a hospital that pays them out as large a share of those profits as possible. This is not to say that it is best for investors to have all profits paid out, spending some money on things like better staff or happier patients could lead to an even more profitable hospital in the long run.

Typically, investors push for their wants by influencing hospital leadership. In a for-profit hospital the hospital leadership (i.e. the Chief Executive Officer (CEO), Board of Directors, and/or other leadership positions) are appointed directly by or with significant input from the investors. Presumably, when appointing leadership investors will put additional weight on characteristics that they believe will further their own interests.

Donors

Donors to a hospital can steer resources within the hospital by making *contingent donations*. This means that money is given to the hospital with strings attached, usually as part of a donation agreement. The effectiveness of a donor at influencing a hospital will depend on how cleverly structured their donation agreement is, as in many cases it is somewhat easy for a hospital to move money around and spend a donation on whatever they want.

For example, if I were the CEO of the hospital, I might want some money to build a better parking garage (one that has room for my very expensive car). This garage would cost the hospital 5 million dollars. At the same time, the hospital might get a 5 million dollar donation that is to be used on new equipment for the hospital's cancer center. If the cancer center already had a 7 million dollar equipment budget, then I could move 5 million dollars out of the cancer center budget and into "CEO Friedson's Awesome Parking Garage Fund" and then put the donation of 5 million dollars into the cancer center budget. Now the donated money is paying for new cancer center equipment as required, but the donation has not actually changed the budget in a meaningful way. This is because money is *fungible* (can be moved around interchangeably). If the donor wanted an increase in the budget to the cancer center, then they would have had to word their donation agreement more carefully.

Hospital Size and Efficiency

One other concern when thinking about hospital resource allocation is how efficient a hospital is, this will help determine how much (if any) profit a hospital makes. Interestingly, the size of a firm (i.e. how much a firm produces) can have a strong influence on how efficient that firm is at producing. When a hospital (or any firm) becomes more efficient as it grows, or in other words has a decreasing cost per unit of medical care produced as it produces more medical care, it is said to have *economies of scale*. When the opposite is true, the hospital has an increasing cost per unit of medical care produced as it produces more medical care, it is said to have *diseconomies of scale*, or becomes less efficient as it grows. Whether an individual hospital exhibits economies or diseconomies of scale will be incredibly important to decisions around whether or not to expand.

Economies of Scale

There are several reasons why a hospital might have economies of scale. One of the most common sources is from *bulk purchasing*. Simply put, larger orders of inputs allow for lower per unit prices for those inputs. Buying one alcohol swab or one hypodermic needle is more expensive per swab or per needle than buying 100 of them, which is more expensive per swab or per needle than buying 10,000 of them. As a hospital (or any firm) buys their inputs in larger orders, they typically get a better price per unit in the order, pushing down their costs and increasing production efficiency.

Another source of economies of scale comes from *fixed costs*. Recall from Chapter 6 that fixed costs are costs of production that are paid once, such as the cost of purchasing a new X-ray machine. If that X-ray machine cost 100,000 dollars and I use it for 1,000 X-rays, then each X-ray has a fixed cost component of 100 dollars.[11] But, if I scale up and produce 100,000 X-rays, then each X-ray has a fixed cost component of only one dollar. The more I produce, the more units fixed costs are spread over, lowering the cost per unit of production.

A third source of economies of scale comes from gains from specialization (another throwback to Chapter 6). A larger firm creates more opportunities for specialization. For example, a smaller hospital may have a single combined intensive care unit (ICU). As a hospital expands it may see enough patients to support having a separate coronary care or cardiothoracic intensive care unit (a CCU or CTU) to specialize in post operative heart attack or heart surgery patients. In the smaller hospital, the ICU would take all of these patients, but as the hospital grows, the new CCU or CTU would allow the relevant medical and line staff to specialize and improve overall hospital productivity. This is not an exhaustive list of potential sources of economies of scale but should hopefully illustrate that these gains from expansion exist and have the potential to be non-trivial.

Diseconomies of Scale

There are also reasons why a hospital (or any firm) might have diseconomies of scale. One of the most common is difficulties in managing a larger and larger workforce. Chapter 8 discussed the concept of workers *shirking* responsibilities, a problem that becomes more pronounced the larger the firm. Larger firms also have more layers of management which become increasingly expensive as there are more people to manage, and larger firms can have larger bureaucratic barriers to making improvements.

Again, this is not an exhaustive list of potential sources of diseconomies of scale but should hopefully illustrate that these efficiency losses from expansion exist and have the potential to be non-trivial. Importantly, a hospital (or any firm) can have some sources of economies of scale and some sources of diseconomies of scale at the same time. The overall situation for the hospital will depend on what the balance of these forces is at any given time. It is possible that a hospital could have net economies of scale up to a point, after which the diseconomies of scale become dominant and it inefficient to grow any further.

---

[11] Each X-ray would also have a *variable cost* which includes things like the labor of the X-ray technician and the electricity used to run the machine. This cost would be paid every time the machine is used.

Economies/Diseconomies of Scope

Related to economies and diseconomies of scale is the concept of *economies and diseconomies of scope*. Whereas scale asks the question "do I become more or less efficient as I produce more?" scope asks the question "do I become more or less efficient as I produce a wider variety?" Economies of scope will depend on natural synergies (or discordance) between different types of services. For example, adding in better imaging services may improve the precision and speed with which certain surgeries can be performed, increasing the efficiency of production via economies of scope. On the other hand, adding different types of surgeries to a hospital's repertoire without increasing the number of surgeons might create a situation where increased task switching (via the same surgeon providing additional types of surgery) undoes some of the existing gains from specialization, reducing efficiency via diseconomies of scope.

Growing Despite Diseconomies?

It is tempting to say that a hospital's rule for growth should be to grow when it has economies of scale and stop growing when it has diseconomies of scale. This, however, loses sight of a firm's primary objective, which is to maximize profits. Economies and diseconomies of scale (or scope) deal with costs, which are only one part of calculating profits. The other part of profit is revenue. A hospital that has diseconomies of scale could still grow and increase profits if it can find a way to increase revenue in a way that outpaces the efficiency loss from diseconomies. For example, a bigger hospital may have the throughput to support the use of less frequently needed but also much more expensive services. On the whole, this could create a situation where a hospital could grow and become less efficient from a cost standpoint, but also more profitable as bigger ticket services are brought into the hospital's repertoire.

Hospital Competition

When there are multiple hospitals in a market they will compete with each other for business. This was alluded to earlier in the chapter when we discussed how patients exert influence over hospital allocation of resources.

Price Competition

Typically, when economists think about firms competing with one another their first thought is about competition based on prices. Firms will undercut each other, offering better deals to attract more business. Think about the hospitals in your area. What do you know about their prices relative to one another? Probably not a lot beyond a vague understanding of which hospitals are "nicer" or "less nice," and a general understanding that nicer things tend to be more expensive. Hospitals do not have a tremendous incentive to compete based on prices offered to patients, as patients rarely pay (or even see) the price of the care. Where hospitals do have an incentive to compete based on price is with insurance companies. Offering a better deal to an insurance company can get that company to push its patients to go to your hospital as the insurer may be able to save itself money by sending patients to the less expensive hospital.

Quality Competition

On the other hand, hospitals have a lot of incentive to compete based on quality. Patients with insurance have a large incentive to shop within hospitals covered by their plan based on quality. So, if a hospital is trying to attract business, it wants to offer deals on price to insurers, but wants to invest in and advertise quality directly to patients, especially quality that patients can discern.

To give a concrete example, one commonly used measure of quality is a high ranking in *US New and World Reports* list of "Best Hospitals." In Denver, one of the local hospitals, *National Jewish Health*, was ranked the number one respiratory hospital on this list. The hospital put a giant banner on the side of their hospital advertising this fact. In fact, I googled their hospital just now as I am writing this and what comes up is "National Jewish Health is the leading respiratory hospital..." When hospitals have ways to signal high quality to patients they want to do so.

Strategic Specialization

The above signaling behavior creates a situation where it becomes expensive for local hospitals to compete based on quality in the same dimension. If one hospital locally is advertised as "the best" at something, then it will take a lot of resources to compete with them for that spot as the best. What may be a better strategy than direct quality competition with that hospital is to invest heavily in a different specialization, and perhaps compete more effectively in that space. If I search for "best cardiac hospital in Denver," "best birthing hospital in Denver," and "best neurology hospital in Denver" I will get a different set of recommendations for each search. This is not to say that hospitals exclusively choose to carve out their own niches and never compete with one another, there is certainly some overlap in the lists.

What I am saying is that strategically choosing areas to invest in can in some cases be a better strategy for quality competition than trying to be "best overall" in a given market.

Hospital Systems

Modern hospitals are decreasingly operated independently but are instead operated as part of a larger "hospital system." This adds an additional layer to decision-making, where a single hospital's leadership may not have the ultimate say over resource allocation decisions if resources are pooled across multiple hospitals (or other affiliated entities such as medical practices) that are part of the single system. In this case, many of the principles of resource allocation used within a single hospital apply but at the larger scale of the system. For example, to the extent that a hospital within the system accounts for more of the overall resource generation, they will likely have additional pull when deciding to how to steer resources.

Hospital systems also provide the firms that are part of the system a benefit in the form of increased patronage. Hospitals and practices that are part of the system can use themselves as preferred destinations for patients needing to be referred elsewhere for care. System-owned medical practices will tend to refer (when appropriate) to system-owned hospitals, who will refer to system-owned clinics, and so forth. This is known as building out a *referral network*. Referral networks are incredibly valuable, as a patient may respond more to a physician's recommendation than to an external quality ranking.

Self-Assessment

1. Consider the statement "Not-for-profit hospitals are better for patients because they aren't interested in making profits." What is correct about this statement? What is incorrect? Write a more accurate statement.
2. Suppose you had the option to go to a hospital where the medical staff was not independent and had to answer to hospital leadership for all decisions related to patient care. Would you want to go to this hospital? Why or why not?
3. Who do you think has the most power over resource allocation within a hospital, and why did you choose hospital leadership as your answer?
4. Who do you think has the second most power over resource allocation within a hospital, and why did you choose the party that you chose as your answer?

5. Consider the example from earlier in the chapter where a donor wanted money to be spent on equipment for a hospital's cancer center. Can you come up with a donation agreement that would prevent the hospital from shuffling around other funds and actually increase the equipment budget with certainty?

6. Explain how an expansion of a hospital laboratory could create economies of scale. Explain how an expansion of a hospital laboratory could create economies of scope.

7. Consider a situation where a hospital purchasing a medical practice would make that practice less profitable. Could it be possible that purchasing the practice could improve hospital systemwide profits more than would be lost from the practice loss of profitability? How?

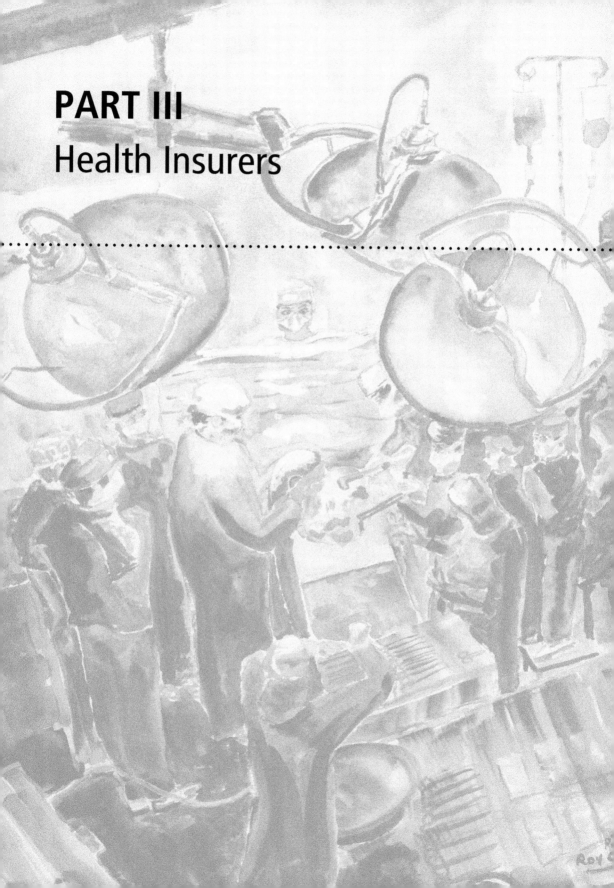

PART III
Health Insurers

10 | Health Insurance as a Product

Health insurance and health insurers sit at the center of the healthcare sector. Incentives generated by insurance and insurers impact decisions made by patients and providers. In this chapter, we will explore some fundamental features of health insurance: what insurance does, why people purchase it, and the business model of a health insurance company.

Insurance

A health insurance policy is at its core like any other insurance policy. So, to understand the workings of health insurance, the first step is to understand insurance in general. The basic concept is that some *assets* (i.e. things that you have) like a home or a car, are both valuable and risky. When I say that the asset has some *risk*, I mean that there is a non-trivial chance that the asset could be significantly diminished in value, for example the house could burn down or the car could have a tree fall on it.[1]

For simplicity's sake, consider two states of the world. One state of the world where your risky asset retains its full value, and one where it is destroyed. You have a house, and it stays as it is, or there is a chance that it burns down. You have a car, and it stays as it is, or there is a chance that it is smashed by a falling tree. Purchasing an insurance policy is protection against the bad outcome. Insurance creates a situation if the bad outcome comes to pass, then you will be returned to the good outcome.

To be a little more detailed, an individual purchases an insurance policy that will pay out a certain amount if criteria are met. A car insurance policy may pay out up to the amount needed to replace the car in the event of an accident, or a home insurance policy may pay out up to the amount needed to replace the home in the event of destruction of the home.

---

[1] The tree would damage or destroy the car. Don't think about a dinky little tree that would barely scratch the car, think about a big tree.

Risk Aversion

Humans like to buy insurance because in most cases they are *risk averse* or have *risk aversion*. This means that a person does not like risk and would prefer to avoid it given a safer option with an equal average payout. Consider two games we could play. In the first game, I flip a coin and on heads you get nothing, but on tails you get $2. If the coin is fair, then the average payout is $1 (50 percent chance of heads and $0, 50 percent chance of tails and $2). In the second game, I flip a coin and then give you a dollar no matter what.[2] Again, the average payout is $1. If you prefer the second game to the first, then you are risk averse in this case. Risk aversion is a common feature for preferences, people tend to not want a choice with risk baked in when there is a less risky (or riskless) option available.[3]

Desire for Insurance

Here is the key question: how much would you be willing to pay to enter a world where an asset retains its value no matter what? If the asset is broken or destroyed, then it is repaired or replaced. If the answer for how much you are willing to pay for this new arrangement is more than zero, then congratulations, you have a willingness to purchase insurance.[4]

How much you are willing to pay for insurance will depend on two things. The first is how much risk you are exposed to. The riskier the asset, the more you are willing to pay to insure it. If an asset can potentially lose a greater amount of value, or loses value with greater likelihood, then you would be willing to pay more to insure it. This is perhaps a little unfair, because as an asset gets riskier you need more "valuable" insurance in the sense that a more generous or more frequent insurance payout is needed to cover it. So yes, you are willing to pay more when you have a riskier asset, but you also get more value in return.

The other factor in willingness to pay for insurance is how much you dislike risk, or how risk averse you are. The more you dislike risk, the more you are willing to pay to avoid it, and the more you are willing to pay for insurance.

---

[2] In this game there was no need to flip the coin, you get paid either way. I just thought it would be fun to flip the coin.

[3] Risk aversion is present whenever a person has *diminishing marginal utility* for something. This is discussed in the end of chapter supplement, but, if this idea piqued your interest, then go ahead and read that now.

[4] Willingness to buy insurance does not mean that you *will* buy insurance, that will also depend on the price of the plan and what the plan offers.

What Does Health Insurance Protect?

Insurance provides protection for an asset against risk. So, does health insurance provide protection for your health against the risk of illness or injury? Your health is certainly valuable, and it is also risky, so presumably you would like to purchase insurance to protect it. The big problem with this way of thinking about health insurance comes from the discussion in Chapter 2: health is not something that you can buy directly, you can only purchase things that impact your health indirectly. So, it is not possible for health insurance to "repair or replace" the asset as other types of insurance do. To illustrate, let's compare health insurance to auto insurance in Table 10.1.[5]

There are a few key differences here. First is that health insurance is paid in situations where there is no "damage" to the value of your health. Health insurance pays for routine and preventative care such as primary care visits and immunizations. This would be akin to auto insurance paying for oil changes and tire rotations. Health insurance also pays for non-illness related elective care such as a vasectomy. This would be akin to auto insurance paying for new rims for your tires.

The second key difference is that the amount of money paid out for health insurance is not tied to the value of health that is lost. If I am diagnosed with a treatable illness, then my health insurance will pay for my treatment. The amount paid by the insurance company will not be determined by how much I value my health but will be determined by the cost of the care. Also, there is no guarantee that the treatment will be

Table 10.1 Auto insurance vs. health insurance	
Auto Insurance	Health Insurance
• Purchase an insurance plan. • In the event of damage to the vehicle, plan pays out money. • Money paid out is enough to repair the vehicle or replace the vehicle (maximum payment determined by value of vehicle).	• Purchase an insurance plan. • In the event of illness or injury, plan pays out money. Also pay out for routine care. Also pay out for non-illness related care. • Money paid out is based on expenditure, which may or may not be sufficient to repair health (maximum payment not determined by value of health).

---

[5] For you auto insurance connoisseurs out there, I'm only talking about the part of the insurance policy that covers damage to your own vehicle, not the part that covers liability due to damage to others or their property, or the part that covers injury to self. A full auto insurance plan is actually a bundle of several insurance products.

effective: health insurance will pay for treatments even when they are not certain to repair the asset (your health), something that auto insurance does not do. There is no auto insurance plan that says, "if your car it damaged, we'll sometimes pay to have it repaired and sometimes pay someone to put some duct tape on it and hope for the best."

Health Insurance as Wealth Insurance

From the previous exercise, it looks like health insurance doesn't fit the mold of a typical insurance plan. But what if health insurance isn't insuring your health? What if health insurance is protecting your wealth against risk generated by your health? Think about it this way:

1. Your wealth is an asset that you value.
2. You are willing to pay quite a bit for medical care, in some cases so much so that you would wipe out all your savings or even go into debt to purchase medical care.
3. Your wealth thus faces risk due to expenditures on medical care.

If we change our point of view from "health insurance protects your health" to "health insurance protects your financial well-being from health-based risk" then suddenly the idea of health insurance makes much more sense as an insurance product. Let's do the earlier comparison again, now thinking about health insurance as insurance for your wealth. This is shown in Table 10.2.

Now, health insurance fits the mold for an insurance plan very well. It is insuring an asset (your wealth) against risk (possible expenditures on medical care), and the protection is sufficient to repair the damage incurred (payments from the insurance restore your wealth).

The big idea here is that health insurance does not protect your health, it protects your wealth from expenditures tied to your health. In fact, this is the same thing that auto insurance does. Auto insurance does not protect

Table 10.2 Auto insurance vs. health insurance revisited	
Auto Insurance	Health Insurance (as Wealth Insurance)
• Purchase an insurance plan. • In the event of damage to the vehicle, plan pays out money. • Money paid out is enough to repair the vehicle or replace the vehicle (maximum payment determined by value of vehicle).	• Purchase an insurance plan. • In the event of an expenditure on medical care, plan pays out money. • Money paid out is enough to repair the damage to your finances from the health expenditure (maximum payment determined by value of care).

your car. If there is a big hailstorm rolling in with golf ball sized hail that will decimate your car, you don't go outside and yell "Stop hail! I have INSURANCE!" and cause the hail to avoid your car. The hail destroys the car, and the insurance pays for the repair or replacement. The damage to the car was not prevented, but the damage to your wealth due to your car was. Likewise, health insurance does not stop you from getting ill or injured. If you do get ill or injured the damage to your wealth due to paying for medical care is repaired.

Bankruptcy as Health Insurance

By the above logic, you get a form of health insurance from bankruptcy protections. That may sound a little crazy but consider what bankruptcy protections let you do. Chapter 7 bankruptcy allows an individual to pay everything that they can by liquidating (selling) all of their assets in order to discharge (i.e. get rid of) their unsecured debt (debt that has no collateral) that is more than the value of their assets. They also get to protect certain assets from this liquidation process, such as their home, vehicle, and other personal effects. So, if the debt is a medical debt (debt on unpaid medical bills), then bankruptcy protects a person's overall assets from dropping below a certain level due to medical expenditures. In other words, it's health insurance.[6]

A Very Quick Math Lesson

In order to understand more about the workings of insurance we are going to need a little more math. The key concept is *expected value*, which comes from probability and statistics. If you have some *random variable X* (which means that X is a variable that can take on different values with different chances, just like the risky asset that we would want to insure), then the expected value is the average outcome for X if you realize X's value many times.

We've already used the concept of expected value a few times in the book already without naming it. When thinking about people making their "best guess" when the outcome is uncertain, usually, that best guess is the expected value. The formula for expected value (denoted $E[X]$, or "expected value of X") is

---

[6] There are some excellent quasi-experimental studies showing people behaving in ways consistent with treating bankruptcy as a form of health insurance. See for example, Mahoney (2015) or Gallagher et al. (2020).

$$E[X] = \sum_i x_i p_i = x_1 p_1 + x_2 p_2 + \ldots$$

where X has several different possible outcomes each denoted $x_1, x_2, \ldots$ and each outcome has its own probability of happening, denoted $p_1, p_2, \ldots$. So the formula is just saying "take each outcome, multiply it by its probability, and then add them all up." In a sense, expected value is a probability-based average of the possible outcomes. If we have a game where we flip a coin, on heads you get \$1 and on tails you get \$2, then the expected value of the game is

$$E[X] = \sum_i x_i p_i = (1 \times 0.5) + (2 \times 0.5) = 0.5 + 1 = 1.5$$

Insurance Companies

The business model for an insurance company is to "smooth out" risk for a large population. An insurance company collects money from the population, and then pays it back out as bad outcomes occur. Everyone who buys insurance pays in, but not everyone needs a payout at once. The idea is that the amount individuals pay for their plans, known as the *insurance premium* or the price of the insurance plan is enough such that the insurance company can cover all the payouts needed. For simplicity, let's assume that premiums paid into insurance plans are for one year of coverage.[7] Then the premium for one year of coverage will be:

$$\text{Premium} \approx E[\text{payout}] + \text{loading}$$

This statement uses a "$\approx$" which means "approximately equal to." It just means that there's a little bit of wiggle room around the equivalence, which we'll come back to in a moment. $E[\text{payout}]$ is the expected value of the payout for someone buying insurance, for the moment, let's assume everyone carries the same risk.[8] Finally, loading is an additional amount that covers the overhead costs for administration of the insurance plan: things like paying for computers and workers to manage collection and payouts. So, taken together, the price of an insurance plan is set such that money in is roughly equal to money out.

---

[7] The discussion to follow will be as if all insurance plans are for one year of coverage. This is not always the case. Plans can vary in terms of length of coverage and frequency with which premiums are paid. I'm discussing things in terms of years because a year is an easier concept than a "generic insurance coverage time period."

[8] When people carry different risks and look to buy the same insurance things can get crazy. This is what most of the next chapter is about.

One thing that may have bothered you about the idea of expected value is that for one person in one interaction with a random variable, that person does not really get the expected value, they get one of the possible outcomes. However, with an insurance company, the logic of expected value is much more appropriate. The insurance company sees many realizations of the random variable: each person that buys an insurance plan has their own outcome. The expected value of the payout $(E[\text{payout}])$ is the average amount paid out per person enrolled in the insurance plan: a number that is extremely relevant to the insurance company's operations.

As there are more and more people in a given insurance plan, there is less variability in $E[\text{payout}]$ due to the *Law of Large Numbers*: the more independent (i.e. uncorrelated – more on this in a bit) draws you have from a random variable the closer the average outcome gets to the expected value. By taking on a larger volume of clients, an insurance company can be more and more certain as to how much will be paid out in a given year.

How Insurance Companies Make Money

If an insurance company is paying out everything that it takes in (minus overhead costs) then how does an insurer make money? The premiums are all paid in when people buy their plans but are paid out over the course of the year. So, there is a lag during which the insurance company is sitting on a large pile of money that will eventually be paid out but that will not be paid out right away. Insurance companies can use that money for short-term investments and keep whatever returns they get. This makes insurance companies like banks. Banks hold on to deposits and make money from using the deposits for investments during the time between deposit and withdrawal. Insurers hold onto premiums and make money from using the premiums for investments during the time between premium payment and insurance claim payout.

Now we can return to the "$\approx$" in Premium $\approx E[\text{payout}] + \text{loading}$. Insurance companies have a little wiggle room in setting premiums depending on market conditions. If a market for insurance is fairly competitive, then an insurer can use some of the profits made from investing to subsidize lower premiums for customers. This allows them to try to undercut the competition and draw in more business. On the other hand, if an insurer faces little competition, then they might be able to set their premiums higher than $E[\text{payout}] + \text{loading}$ and make additional profit by keeping some of the money paid in.[9]

---

[9] Trish and Herring (2015) present some associational evidence consistent with this behavior. Markets where there is more health insurance concentration relative to the parties that the insurers are selling to have systematically higher premiums.

Correlated vs. Uncorrelated Risk

For the above business plan to work well, insurers want to cover risks that are *uncorrelated*. This means that one person having a particular outcome does not impact the probability of another person having a bad outcome and needing a payout. The opposite of uncorrelated risk would be *correlated* risk, or when one person getting a particular outcome influences the chances of others having a bad outcome.

Insurance works because a lot of people pay in, and only some people get payouts in a given year. In the case of correlated risk, you have a situation where one person getting a payout could increase the likelihood of others getting payouts. This means that there can be a cascade of unanticipated payouts that in total overshoot the amount that the insurance company collected. In other words, correlated risk greatly increases the possibility of big swings in total payouts due to clusters of related payments.

An example of correlated health risk is a communicable disease. One person getting infected and needing additional care (and thus having additional expenditures that are covered by their health insurer) increases the chance of others having the same need due to one infection increasing the likelihood of another infection.[10] In general, insurers like to be able to accurately predict their payouts so they do not run the risk of not having enough money collected to cover their responsibilities, and thus try to avoid correlated risk. Uncorrelated risks allow insurers to more accurately predict payouts and set their premiums accordingly.

Group Insurance

One way that insurers attempt to avoid correlated risk is to try to sell insurance to large groups that have come together for a reason other than purchasing insurance. The reason for the last stipulation is the worry that a group that comes together for the purpose of buying insurance may have done so for a reason, and that reason may be a correlated risk.[11] Groups that health insurers have traditionally sought out for this purpose are employers, as employees are assembled for the purpose for running a business and not due to any underlying correlated health risk.

---

[10] Correlated risk can also generate windfall profits for insurance companies if one person having below normal payout decreases the payouts of others. For example, COVID-19 may have generated windfall profits for auto insurers who collected premiums based on pre-pandemic driving patterns and then paid out claims based on accidents that happened with lower frequency as fewer people drove.

[11] That's not to say that insurers never sell to groups that come together for the purpose of purchasing insurance, just that they give preference (and presumably better prices) to large groups with a lower likelihood of correlated risk.

Experience Rating

As a lead-in to the next chapter, let's think about what happens when people looking to buy insurance have different underlying risk. How does an insurance company know how much to charge? One solution is to charge each person based on their individual risk. An insurer would charge each person an individualized premium that is based on their individual expected payout. Riskier individuals would have to pay more for insurance and less risky individuals would have to pay less for insurance. This process of setting premiums based on individual risks is known as *experience rating*.

Experience rating is common for some forms of insurance. For example, for auto insurance there is experience rating based on driving history: if you get into an accident, typically your premiums increase as the insurer considers you to be a riskier driver to insure. Experience rating also existed for a long time in the US health insurance market based on diagnoses that were already known. This was differential pricing based on "pre-existing conditions." If an individual had a known diagnosis prior to buying health insurance, then a health insurer would experience rate and charge them a higher premium.

Moral Hazard

One final point to make when thinking about health insurance is to bring up the idea of *moral hazard*. Moral hazard is a form of asymmetric information where one party in a transaction has information that other parties do not. In this case, the hidden information is an action that is taken. The insured person engages in their day-to-day behavior which is not viewed by the insurance company. The idea of moral hazard is that when you have insurance, you may not be as careful with your behavior as you would be in the world where you did not have insurance. A person with auto insurance may drive more recklessly than they would otherwise, and a person with health insurance may not take as good care of their body as they would otherwise.

This concept can expand to thinking about health insurance (or any insurance for that matter) as wealth insurance. When you have cost sharing you may be more cavalier about spending than you would if you bore the full cost yourself (this was shown in Chapter 4 theoretically and Chapter 5 empirically). Thus, you can then view increases in medical spending due to insurance as a form of moral hazard: once you have insurance that protects your wealth you are not as financially prudent as you would have been in the absence of the insurance.

Self-Assessment

1. Insurance tends to cover "big ticket" assets with higher value. Why do we not see insurance markets for lower value items such as "ice-cream cone insurance?"

2. Some individuals are willing to pay for risk in some instances. Economists call this "risk-loving" behavior. Would a person who exhibits risk-loving behavior be willing to purchase insurance? Why or why not?

3. Life insurance pays out money when somebody dies. What does life insurance protect?

4. Consider the statement "Bankruptcy is insurance for everything." Do you agree? Why or why not?

5. If there was a systematic increase to the health risk of the majority of the US population (e.g. due to increasingly poor lifestyle choices), what would happen to health insurance premiums?

6. If technology improves to make the cost of medical procedures lower, what will happen to health insurance premiums?

7. If technology improves to make illnesses treatable that were not previously treatable, what will happen to health insurance premiums?

Supplement. A Math-Based Way to Show Desire to Purchase Insurance

· ·

What I am going to show you here has more math than the rest of the book, so fair warning that I am about to jump down a bit of a math rabbit hole. I think it's worth taking a moment to do this exercise because it cleanly and simply shows why people are willing to purchase insurance. All that you need is *diminishing marginal utility*, the idea that you get more utility from the first unit of something than you do from the second than you do from the third and so forth. As long as someone's utility function has that feature, then they will be *risk averse* and willing to purchase insurance. That's it. That's all you need. OK, that and an understanding of expected value, which we have from earlier in the chapter.

All that is to follow is plotted in Figure 10.1. Here's the setup. You have a risky asset X. X can take on two possible outcomes, X_1 and X_2, where X_2 is the "good" higher value outcome and X_1 is the "bad" lower value outcome. To keep things simple, we'll say that each outcome has a probability of 0.5 (or a 50/50 chance) of occurring. This exercise works with any non-certain (zero or one) probabilities, but 0.5 is nice because it makes the expected value $E[X]$ exactly halfway between X_1 and X_2, which makes Figure 10.1 easy to see.

With this risky asset, you never actually get the expected value $E[X]$. You get the outcome that you land on and the utility associated with that

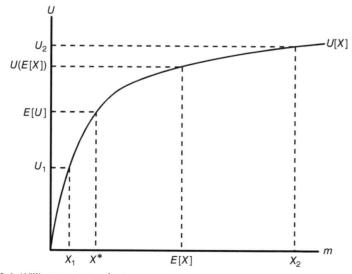

Figure 10.1 Willingness to pay for insurance

outcome. If you get the good outcome and the asset is worth X_2 then you get the higher utility U_2, and if you get the bad outcome and the asset is worth X_1 then you get the lower utility U_1. So, if you have a 50/50 chance of getting either utility, then your expected utility $E[U]$ is halfway between U_1 and U_2. Notice (and this is the important part), that the expected utility $E[U]$ is lower than the utility you would get if you received the expected value of the asset with certainty, $U(E[X])$. This means that you are less happy with the risky asset than you would be if you got the expected value with certainty. You are getting the same utility that you would if you had a riskless asset valued at X^* as opposed to a risky asset valued at $E[X]$. So how much are you willing to pay to eliminate the risk in your asset and get $E[X]$ with certainty? $E[X] - X^*$, which is referred to as a *risk premium* or the maximum amount you are willing to pay to eliminate risk. If you have a risk premium, then you have willingness to buy insurance.

This all comes from $U(E[X]) > E[U]$ which is true in any situation where there is diminishing marginal utility (which is represented by the curve in the utility function). If you want to do a really big math dive (sorry to nerd out for a second) this is actually an application of *Jensen's Inequality* which defines relationships between expected values based on how functions curve. The bottom line is that under simple assumptions about people's utility (early units are more valuable than subsequent units), individuals are risk averse and willing to purchase insurance.

11 | Adverse Selection

This chapter unpacks the *adverse selection problem* in health insurance markets, which in popular culture is sometimes referred to as the *death spiral*. Adverse selection is a form of *asymmetric information* where one party has information that another does not, and that information is leveraged in a way that causes problems for the market.

In an adverse selection problem, the hidden information is an underlying characteristic. One party (in our case the potential insurance customer) has some knowledge of their underlying risk that the other party (the insurance company) does not. Once this information is hidden, everyone acts rationally, which can lead to the outcome of the market unraveling in spectacular fashion.[1]

Later in this chapter, we'll walk through exactly how and why this happens. Before we do that, I want to examine the question "why not let insurance companies have all of the information?" If hidden information is a problem, then why not make it illegal to hide information in the first place? As it turns out, full information can lead to undesirable outcomes in the health insurance market as well.

To give a quick outline of where we're going in this chapter. We'll look at:

1. problems that arise in the health insurance market when information is shared
2. problems that arise in the health insurance market when information is not shared
3. policies that attempt to solve both sets of problems and the tradeoffs that come with these policies.

Uninsurable

There are some individuals for whom the price of health insurance (the premium) is so high that it defeats the purpose of the financial protection offered by the insurance. These individuals are referred to as *uninsurable*.

---

[1] That's why it's called "the death spiral" and not "the minor inconvenience."

I am not saying that these are people for whom the price of health insurance is a little too high. This isn't a case where someone looks at the premium and says, "that's just a teensy bit too pricy for my liking, I'm going to choose not to buy it." These are cases where the premium is sufficient to wipe out the very finances that the insurance is aimed at protecting.

Who Is Uninsurable?

One way to be uninsurable is to have a high chance of needing a large payout from the health insurance company. If the premium is set such that Premium $\approx E[\text{payout}] + \text{loading}$, then a large $E[\text{payout}]$ will generate a high price for an individual when an insurer is allowed to experience rate. If you have cancer and want to buy new health insurance, then under experience rating, the price that the health insurer charges you will be reflective of the expenditures you will likely have on expensive cancer drugs. Potential expenditures on care are both large and likely, which will generate a high premium. If that premium is high enough to defeat the purpose of financial protection, then the cancer has made you uninsurable. This example works for any situation where future expenditures are predictably large and likely. Being uninsurable is particularly common for individuals with chronic illnesses.

It is also possible that a more modest $E[\text{payout}]$ could generate a premium which defeats the financial protection goal of insurance. This is the case when an individual seeking insurance does not have much financial security to begin with. If an individual is poor, then even a relatively small insurance premium could be sufficient to defeat the financial protection purpose of health insurance.

Public Health Insurance and the Likely Uninsurable

In the United States, there are several forms of public health insurance that cover individuals who have an increased likelihood of being uninsurable. For individuals with limited financial resources, there is Medicaid, a program that offers health insurance to certain classes of individuals with incomes under specific thresholds. Similarly, Medicare covers all individuals aged 65 or older, as well as individuals with certain disabilities or end-stage renal disease.[2] As people are more likely to develop chronic illnesses as they age, Medicare covers many individuals who would likely be uninsurable if they had to purchase insurance on their own. The Department of Veteran's Affairs and the Department of Defense offer insurance for veterans and armed service members, respectively, many of whom are at

---

[2] Medicare and Medicaid are discussed in greater detail in Chapter 14.

elevated risk for needing large health insurance payouts due to the nature of their current or previous work.

The Remaining Uninsurable

There are still a large number of people who can be considered uninsurable who do not qualify for publicly provided insurance in the United States. Individuals with "pre-existing conditions," or any ailment that exists at the time that they seek to purchase insurance run the risk of being uninsurable when insurers can experience rate. If the condition does not qualify them for a subsidized (or free) public insurance plan (as is the case, e.g. for certain permanent disabilities under Medicare), then an individual with the condition becomes uninsurable if their $E[\text{payout}]$ is sufficiently large that the insurance premium it generates defeats the financial protection purpose of the insurance.

Prior to the Patient Protection and Affordable Care Act (ACA), which makes it illegal for health insurers to charge different premiums based on pre-existing conditions (i.e. to experience rate based on existing diagnoses), individuals with these conditions were regularly placed in situations where they could either go without health insurance and be financially crushed by high medical bills, or purchase health insurance which had a premium large enough to financially crush them directly.[3] One of the main goals of the ACA was to alleviate this problem of uninsurable individuals, to avoid having situations where individuals face financial hardship because of diagnoses that are beyond their control. However, this restriction comes with a cost. When you eliminate experience rating, you open the possibility of the adverse selection problem taking effect.

The Adverse Selection Problem

The adverse selection problem in health insurance arises when insurers cannot experience rate. All we need to demonstrate the problem is the formula for calculating an insurance premium, $\text{Premium} \approx E[\text{payout}] + \text{loading}$, and a line.

We are going to use the line in Figure 11.1 to represent all individuals in a health insurance market. It shows people in order of their risk of a large payout as represented by their individual value of $E[\text{payout}]$. The left side of the line is less risky, with lower values of $E[\text{payout}]$ the further

---

[3] They also had the third option of buying cheaper insurance with less coverage, and they could then be financially crushed by a little bit of both.

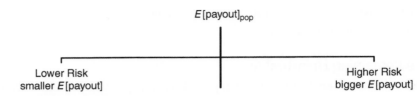

Figure 11.1 Individuals in a health insurance market

to the left you go, and the right side is more risky, with higher values of $E[\text{payout}]$ the further to the right you go. In the middle is $E[\text{payout}]_{\text{pop}}$ which is the expected value for the entire population in this market.

Regardless of whether or not a health insurance company can experience rate, the insurance company will want to maintain a situation where the money brought into the company via premiums is enough to cover payouts. Under experience rating, an insurer does this at the individual or group level, generating individualized or group-based premiums that balance cash into the insurer and cash paid out. When experience rating is not available, the insurer still needs to balance money in with money out and will charge a single premium to the entire market based on the expected payout for the entire population of that market. This means that for the market where individual risk is not observable (or is observable but cannot be acted upon) by the insurer the premium is set such that $\text{Premium} \approx E[\text{payout}]_{\text{pop}} + \text{loading}$.

Once this new premium is set, some individuals are being offered prices based on a value of $E[\text{payout}]$ that is quite different than their own. If a person is very risky, and is on the right side of the line, then their individual risk is potentially much greater than the average population risk, or in math terms, $E[\text{payout}]_{\text{pop}} < E[\text{payout}]_{\text{ind}}$. These people are getting a good deal. Insurance is meant to be pricier the more risk that it is covering, and these people are covering a lot of risk for a disproportionately low price. On the other side of the line, if a person is not very risky, then their individual risk is potentially much less than the average population risk, or in math terms $E[\text{payout}]_{\text{pop}} > E[\text{payout}]_{\text{ind}}$. These people are getting a bad deal. Insurance is meant to be less pricy the less risk that it is covering, and these people are covering little risk for a disproportionately high price. Figure 11.2 shows who is getting a good deal and who is getting a bad deal based on our line.

What can happen at this point is that some of the population that is getting a bad deal can choose not to purchase insurance. They can say "you know what, this just isn't worth the money considering what I am getting in return," and decide not to purchase health insurance.

Figure 11.2 People getting good and bad deals with no experience rating

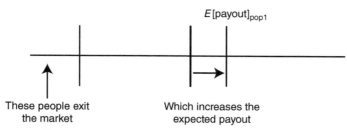

Figure 11.3 People getting bad deals exit the market

When this happens, $E[\text{payout}]_{\text{pop}}$ is no longer the expected value for the population participating in the market. The bottom part of the risk distribution is no longer part of the market, so the market now has a new, larger expected payout $E[\text{payout}]_{\text{pop1}}$. This is similar to taking an average over a bunch of graded homework assignments. If you drop the lowest assignment grade from the average, then the average increases. In this case we have dropped the least risky people from the insurance pool, so the average risk (i.e. the average payout) has increased. This change is shown on our line in Figure 11.3.

The problem is that we have returned to the situation that we were just in. Under the new expected payout $E[\text{payout}]_{\text{pop1}}$ there is a new, higher premium for this market due to the formula Premium $\approx E[\text{payout}]_{\text{pop1}} + $ loading. In this new market position, there are once again people getting good deals and people getting bad deals. Further, the people getting bad deals once again have the option to say, "you know what, this just isn't worth the money considering what I am getting in return," and decide not to purchase health insurance.

When this happens, $E[\text{payout}]_{\text{pop1}}$ is no longer the expected value for the population participating in the market. The bottom part of the new risk distribution leaves the market, so the market now has a new, even larger expected payout $E[\text{payout}]_{\text{pop2}}$. This second change in the market is shown for our line in Figure 11.4.

This process can repeat over and over and over again, with the lowest risk people getting a bad deal and exiting the market, the insurer adjusting

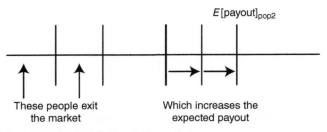

These people exit
the market

Which increases the
expected payout

Figure 11.4 People getting bad deals exit the market again

premiums to match the new market risk profile, and a new group of people deciding that the price isn't worth it and exiting. The price of health insurance spirals upwards and the market unravels until all that is left are high-risk (and likely uninsurable) individuals being charged prices that defeat the financial protection purpose of insurance. Bummer.

If you do not want health insurers to experience rate, then you need to find a way to avoid the adverse selection problem. In other words, you need to keep the people with the lowest risk of leaving the market. There are a few ways that governments have done this, each with its own tradeoffs. Next, I will present two different approaches and explain how they work. Again, the key objective in both situations is to prevent low-risk individuals from exiting the market.

Avoiding the Adverse Selection Problem: Single Payer Systems

One way to avoid the adverse selection problem is to have a system where there is only one universal insurance company: the government. Some examples of this type of system can be found in Canada, Denmark, Norway, and the United Kingdom. There is no ability to exit the market, because there is no market in a traditional sense, individuals do not purchase insurance they are provided it as a benefit from the government.

In a sense, everyone pays a premium in the form of taxes, but this "premium" is not necessarily tied to an individual's risk of needing medical care but is instead determined by the national tax code. To follow the logic of taxes as a premium a bit further, everyone is compelled to "purchase" insurance in these countries in the same way that they are compelled to "purchase" things like roads, bridges, and national defense in the United States: failure to pay your owed taxes is illegal.

Single payer systems sidestep the adverse selection problem. Premiums are not determined by risk, and further, low-risk individuals remain in the pool of insured because they are provided insurance without having to go out and purchase it. There is no private market for insurance, so there is no adverse selection problem.

Avoiding the Adverse Selection Problem: Market-Based Systems

Another way to avoid the adverse selection problem is to have the government intervene in the market. This is what was done with the ACA. The government offers incentives, positive or negative, to try to convince low-risk individuals to purchase insurance and avoid setting off a cascade of low-risk individuals exiting and subsequent premium increases.

Specifically, the ACA does this with a mix of "carrots" and "sticks" (i.e. positive and negative incentives). The primary carrot is subsidies for purchasing health insurance. This lowers the price paid by low-risk individuals (actually it lowers the price for all individuals who qualify for the subsidy, which is determined by income not by risk), making it less likely that they will choose to not purchase insurance. Prior to 2019, the ACA also had a stick called the *individual mandate*, under which people were required by law to have health insurance or else they would have to pay a tax penalty (as of 2019 this penalty was reduced to $0). The ACA also includes the establishment of "health insurance exchanges," websites where individuals can group together to purchase health insurance, which lowers both the price (as groups can get a better price than if the group members were to shop as individuals) and also lowers other non-cash economic costs such as the time spent searching for an insurance plan.

An Aside on the General Strategy of the ACA

One way to view the ACA is as having the primary goal of solving the problem of individuals being uninsurable due to pre-existing conditions. The ACA made it illegal for insurance companies to charge these people different prices. Most of the rest of the ACA was aimed at solving problems that spin off from the solution this primary goal.[4] Disallowing experience rating

---

[4] Not all of the rest of the ACA was aimed at this, the ACA is a big law with many different parts. For example, one part of the ACA established a "pay for performance" system for hospital payments from Medicare, which was aimed at increasing care quality.

based on pre-existing conditions creates an adverse selection problem, so the ACA includes a series of incentives to keep low-risk individuals in the health insurance market. Some of the incentives (in particular the individual mandate) required people to purchase a product which they may not be able to easily afford or suffer tax consequences which they also may not be able to easily afford, so the ACA included federally funded expansions to public insurance for the poor (Medicaid).

Interestingly, much of the US policy debate around the ACA has not been about the primary goal: the idea that individuals should not have to pay an unaffordable price for health insurance (or medical care) due to pre-existing conditions has broad support across the US political spectrum. Most of the political debate has been over the correct mix of carrots and sticks that should be used to prevent the adverse selection problem, and the extent to which public insurance programs should (or should not) be expanded.

Single Payer vs. Market-Based Insurance: Which Is Better?

As a health economist, I am frequently asked whether a single payer system or a market-based system is better. What follows is my honest opinion on the matter and is by no means the settled opinion of economists writ large (although I'm sure there are a non-trivial number of economists who would agree with me).

Neither is inherently a better system. Single payer and market systems are the base scaffolding upon which the entirety of a healthcare sector is built. All of the details of each system creates incentives for the various actors, and it is the aggregation of these details (and the behaviors they promote) that influence how successful a given healthcare system is on any given measure of quality.

There are natural advantages and disadvantages to either choice. A single payer system provides a simpler solution to the problem of uninsurable people and to the adverse selection problem, in this dimension, it is an easier system to get right. However, in the end, any system can perform poorly if incentives exist that drive individuals to undesirable behavior. One of the primary goals of this book is not just to highlight places where these incentives arise, but also to teach the economic thinking that allows you to identify weird incentives in the wild. Details of an institution matter, and it is those details that will determine the ultimate success (or failure) of a system.

Self-Assessment

· ·

1. As new technologies are developed that make treatable illnesses less expensive to treat, what will happen to the percentage of the population that is uninsurable?
2. As new technologies are developed that make previously untreatable illnesses possible to treat, but the treatments are very expensive, what will happen to the percentage of the population that is uninsurable?
3. There is not a law preventing experience rating in the auto insurance market. Why do you think that is?
4. One idea for fixing an adverse selection problem is a "high-risk pool" where the highest risk individuals in an insurance market are either given public insurance or a public subsidy on their private insurance. What are some benefits of high-risk pools? What are some costs of high-risk pools?
5. Describe a situation where a government uses a high-risk pool to attempt to avoid an adverse selection problem and then the adverse selection problem happens anyway.
6. If insurance exchanges did nothing to lower health insurance premiums, would it still be possible for them to help keep low-risk individuals in the health insurance market?

Supplement. Why Do the US and UK Have Different Health Insurance Systems?

The United States and the United Kingdom (UK) are countries that have a lot in common culturally, politically, and economically. A question that arises is why do they have such different health insurance systems? The United States has a largely market-based system with many different insurance companies that compete for business (as well as a sizable government insurance presence for certain populations). On the other hand, the UK has a single payer system where public healthcare is available to all permanent residents, provided by the National Health Service (NHS).

One possible reason for the divergence in systems has to do with World War II. During the war, both countries enacted programs to prevent prices from rapidly increasing (which can happen when a country pushes production very hard as was done for the war effort). The United States took the approach of regulating prices by establishing the Office of Price Administration, which directly controlled prices in many markets, including labor markets. With prices in labor markets (i.e. wages) fixed, businesses in the United States found a workaround to attract talented labor to come to work for them: they offered increasingly generous benefits. One of the most common and popular benefits offered was employer-sponsored health insurance.

On the other hand, the UK opted to control prices by regulating the quantities that could be purchased in private markets (as opposed to prices). This was done via rationing. People were issued ration books, which were books of coupons that entitled individuals to be able to purchase certain items. Both systems were able to keep down prices, one by preventing runaway demand (rationing), and one by controlling the prices directly.

However, at the end of the war, this left the countries in two very different places. The United States had undergone a rapid expansion of the health insurance sector, with health insurance companies having grown in size and power due to the influx of enrollees during the war. On the other hand, the UK had no such expansion of the sector. So, there was little opposition from the private health insurance sector when the UK established the NHS. On the other hand, establishing a similar program in the United States would have involved closing down a large industry that enrolled almost a quarter of the US population and was continuing to grow.

12 | Prices

Prices are central to any functioning market. Prices help determine how resources are allocated in the economy. In a perfectly competitive free market, prices are arrived at through natural interactions between buyers and sellers. The standard explanation in an economics textbook goes something like this:

> At any given price, buyers have an amount that they are willing to purchase of a good (represented by demand), and at any given price, producers have an amount that they are willing to produce (represented by supply). The higher the price, the less buyers will be willing to buy and the more sellers will be willing to sell.
>
> There is an *equilibrium* price at which the amount produced is equal to the amount demanded. Markets naturally move to equilibrium: when the price is too high, sellers will compete by lowering prices to undercut each other and, when the price is too low, buyers will compete by outbidding each other and push up the price. Once a market has reached equilibrium lots of great things happen, which is why we love the free market...and so on...

This explanation of an equilibrium is illustrated in Figure 12.1 and makes up the basis for understanding a great deal of the markets in the US (and world) economy. Importantly, this model for understanding a market relies on price as its centerpiece. Price serves not only as the amount needed to conduct a transaction, but also, and perhaps more importantly, as a signal of the value of the good or service being provided to everyone in the market. Based on this signal, buyers decide how much they want to purchase and sellers decide how much they want to provide. What makes medical care fundamentally different from many other markets in the economy is that, for most participants in this market, prices pass through an intermediary (the health insurer) and are broken apart into separate signals for buyers and for sellers.

Different prices for buyers and sellers are not a completely unheard of feature of a market. Many markets have sales taxes, where the buyer price and the seller price are slightly different as a portion of the paid price is siphoned off to the government. While sales tax rates are readily known and transparent, what is different in health care is that the information on price is siloed, and in many cases different from person to person. Buyers

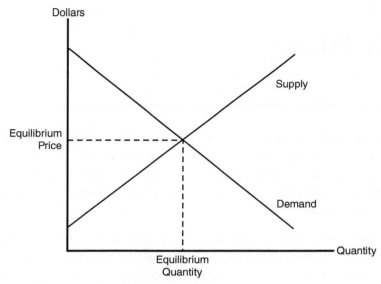

Figure 12.1 Picture from a standard economics textbook

do not always know the prices paid to sellers, and sellers do not always know the price paid by buyers. Additionally, a single seller (e.g. a hospital) may serve many different buyers (patients) who all experience different prices for the same service as they may all have different insurance plans. This means that the signal of value that drives the fabled "invisible hand" to allocate resources is sending different messages to different actors, creating a situation where one part of a market may be getting different information than another.[1]

Prices in Healthcare

The price of a specific medical service may differ depending on which party in the transaction you are talking about. Due to the presence of health insurance, the price felt by a patient and the price felt by a provider might be quite different.

Prices Felt by Patients

The price felt by a patient is the out-of-pocket cost of the care being purchased. In the case of an insured individual, this is the cost sharing component

---

[1] To push the metaphor further, it is as if there are two invisible hands, a right hand and a left hand allocating resources on different sides of the market. In this case, healthcare can be a situation where one invisible hand does not know what the other invisible hand is doing.

of their insurance plan. As discussed in Chapter 4, if their plan has a fixed copay, then the price they feel is the copay. If their plan has coinsurance, then the price they feel is the price of the care multiplied by their coinsurance percentage. If they have a deductible, then the price is different depending on whether or not they have paid their deductible for the year. Notice that all of these prices are influenced in some way by the health insurer and are not completely a result of interaction between buyer and seller.

Further complicating matters are uninsured individuals, who pay providers directly without an insurance company serving as an intermediary. For them, the price listed by a provider is the price that they are responsible for paying. This creates a dichotomy in pricing between the insured and uninsured that we will return to later in this chapter.

Prices Felt by Providers

The price felt by a provider is the payment received for goods or services rendered. This includes all money received from different payers for the same thing. So, if a patient has 20 percent ($C = 0.2$) coinsurance and pays $20 out-of-pocket for an office visit that is priced at $100, the price felt by the provider is $100, as the insurance company is also paying $80 toward the care.[2] In a situation where a patient is paying a fixed copay, the copay amount could be completely different than the amount that is actually paid to the provider. For a copay of $50 the payment to the provider could be $100, $500 or even $5,000 (or any other amount) as the total payment amount to the provider would be determined by a separate process than the process that determines the copay amount.

The Lifecycle of a Medical Bill

A good way to understand prices within the healthcare sector is to follow the life of a medical bill. The process by which a bill is handled, who pays, how much, and when explains a lot about how prices differ from party to party as well as how these differences arise.

The Chargemaster

Medical bills begin with a document called a *chargemaster*. Each provider maintains a chargemaster, which is a list of all goods and services that

---

[2] Recall from Chapter 4 that the price paid by a patient under coinsurance is $(C \times P_m)$, and the price paid by the insurer is $(1 - C \times P_m)$, meaning that for a price of $100 to the provider, the patient only experiences a price of $20.

they provide as well as the price they charge for each good or service. The chargemaster is a master list that is used to construct medical bills, each service that was rendered has a counterpart (or counterparts if there are multiple components to the service) on the chargemaster, and each one is looked up and transcribed onto the medical bill. So, a medical bill will consist of a list of each service provided (each individual service listed on the bill is referred to as a *line item*), as well as each of their prices from the chargemaster (referred to as *charged amounts*), and then a grand total.[3] The grand total on the bill will be adjusted down by any amount paid at the time care was delivered (such as a copay collected by the provider) and then is sent off to whoever is responsible for paying. When the bill is sent to an insurance company, it is often referred to as a *medical claim* or simply as a *claim*, which is an insurance term for a case that is trying to collect against an insurance policy.

A question that naturally arises is "how do providers arrive at chargemaster prices?" This is not a question with an obvious answer. Chargemasters generate medical bills but are not necessarily the amount that a provider will eventually be paid for the service by any given payer. Because of this, there is reason to believe that providers may set their chargemaster prices strategically to maximize profits as opposed to treating the chargemaster as a "true" list of prices they expect to be paid. We will return to this idea shortly.

Medical Bills and Insurers

Once a medical bill is sent to an insurance company, the insurer will go through each line item and look up (a) how much they have agreed to pay the provider for that item, as well as (b) how much of that amount the patient still owes. They will then send payment to the provider for the bill, and, if appropriate, notify the patient of their need to pay the balance. The amount paid to the provider for a given line item is referred to as an *allowed amount*, or sometimes as an *allowed payment*.

Allowed amounts are typically much lower than charged amounts and are pre-negotiated between providers and insurers. A health insurance company will negotiate each service's payment prior to entering into an agreement to cover their enrolled patients at a given provider and will periodically renegotiate and update their payment agreements. So, the

---

[3] Chargemasters as usually organized based on standardized numerical codes. These codes create a common classification for all known medical procedures and are updated as new procedures are added. The overarching coding system used in the United States is the "Healthcare Common Procedure Coding System" or HCPCS (pronounced "hick picks"). The codes are maintained by the Centers for Medicare and Medicaid Services (CMS).

allowed amount for any given service will depend on the outcome of this negotiation.

This is where characteristics of a given provider and a given insurer become important. As one party in the negotiation gains *bargaining power* relative to the other, they become more able to push for allowed amounts that they find favorable. To put a finer point on it, providers are looking to be paid more for services, and insurers are looking to pay out less.[4] So, a provider with more bargaining power will be able to negotiate larger payments, and an insurer with more bargaining power will be able to negotiate lower payments.

Arriving at Allowed Amounts via Negotiation

One problem that arises when negotiating allowed amounts between providers and insurers is that the number of procedures that a provider might perform and be billed for is quite large. For any given provider, there might be tens of thousands of different distinct products and services to negotiate, as even what we may think of as a single procedure may have many different ways of being billed.

To give an example, billing for medical and surgical procedures is done using numerical codes called "Current Procedure Terminology" (CPT) codes.[5] For coronary artery bypass graft (CABG) surgery (a.k.a. a heart bypass) there are over a dozen different CPT codes that could be used, each with its own chargemaster price. CPT code 33510 is used when the surgery bypasses a single artery using a single harvested vein (the surgeon takes a vein out of you, most commonly from the leg, and puts it in your heart to go around a clog), which should not be confused with CPT code 33533 which is used when the surgery bypasses a single artery using a single harvested artery (the surgeon takes an artery out of you, most commonly from the arm or chest, and puts it in your heart to go around a clog). There are different codes for each number of clogs bypassed, as well as a separate subset of codes used when there is a mix of both arteries and veins used to do the bypassing. There are also separate codes (each, of course, with their own price) for harvesting each vein or artery used in the bypass, as well as separate codes for putting a scope into your body to look at the veins or arteries when harvesting them. The point here is that the chargemaster gets long and complicated very quickly and that each line of the chargemaster must be negotiated.

---

[4] Recall from Chapter 10 that $Premium \approx E[Payout] + loading$, so a health insurer that is able to negotiate lower payments pushes down $E[Payout]$ by paying less for services and is able to better compete for customers by offering lower premiums.

[5] CPT codes are themselves a subset of HCPCS codes.

To make things easier, negotiations can be based off a set of benchmark prices set by the Centers for Medicare and Medicaid Services (CMS) for making payments under Medicare. Rather than negotiate each service's price individually, negotiations can be over a markup to the Medicare payment, such as "should we pay Medicare's price plus 10 percent? Or Medicare's price plus 12 percent?" Presumably, these negotiations would be over payments that are higher than the Medicare payment, as Medicare is the largest insurer in the US market, and thus has the most bargaining power.[6] After pegging most payments to a percentage markup over the Medicare payment, this then leaves insurers and providers free to do more focused bargaining over the price of a smaller subgroup of services for which they have strong opinions on what the specific payment should be.

There is evidence that the market for private health insurance payments follows this pattern of negotiating based off Medicare as a starting point. Clemens and Gottlieb (2017) showed that when Medicare changed its payments for one set of specialties, but not another, private health insurance payments subsequently changed following the same pattern. Likewise, when Medicare reshuffled its payments based on location (they updated geographic boundaries for location-based differences in payments, as different places have different costs of inputs such as office rents), private health insurance payments again changed following the same pattern. This is behavior that is consistent with negotiating using Medicare as a starting point.

Denial of Payment

The other thing that can happen after a bill is sent to a health insurer is that the insurer can refuse to pay. This can be thought of as sending back an allowed payment of zero dollars. There are many reasons why an insurer may do this. Some are administrative: the provider filled out the wrong paperwork or filled out paperwork incorrectly. However, it is possible that denial of payment could be used as a negotiation tactic to push providers to accept lower payments on average by being intentionally difficult in medical claim processing.

A Sample Medical Bill

To illustrate how this process works, Table 12.1 is a simplified version of a medical bill. This is based approximately off the actual bill I received for the birth of my daughter.

---

[6] Medicare can set its own prices for procedures, and providers do not get to negotiate other than "take Medicare patients" or "don't take Medicare patients." This is discussed more in Chapter 14.

Table 12.1 Baby Girl Friedson's birth medical bill	
Charged amount	$17,000
Negotiated payment	$10,000
Insurer pays	$9,750
You pay	$250

I have collapsed all of the line items (procedures) into a single line. If you were to add up the chargemaster prices for all of the services rendered during the birth (i.e. delivery of a baby, anesthetic for mom, an overnight stay in a hospital room, nothing for dad because he totally did not faint), it adds up to $17,000. Then, for all those procedures, just by having the insurance company negotiating prices on my behalf, the payment that needed to be made for the hospital to be satisfied was knocked down to $10,000. That is $7,000 **less** than what was listed on the chargemaster for that care.

Then the remaining $10,000 to be paid to the hospital was split between my insurer and myself based on our cost sharing as laid out in my insurance plan. In this case, I had a single copay of $250, and the insurer was on the hook for the remainder ($9,750). The price difference as felt by different parts of the market becomes incredibly apparent here. From the hospital's point of view, that childbirth carried a price tag of $10,000. However, from my point of view, childbirth carried a price tag of $250.

Medical Bills and the Uninsured

The process of paying a medical bill for individuals not using health insurance is slightly different. In this case, the provider will send the bill to the patient directly, and the patient (who likely has not pre-negotiated payments with the provider) will be responsible for the full amount on the bill – which is the amount from the chargemaster. Uninsured individuals thus are charged significantly more for the same service as compared to insured individuals.[7]

Note that there are two reasons for this price discrepancy. First, the uninsured individual is not cost sharing with anyone, the full cost of what is

---

[7] This is not to say that all uninsured individuals always pay this full amount, for example, some hospitals have programs for individuals with no insurance and limited ability to pay. In general, the uninsured start from a sizable disadvantage when arriving at amounts to be paid.

listed on the bill is their responsibility. Second, due to their lack of nego-tiation, uninsured individuals are charged the full chargemaster price and receive no discount off the chargemaster.

These differences are significant. To illustrate again with the example of my daughter's birth, had I been uninsured, and had my wife and child received the same care, we would have been charged $17,000 instead of $250, an increase in the price of $16,750 (or an increase of 670 fold).[8] Of that price increase, $9,750 would have come from no longer cost sharing with another party and $7,000 would have come from no longer having someone (with a lot more bargaining power than we had as one family) negotiating with the hospital on our behalf.

Where the Chargemaster Comes From

In the context of how payments are made, we can now return to the question of where chargemaster prices come from. This is not a ques-tion that has an immediately obvious answer due to the multiple uses of the chargemaster prices. Providers have multiple incentives that they face when setting chargemaster prices, which do not necessarily agree. On one hand, the chargemaster is an opening bid in a negotiation between providers and health insurance companies. On the other hand, the chargemaster is the list of prices that will actually be paid by indi-viduals without insurance and may be a point of competition if these people shop around based on price. There are thus competing interests for providers when choosing what numbers to list on the chargemaster: the prices that will get the best outcome for negotiations with health insurers may not be the ideal prices for dealing with the uninsured (and vice versa).

The process for setting the prices on the chargemaster is best described as "murky." When interviewed by reporter Steven Brill for a *Time* magazine article on medical bills, the Senior Vice President of Payer Relations at a major US hospital remarked that he "didn't know exactly" where the num-bers came from, and later returned with the answer that the chargemaster was "a historical charge, which takes into account all of our costs of run-ning the hospital." This seems to suggest that there may be other factors at play when setting chargemaster prices, such as spreading out other costs in the hospital (e.g. hospitals might be using profitable services to subsidize less profitable services).

---

[8] The value of this price increase represents over 25 percent of the median household income in Colorado in 2017 – the state and year in which my daughter was born (Guzman 2018).

Prices, Search, and Competition

One function of a price in a perfectly competitive market is to serve as a point of comparison for competing goods. If I want to fill up my car with gasoline, or if I want to buy a sandwich for lunch, then I can look at prices and shop around for the best deal. This becomes much more difficult when purchasing healthcare as chargemaster prices are not always immediately available, immediately understandable, or representative of the price that will ultimately be experienced by a patient.

When deciding where to get medical care, especially when individuals have insurance that drastically lowers the price experienced, people may care much more about features other than the price of the care when deciding between competitors. If you are in the back of an ambulance, experiencing a medical emergency that requires immediate medical attention, you are extremely unlikely to yell to the driver, "take me to the other hospital that is further away, they have better deals on emergency heart bypass!"

In the previous example, you as the patient most likely cared about the hospital that is the closest as opposed to the hospital that was the least expensive. In many (if not most) other situations, individuals will want to shop around based on quality rather than based on price, especially if they have insurance. Imagine that you were given a card, that when presented to a restaurant, any sandwich cost you $5 (the sandwich maker would still get paid their menu price for the sandwich, so you don't have to worry about them doing a bad job making it). Would you shop around for the most affordable sandwich? I wouldn't. I would shop around for the most delicious sandwich.[9]

Shopping Based on Quality

If individuals with insurance care less about price, then they might want to shop around based on quality. This is not necessarily an easy thing to do. Imagine that you need to have a risky surgery where you might not survive. You would then want to shop around for the hospital that would maximize your likelihood of survival. What information would you use to find the best choice?

One thing you could do is look at how often people getting your surgery survive, and then go to the hospital with the best survival rate. However, this will not necessarily get you your best chance at survival: a hospital with the best equipment, and the best staff, and the best medical practices

---

[9] If you haven't guessed already, in the previous example the sandwich card is your health insurance, and the sandwich is medical care.

may actually have a lower survival rate for their patients because they might attract the sickest and riskiest cases. This is referred to as *selection bias*, where a group with a given characteristic (in this case how likely they are at baseline to die during surgery) appear in a sample (in this case the people treated at a given hospital) with exaggerated frequency, causing it to not be representative of the general population.[10]

Selection bias makes shopping around based on previous experiences of hospitals (or other providers) difficult. A hospital performing poorly could be an indicator that they are not a good hospital but could also be an indicator that they treat a very sick population. When publicly reporting quality metrics, agencies such as CMS use a process called *risk adjustment*, which attempts to statistically correct quality metrics for differences in the underlying patient population and allow for more "apples to apples" comparisons between providers. While it is difficult to do risk adjustment perfectly (as it is difficult to capture every characteristic of a patient population that is relevant to health outcomes), this process does make providers more comparable than if it was not done.

One final way that providers can compete with each other based on quality is to do so on dimensions of quality that have little to do with the actual care. If you are going to have a surgery that is not risky (i.e. the surgery has a near 100 percent chance of success, and few risks), but does require a hospital stay of two days, and you bear very little of the cost due to insurance, you may shop around based on creature comforts of the facility. Does the hospital have good food? Private rooms or shared rooms? A big TV and lots of streaming options in the room? All of these could be deciding factors for a patient when price is not relevant and are thus dimensions along which providers might compete with one another for customers.

Price Transparency

One idea for improving the patient experience in healthcare is to create a system where prices are easier to assess and compare across providers. This is often referred to as "price transparency." There are various laws aimed at improving price transparency at both the state and federal level. For example, as of January 1, 2021 CMS required all hospitals in the United States to provide machine readable price lists and to display prices for at least 300 shoppable services in a consumer friendly format (Department of Health and Human Services 2020).

---

[10] Selection bias is form of *latent variable* problem as discussed in Chapter 5. Because we cannot observe the illness level of the patients going into the hospitals (the latent or omitted variable), we arrive at an incorrect assessment of the hospital quality.

In theory, price transparency has the ability to lower prices for care for patients if it enables patients to effectively shop around for services looking for the best deal. That said, price transparency initiatives come with two caveats. The first is that patients shopping around will only be effective at spurring competition (and lowering prices) if price is what patients care about. For example, if the same service has differences in quality across providers, and patients care more about quality than price, then an increase in price transparency may not cause more competition between providers. Whaley (2019) provides some evidence of this: when a price comparison tool was rolled out to different healthcare markets, markets that saw larger increases in the use of the tool saw larger decreases in the prices of healthcare services that are fairly standard across all providers (such as laboratory tests), but little change in the prices of healthcare services that might be billed as the same thing but have significant quality variation (such as office visits).

The second caveat to price transparency has to do with the negotiated nature of prices. In a negotiation, information can be leveraged into bargaining power. If you're trying to buy a used car from me and I know that you are willing to pay $5,000 for it, then I am unlikely to accept an opening bid of $2,000. But if I have no idea how much you are willing to pay, then I might accept the $2,000 bid.

The same applies to negotiations between providers and insurers. If a provider knows that an insurer is paying more to someone else, they may be better able to push for higher payments, meaning that price transparency has the ability (at least in theory) to increase prices.

Self-Assessment

1. Different patients may pay different amounts for the same the same service from the same provider. What will influence how much each patient will pay?
2. Different insurance companies may pay different amounts for the same service from the same provider. What will influence how much each insurance company will pay?
3. If you were a hospital administrator who was in charge of setting prices on the chargemaster, and could set any price that you want with the goal of making as much profit as possible for the hospital, what are some of the factors that would influence your decision? Why would these factors matter?

4. Why are prices paid by Medicare a useful starting point for negotiations over payment amounts?

5. Not having insurance increases a patient's out-of-pocket payments in two distinct ways, what are they?

6. In many cases, price is not the primary concern for patients shopping around for medical care. If not price, then what do patients care about?

7. Consider the statement "Price transparency will always lead to lower prices for medical care." What is correct about this statement? What is incorrect? Write a more accurate statement.

13 Managed Care

One way that health insurance companies compete with each other is by offering lower premiums for the same level of coverage. However, insurers are limited in the amount that they can price compete with each other because they are bound by the formula Premium $\approx E[\text{payout}] + \text{loading}$. There is a little bit of wiggle room for an insurer to cut the premium by shifting profits toward cutting prices, but unless insurers find a way to lower $E[\text{payout}]$ or loading it can be difficult to make large changes in premiums. Cutting premiums too much could leave an insurer in a situation where they do not have enough money to make the payments that they are obligated to under their contracts (the policies sold to customers).

Enter the *Managed Care Organization (MCO)*. An MCO is an insurance company that uses its ability to create incentives for players in the market for medical care to push down $E[\text{payout}]$ and with it offer lower premiums. The goal of an MCO is to create incentives that lower the amount of medical care used (or the cost of the medical care used), while at the same time offering similar quality of care (i.e. maintaining the health outcomes of their customers). The sales pitch goes like this: "I can offer you an insurance plan that has a 10 percent lower premium and delivers you the exact same health as your current plan." Sounds like a good deal right?

The strategy of an MCO is predicated on the existence of "waste" to squeeze out of the system. That somewhere, there is enough valueless (or low value) overuse of care, that proper use of incentives can eliminate the extra care and make both the patient and the insurer better off.[1] Where is this waste? It's in Chapter 2, sitting on the flat of the curve. Figure 13.1 shows the key picture again to save you having to flip back.

The flat of the curve is a place where you can decrease the amount of medical care (m) used and not change health outcomes (H). Less medical care used on the flat of the curve directly lowers $E[\text{payout}]$ and with it the premium, and, on the flat of the curve this does not decrease health.

The rest of this chapter will explore the specifics of how MCOs do this, both from an organizational standpoint (how you set your insurance company up

---

[1] Or at least make one of them better off and the other no worse off.

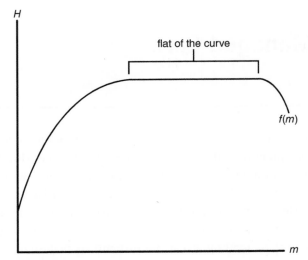

Figure 13.1 The flat of the curve

to best leverage your incentive making abilities) and from an operational standpoint (what types of incentives an insurer uses to accomplish this aim).

MCO Structure

Before digging into the "playbook" for managed care, it's useful to take a look at how insurance companies organize themselves. To this point, much of what has been discussed has set insurers up as an intermediary between patients and providers when it comes time to pay medical bills, but there are features of an insurer's overall structure that change the nature of this relationship.

Health Maintenance Organization

The most extreme example of the importance of insurance company organizational structure is the Health Maintenance Organization (HMO). An HMO is a situation where the insurer and the provider are the same entity. To put a finer point on it, the insurance company owns and operates their own medical practices, hospitals, clinics, and so forth. Everything is offered under one umbrella, so patients deal with the same entity for both scheduling and payment, and the healthcare providers are employed directly by the HMO.

One of the most prominent examples of an HMO in the United States is Kaiser Permanente. Kaiser Permanente runs health plans in several metro areas, including Denver, Colorado. In Denver, they operate multiple health facilities, and employ the physicians (and line staff) that work in those facilities directly. Kaiser Permanente enrollees can receive primary and specialty care directly from Kaiser, having almost all medical needs met without going outside of a Kaiser Permanente facility.[2]

There are some big benefits that come from HMO structure, the most prominent being the degree of control that the insurer has over care decisions when they are also the provider (or the direct employer of the medical staff doing the care provision). There is also an additional degree of control that HMOs have over patients as the HMO oversees scheduling for services. HMOs enjoy some baked in cost savings in the loading part of the Premium $\approx E[\text{payout}] + \text{loading}$ formula. A typical health insurer may need to spend a non-trivial amount of resources sending information (and money) back and forth between them and various different providers. An HMO is both the insurer and provider and is thus able to save on these costs by using a single integrated system.

Preferred Provider Organization

A Preferred Provider Organization (PPO) is a more "traditional" health insurance company structure. Patients choose which providers they want to see, and the insurance company acts as intermediary, paying the medical bills (or the part of the medical bill that is their responsibility due to cost sharing). The big difference between a total free for all and a PPO is the "network." A PPO keeps a list of providers (facilities, physicians, etc.) and these providers are "in-network." Any other provider is "out-of-network." Patients are free to go to whichever provider they would like, however, the terms of the insurance policy (such as the cost sharing) are much more generous (in the patient's favor) when the provider is in-network. Patients have the flexibility to choose their providers but are heavily incentivized to pick providers that are in-network.

PPOs engage in heavier negotiation with in-network providers and strive to include providers in their network that practice in ways that are consistent with the "avoid care on the flat of the curve" mission of an MCO. That said, PPOs have less control over their providers as unlike an HMO which employs the providers directly, a PPO enters into a payment agreement with a provider which is not necessarily that provider's sole source of revenue.

Point of Service

A Point of Service (POS) plan is a hybrid between an HMO and a PPO, sharing some features of both.[3] A POS plan builds a network like a PPO

---

[2] More on the "almost" in a moment.

[3] My grandfather referred to all health insurance plans as POS plans, but he was not an economist nor a healthcare expert, and likely meant something entirely different.

and runs it like an HMO. Under a POS plan, there is usually a centralized scheduling and management authority, but the providers contract with the insurer as opposed to being employed directly. It offers a middle ground between HMO and PPO with some (but not all) of the control advantages of an HMO and some (but not all) of the flexibility advantages of a PPO.

Not every insurer will fit neatly into one of the previously discussed structures.[4] It is perhaps better to think of insurance plans as bundles of features, some of which may more closely align with different organizational structures. For example, even the most integrated HMO will make out-of-network payments in some cases. If a patient is having a heart attack, then the closest hospital might not be operated by the HMO. Due to the medical necessity of acting quickly to save the patient's life, the HMO will cover the care provided by the closest emergency department, even if the HMO does not own or operate it.

Tools Used by MCOs

MCOs have a wide variety of "tools" at their disposal to try to bring down costs. The list that follows is not exhaustive but illustrates some of the most commonly used. They are organized based on who the MCO is trying to influence, the patient or the provider.

Everyone: What Is Covered (and Denial of Payment)

One of the simplest ways to incentivize (or disincentivize) care is to choose to cover it (or not cover it) under the insurance plan. From the patient's point of view, they are responsible for the charged amount for any care that is not covered by the insurance plan. The charged amount is usually a much higher price than what they would be responsible for under insurance and cost sharing, so not covering a type of care creates a powerful financial incentive for a patient to not get that type of care, or to find a substitute type of care that is covered.

This is particularly salient to patients when dealing with prescription drugs. In the case of prescription drugs, insurance companies usually have a list of specific drugs that they cover called a *formulary*. Putting drugs on the formulary (or leaving them off) is the equivalent of saying that you cover them (or do not cover them). For example, a common practice

---

[4] This is also not an exhaustive list of every abbreviation that could be used to describe an insurance company setup. This list is just meant to help organize how we think about the most commonly observed types of MCOs.

is to leave name-brand drugs off the formulary when generic brands are available. Generics are bioequivalent compounds made by a different manufacturer than the name-brand drug and are far less expensive.[5] So, by leaving the name-brand drug off the formulary and putting the generic on the formulary the insurance company saves money by shifting people to a less expensive drug while maintaining health outcomes (as the two drugs are the same compound).

Covering and not covering types of medical care also influences providers. Providers want to be paid for their services and will usually not want to provide a service that they will not be paid for. If there are two possible treatments (A and B), both of which will solve a patient's problem with equal likelihood then a provider will want to pick the treatment that they will be paid more for. If an insurer says that they will not pay for one of the treatments (treatment B), then the provider is left with the choice of "get paid with (close to) certainty by the insurer for one treatment (treatment A)" or "possibly get paid by the patient for the other treatment (treatment B)." This incentivizes the provider to choose to offer the treatment that is favored by the insurance company.

Not covering a service can sometimes manifest in extreme fashion, called *denial of payment*. In this case, the insurer is asked to pay for something and they respond with "nuh uh, I am not paying for that" or something similar. When this happens after care has already been provided it is incredibly disruptive to patients and providers and is an extremely strong (and unpleasant) disincentive for that type of care.

Everyone: Prior Authorization

A tool that is related to, but not quite denial of payment is *prior authorization*. Under prior authorization, payment is automatically denied unless it is given authorization. In other words, the insurer needs to give the OK before the care is provided in order for them to pay for it.

To illustrate, consider two different payment schemes for a hospital stay post-surgery. In the first scheme, a person gets the surgery and the insurer will pay for up to ten days in the hospital. Under this scheme, even if the patient is mostly recovered on day six, then it is easy for the patient or the hospital to extend the stay an extra day or two "just in case." The cost to the patient is low (depending on the cost sharing and their individual opportunity cost) and the hospital is usually happy to be paid for additional patient-days. There are incentives to stretch the hospital stay out onto the flat of the curve.

---

[5] More on name brand and generic drugs can be found in Chapter 15.

The second scheme, which uses prior authorization is this: a person gets the surgery, and the insurer will pay for four days no questions asked, after four days, the insurer will cover up to six additional days provided that before each day they get documentation from the provider that the additional day is needed. This allows the insurer to stop payments when there is no longer a defensible reason to keep the patient in the hospital. In this example, the patient would likely be discharged after six days and not spend the extra two "just in case" days.

One downside of prior authorization is that it creates a lot of additional work for the insurer the provider, and the patient. While some of the cost of this work may be recovered by insurer in the form of cost savings due to fewer payments, the extra costs borne by the provider and patient are not compensated.

Everyone: Behavioral Interventions

An increasingly common way for MCOs to steer patient or provider behavior is to use behavioral interventions, sometimes referred to as "nudges." These types of interventions are discussed in greater detail in the supplement to Chapter 8, but the general idea is that the insurer provides information in such a way that a desired choice is more likely to be chosen, without actually limiting people's choices. A classic example is that people have a cognitive bias where they are disproportionately likely to pick the first item on a list. So, when offering different appointment types to patients or treatment possibilities to providers an insurer can simply list their most desired option at the top of the list a receive a slight boost to its use. One thing to think about with regards to MCOs and nudges is that different MCO structures will have different opportunities to deploy them. An HMO will have a different set of "touch points" where they transmit information to patients or providers than a PPO will.

Patients: Gatekeepers

A gatekeeper is a first level provider that you need to get a referral from before you are allowed to see a second level provider. The idea behind gatekeepers is that (a) some types of care are much more expensive than others, and (b) patients may be bad at knowing what type of care they need.

One of the most commonly used places for gatekeepers is when booking appointments with specialists. Specialist appointments tend to cost more than primary care appointments, sometimes tremendously more. If many of the issues that patients go to specialists for could be handled by primary care, then a system where patients must get a referral from a primary care provider before going to a specialist could be a cost saver. The primary care provider is then serving as "gatekeeper" preventing patients from using expensive specialist visits in cases where inexpensive primary care visits would be sufficient and allowing through patients who truly need the more expensive specialist visits.

Gatekeepers create two new costs. The first is that while gatekeepers save money in the case where an unnecessary specialist visit is avoided, they add in the cost of an additional primary care visit in the case where the specialist visit was indeed needed. It is possible that a gatekeeper program could lose more money from additional primary care visits than it saves on avoidable specialist visits. Fortunately, there is an easy way for insurers to test for this: an insurer can simply try the program and keep track of the types of visits used and their costs. If the program saves money, then the insurer should likely keep the program and if it loses money, then the insurer should discontinue the program.

The second cost is borne solely by the patient. For patients that really did need the specialist, the insurer has added in an additional cost from going to see the primary care doctor. Even if that visit has zero cost sharing on the part of the patient, there are still relevant economic costs in terms of time spent. The insurer has created what is sometimes referred to as "red tape" that the patient needs to get through before they can access the care that they need.

Patients: Second Opinion Programs

Second opinion programs are similar to gatekeeper programs, so much so that some would consider second opinion programs to simply be a subset of gatekeeper programs. The idea behind a second opinion program is that some procedures are (a) expensive and (b) not the only (or the correct) course of action. Under a second opinion program, before a procedure that is part of the program is scheduled, a patient must receive a second opinion: a second provider must see the patient and concur with the recommended course of action.

Much like gatekeeper programs, this creates a second visit that will only be worthwhile if the cost of the new visits are more than covered by the cost savings from avoided procedures. Also, like gatekeeper programs, second opinion programs create a cost in the form of "red tape" that is borne by patients. Unlike gatekeeper programs, second opinion programs have an additional weakness: depending on the relationship between the providers, the second opinion provider may not feel comfortable undermining the decision of the first provider. There can be power dynamics and professional relationships at play that can limit the effectiveness of a second opinion program that are not present in the case of gatekeeper programs more broadly.

To give a concrete example: if you are a senior surgeon who gets paid when you perform surgeries, and patients are being sent to a junior surgeon who works in your department for a second opinion, then the junior surgeon may not feel comfortable undermining your decision to operate. You might have some sway over the junior surgeon's future in the profession which makes them feel uncomfortable giving a contrary opinion to yours.

Patients: Cost Sharing Manipulation

MCOs can influence patient behavior based on the cost sharing in an insurance plan. If an MCO would like patients to use less of a certain type of care, then the insurer can increase the cost sharing on that care. Likewise, if an MCO would like patients to use more of a certain type of care, then the insurer can decrease the cost sharing on that care.

An example of this is low-cost preventative care that can potentially prevent high-cost interventions down the road. I have not had to pay anything out-of-pocket for vaccinations for as long as I can remember. Flu shots? Zero cost sharing. Vaccines for my children? Zero cost sharing. Why? Vaccines are low cost and prevent the need for care for serious illnesses down the road. A free flu shot for all enrollees in an MCO is likely less expensive than additional hospitalizations due to severe bouts of flu that deteriorate into pneumonia, even if the hospitalizations only occur for a small number of enrollees.

In a similar way, MCOs can disincentivize lower value care by increasing the cost sharing. Here's another example from my actual insurance plan: if I have an emergency and go to an emergency department at a local hospital, then I have to pay a larger copay than if I go to an urgent care center run by my HMO. Why? The emergency department has a lot of overlap in services with urgent care but charges a lot more. If there is a type of emergency care that can be done at both places, the insurer would prefer that I go to their urgent care facility which costs them less than an emergency department visit. So, the insurance plan gives me a financial incentive to do just that. The only situation in which I will choose to go to the emergency department is when I think that the emergency department can provide the service that I need and that the urgent care cannot.[6]

Providers: Choice of Providers to Interact With

One place where MCOs have a lot of leverage with regards to provider behavior is when deciding which providers to interact with. For a PPO this

---

[6] I may also be concerned with other relevant costs such as travel time, especially if there is a lot of blood.

is a question of which providers are included in-network and which are left as out-of-network. For an HMO this is a question of which providers are hired directly. When choosing a set of providers to interact with, an MCO will want to consider how that provider has behaved historically (if that information is available) and what type of general practice patterns the provider tends to use. An MCO will try to gauge how well the provider conforms with the strategy of "lower payouts, same health outcomes."

A PPO or POS may also care a lot about the size of the providers that they contract with, or at least the size of the provider's practice relative to the market. Smaller providers may have less bargaining power than larger providers, allowing insurers to get to lower payouts by leveraging their bargaining power in payment negotiations and pushing down the price they pay to the providers.

Providers: Payment Manipulation

Another place where MCOs can create incentives for providers is in how much the providers are paid, and what scheme is used for payment. Think back to Chapter 8: how a person is paid makes a big difference in how they perform their work duties. A provider who is paid via fee-for-service is incentivized to produce as much as possible, whereas a provider who is paid via salary has no such incentive. It should thus be no surprise that when HMOs hire physicians directly, it is common practice to hire them into salaried contracts.

This is not to say that there is no room for payment to be used as an incentive in fee-for-service systems as are commonly used in PPOs. When negotiating with providers over allowed amounts, insurers can be as difficult as possible in some parts of the negotiations and strategically relent in others. An insurer could choose to fight as hard as possible on compensation for care that they believe is on or close to the flat of the curve. The insurer could also choose to relent and give more generous compensation for types of care that they consider to be higher value (i.e. care that they want to incentivize). This would create a situation where compensation is slightly more generous or slightly less generous based on the types of care that the insurer would or would not like to incentivize.

Providers: Capitation

Another payment scheme that an MCO can use is *capitation payment*, meaning a flat payment to care for a given patient for a given time frame. Capitation creates a unique incentive to provide the "appropriate" amount of care for a patient. The trick to capitation is that after accepting the capitation contract, the provider is on the hook for all relevant care that the patient needs for a given episode.

Under capitation, a provider does not want to do too much. If a provider does more for a patient than is necessary then they have spent resources on care that they did not need to spend, meaning that they could have made more profit by doing less. If a provider does too little for a patient and the patient deteriorates and needs additional care, then the provider is on the hook for the cost of that additional care and will not receive a payment above and beyond the original capitation payment. This means that the provider could have made additional profit by doing more. Capitation creates an incentive to not do too much, and creates an incentive to not do too little, putting provider incentives into a "Goldilocks Zone."[7]

Providers: Bonuses and Holdbacks

MCOs can also incentivize behaviors in providers by setting specific goals and then making additional payments to the providers if those goals are met. If the payment is above and beyond the contracted payment amount, then this is called a *bonus*, and if the payment is part of the contracted payment amount that is "held hostage" unless the goal is met, then this is called a *holdback*. By setting goals that trigger the bonuses or holdbacks in such a way that they match with the "lower payouts, same health outcomes" strategy of the MCO, the insurer can create a provider incentive that is in line with their game plan.

MCO Control and Patient Choices

One question that arises from the discussion in this chapter is "if HMOs are more centralized and can better take advantage of incentives to lower costs, then why isn't every plan an HMO?" Put differently, "why isn't it the case that the only competitive plans are the lowest premium plans with the most aggressive use of MCO tools to get there?" The answer is: because the price isn't the only cost that people care about.

MCOs can lower the price of insurance, but many of the incentives that they use create other costs in the form of inconvenience and lack of flexibility. HMOs have not completely taken over the market because

---

[7] This is a reference to the story "Goldilocks and the Three Bears" where Goldilocks doesn't want food that is too hot or too cold but prefers the food that is just right. I'm borrowing the term "Goldilocks Zone" from astronomy where it is used to describe the distance from a star where water on a planet is not so hot that it boils off and not so cold that it is all frozen. This is an apt term for capitation payment incentives, where the incentive is not to do too much and not to do too little.

consumers want lower prices but also want convenience and flexibility and are willing to pay higher prices to get them. The general MCO strategy is powerful and has worked its way into most modern insurance plans in some way, but there is still a balance between prices and convenience that needs to be struck.

Self-Assessment

1. If all care that was delivered was to the left of the flat of the curve, would MCOs still exist? Why or why not?
2. Some PPOs differentiate themselves by how "wide" their networks are. A "wider" network means that the network has a larger set of providers to pick from. Similarly, "narrow" networks have a smaller set of providers to pick from. Would you expect a narrow network PPO to have a larger or a smaller premium than a wider network PPO? Why?
3. If you were a physician working at a hospital, how would you feel about an insurance plan that required prior authorization for extending hospital stays?
4. Can you think of a situation where a gatekeeper program would cause overall payouts (and with them, premiums) to increase? What would that situation look like?
5. Can you think of a situation where a second opinion program would cause overall payouts (and with them, premiums) to increase? What would that situation look like?
6. Imagine you are an MCO that is preparing for negotiations with a hospital over payments. You have been given the hospital chargemaster. The chargemaster contains over 10,000 different procedures and their potential payments. Your job is to decide which procedures are worth bargaining aggressively over. How would you go about figuring out which procedures matter to you?

14 | Public Insurance

One of the largest health insurance providers in the United States is the government. This chapter discusses the size, structure, and programmatic details of government insurance programs. Many of these plans are large, complicated, and have details that change somewhat frequently. This chapter is meant as a broad introduction to public insurance in the United States and not as a definitive guide. The goal is to unpack what the major insurance programs are and how they work.

The majority of the chapter will deal with the largest programs: Medicare, which is public insurance for those aged 65+ or who have certain permanent disabilities, and Medicaid, which is public insurance for those with low income. This chapter will also discuss other forms of government insurance such as programs run by the Department of Veteran's Affairs, Department of Labor, and other programs provided by the Department of Health and Human Services (which also oversees Medicare and Medicaid).

How Big Are These Programs?

A first question to ask is "how much of the health insurance sector is run through the government?" There are a few different ways to measure this, but the answer is generally "a sizable chunk." Keisler-Starkey and Bunch (2020) provide estimates of how much of the US population receives health insurance from different insurers using data from the US Census Bureau. They estimate that around 110 million people received health insurance from Medicare or Medicaid in 2020.[1] That represents just a shade over a third of the 2020 US population. Just under another 3 million people received health insurance through the Department of Veteran's Affairs (another almost 1 percent of the US population), and another 9.2 million through the US military (or almost another 3 percent).

According to the Centers for Medicare & Medicaid Services (CMS), which is a part of the Department of Health and Human Services and is the

---

[1] This counts the population that was enrolled in one or both programs. If you're in both programs (which is possible) you're not counted twice.

federal administrator for Medicare and Medicaid, there was $829.5 billion in Medicare spending and $671.2 billion in Medicaid spending in 2020. Together, these account for 36 percent of national health expenditures, or roughly 7.2 percent of the GDP of the United States in 2020 (Centers for Medicare & Medicaid Services 2022a).

The enrollment in these programs has generally been growing over time. Proctor (2016) provides estimates of public insurance similar to Keisler-Starkey and Bunch (2020) covering 1987–2010. In 1987, Medicare and Medicaid covered 18.9 percent of the US population. By 2000, this had grown to 21.2 percent of the population, and by 2010 this had grown again to 26.8 percent. Recall (or just go back a few paragraphs) that in 2020 just over a third of the population was enrolled. Over 30 years, these programs took in an additional 12 percent of the US population.

Medicare

Medicare was signed into law in 1965, and covered individuals aged 65 and older. The original plan included Part A, coverage for hospital inpatient care, and Part B, medical insurance. In 1972, the program was expanded to include coverage for those under age 65 with long-term disabilities as well as for individuals with end-stage renal disease. Then, in 1982, coverage was again expanded to include coverage for hospice care. The 1997 Balanced Budget Act added Part C to Medicare, which allows individuals to purchase approved third-party MCO coverage in lieu of using Medicare Part B. Part C has been rebranded several times, it went by "Medicare+Choice" or "M+C" before being rebranded as "Medicare Advantage" in 2003 as part of the Medicare Prescription Drug, Improvement, and Modernization Act of 2003 which also introduced Part D, Medicare's coverage for prescription drugs.

What follows is a brief description of how the different components of Medicare look from the point of view of an enrolled individual. Plan details (such as the size of deductibles) may vary from year to year, so for the most up-to-date information on plan characteristics, check Medicare.gov. That said, the general structure of the plans is as follows and all specific dollar amounts are current as of 2022.

Part A

Part A covers inpatient stays in hospitals or skilled nursing facilities. For a given "event," which starts when a patient is admitted as an inpatient and ends when a patient has not received inpatient care for 60 days in a row, all patients pay a deductible which is set at $1,556. For the first 60 days, the patient pays no cost sharing (other than the deductible), and then pays $389 for each day from day 61 to 90. Each patient also has a "lifetime reserve" of 60 days that can be spent after the 90th day of inpatient care, where the patient pays $778 per day. The lifetime reserve is used across all inpatient stays, so if a patient stays for 95 days, which is 5 days over the 90 you can use before tapping into the lifetime reserve, then there would be 55 (60–5) days left in the reserve. Once 90 days have been spent and the lifetime reserve is exhausted, then the patient is responsible for 100 percent of inpatient costs, in other words, Medicare is done spending on that patient for that inpatient stay and the patient is on their own.

Part A is interesting in that it offers generous coverage for shorter hospital stays but has a complete lack of coverage for catastrophic situations where a patient needs long-term hospitalization. For individuals looking for financial protection against catastrophic inpatient expenditures, Part A is not a solution.

Part B

Part B covers what Medicare refers to as "medically necessary services" and "preventative services" that do not fall under the umbrella of services covered by Part A. This includes a limited subset of prescription drugs (with the majority of prescription drugs covered under Part D). Unlike Part A, Part B has a monthly premium which starts out at $170.10 per month but scales up based on income (higher income individuals pay a higher premium), as well as an annual deductible of $233.

Part B operates under a 20 percent coinsurance model for most services but has zero cost sharing for specific services such as clinical laboratory services, home health care services, and depression screening. The 20 percent coinsurance is off of the amount that Medicare pays the provider, not the amount that is charged to Medicare. In fact, the amounts that Medicare pays to providers are tightly controlled in most cases, this is discussed later in the chapter.

Part C (Medicare Advantage)

Medicare Advantage is an alternative to traditional Medicare. These plans are offered by private insurance companies but follow rules set out by Medicare as to what must be covered under the plans and what cost sharing is allowed to look like. Medicare Advantage plans usually replace Part A and Part B, but some Medicare Advantage plans also replace Part D.

After you choose a Medicare Advantage plan, Medicare pays the insurer a fixed amount each month. As a patient you are still responsible for your Part B premium even though your Medicare Advantage plan "replaces"

Part B. Some Medicare Advantage plans charge an additional premium (this can be seen as a higher total price), these plans tend to have more generous benefits. Some Medicare Advantage plans send money back to Medicare and pay part or all of your Part B premiums for you (this can be seen as a lower total price), these plans tend to have less generous benefits. Medicare Advantage plans are free to use different cost sharing structures (they are MCOs after all and want to do MCO things), but are subject to an annual limit for patient out-of-pocket costs for services covered by Part A or Part B.

Part D

Part D offers coverage for prescription drugs but is an optional part of Medicare. Individuals can choose to enroll in Part D but can also instead choose to purchase their own prescription drug insurance. Part D is either offered as standalone coverage or as part of a Medicare Advantage plan. Under the "standard" Part D plan, enrollees have a $480 deductible. After the deductible, there is 25 percent coinsurance for the next $3,950 spent on drugs. After a total of $4,430 ($3,950 + $480) is spent, the plan changes, but not tremendously for the patient. The patient continues to pay 25 percent of costs, but is also responsible for small pharmacy dispensing fees (in the range of $1–$3 per prescription), the big change is on the insurer end, where for generic drugs the insurer pays 75 percent but for name brands the insurer pays 5 percent and the drug manufacturer covers the remaining 70 percent by reducing the price (i.e. giving a discount).[2] Once a total of $7,050 is paid by the patient out-of-pocket in a year, the plan enters a final, "catastrophic coverage" phase, where from that point on the patient pays the greater of 5 percent coinsurance or a flat copay of $3.95 for generic drugs or $9.85 for name-brand drugs. The plan resets at the start of each year.

Gap Plans

You likely noticed that in the above plans there is significant cost sharing, in some cases cost sharing that may defeat the purpose of the insurance (e.g. Part A when you have a large number of inpatient days). There are private insurance plans that offer "gap" coverage sometimes referred to as a "Medigap" plan or as "Medicare Supplemental Insurance," which are insurance plans that cover the places that Medicare leaves open to patient

---

[2] This middle section of Part D coverage used to shift significant costs to the patient and was referred to as the "donut hole." The idea is that there was delicious coverage before and after this part, but a hole (with less delicious coverage) in the middle of the plan, much like a donut.

cost sharing. Of note is that while gap plans are allowed to cover services not covered by Part A and Part B, gap plans are not allowed for Part D. You can forego Part D and buy a gap plan that covers drugs but cannot have Part D and a gap plan that covers the Part D cost sharing.

Medicaid

Medicaid was created at the same time as Medicare, as part of the 1965 Social Security Act. Aside from the obvious difference of Medicare covering individuals largely based on age and Medicaid covering individuals largely based on income, there are some big differences in how Medicare and Medicaid work. This is due to the fundamental structure of the programs. While Medicare is a single program run by the federal government, Medicaid is a federal-state partnership. While there is a single federal Medicaid program, each state has its own Medicaid program with its own rules.

The Federal-State Partnership

Medicaid is paid partly by states and partly by the federal government. This is done through a *matching grant*, which means that for each dollar spent by a state, the federal government pays $X. The federal government sets minimum standards that a state Medicaid program needs to meet in order to get any funding, and then matches (the $X paid by the federal government per dollar spent by the state) can be more (or less) generous depending on the features of a state's Medicaid program and a state's demographics.[3] In general, states with lower income per person receive more generous matches from the federal government, but there are exceptions.[4]

Once it meets the federal minimum standards, a state can then choose to be more generous in their coverage along two dimensions. First, a state can choose to cover services more generously. This can be either a wider set of services covered than the federal minimum, or a more generous (more in the patient's favor) cost sharing than the federal minimum. Second, a state can choose to have broader program eligibility than the federal minimum. States also have the option to name their program something other than "Medicaid," even though it is a state Medicaid program. The majority of states but not all states do this, and program names include "Medi-Cal" in

---

[3] For a deeper discussion on the nature of the federal-state partnership and structure of Medicaid, see Rudowitz et al. (2016) and Artiga et al. (2017).

[4] For example, states that expanded Medicaid as part of the ACA received a temporary very generous match for funds used on the newly enrolled.

California, "SoonerCare" in Oklahoma, "MedQuest" in Hawaii, and "Apple Health" in Washington.[5] There is a tremendous amount of state by state variability in Medicaid characteristics, what is discussed next are some examples to give a sense of how programs vary, but for a more detailed explanation I would recommend the dashboards kept by the Kaiser Family Foundation, which allow you to see differences in programs across many dimensions and across time (www.kff.org/state-category/medicaid-chip/).

Variation in What Is Covered

State Medicaid programs are required to cover certain minimum benefits. These include hospital services, nursing facilities, home health services, and laboratory tests.[6] States can also choose to add other forms of coverage such as prescription drugs, dental services, prosthetics, and hospice care. For example, as of 2018, 36 state Medicaid programs covered dental services. Then, across these states that did cover dental, there were differences in how generous the plan characteristics were. Both Colorado and Delaware offered Medicaid dental plans that did not include cost sharing for up to $1,000 of expenditures but had different limitations as to which services were acceptable for these payments. On the other hand, Michigan required a $3 copay for dental services with no payment limit, but also required that certain types of dental care receive prior authorization.

This variation in coverage extends into mandatory services as well. All states are required to cover inpatient hospital services, but there is still variability in cost sharing from state to state. For example, Arizona and Maryland do not require any patient copayment, whereas Massachusetts has a $3 per admission copay and Virginia has a $75 per admission copay.

Variation in Who Is Covered

In a similar manner to the services covered, states can extend their Medicaid programs to cover individuals who are not covered based on the federal minimum requirements. For example, while states are required to cover children in families with incomes below 138 percent of the Federal Poverty Level (FPL) in order to receive federal funding, there are considerable state by state differences in eligibility. Oregon's Medicaid covers infants aged 0–1 with families below 190 percent FPL, and then children aged 1–18 with families below 138 percent FPL. Colorado's Medicaid covers all children

---

[5] This is not to be confused with the "Apple Health App" which is on many Apple devices. These are not related.

[6] For a complete accounting of mandatory and optional services for state Medicaid programs to cover, see www.medicaid.gov/medicaid/benefits/mandatory-optional-medicaid-benefits/index.html

through age 18 with families below 147 percent FPL, whereas Connecticut covers all children through age 18 with families below 201 percent FPL.

How Providers Are Paid by Medicare and Medicaid

From Chapter 8, we know that the pay structure used to compensate providers is important for determining provider behavior. We will next look broadly at how Medicare and Medicaid pay providers. In the case of Medicare, the payments come from CMS, and in the case of Medicaid, the payments come from the state Medicaid office and the federal government pays the state for the federal component of the costs. What follows has a few caveats. First, this is the broad structure of payments, the exact formulas can get quite detailed based on the specifics of the type and location of the service (we'll discuss this in slightly more detail in a moment). Second, this is not how payments are done under Medicare or Medicaid managed care plans (such as Medicare Advantage or states that employ Medicaid sponsored MCOs), in those cases the government pays the MCO to cover the patients, and the MCO pays the providers based on their own plan structure.

Inpatient Payments

Inpatient hospital services are paid on a capitation basis. Patients are put into classifications based on the illness that they are diagnosed with and their reason for being at the hospital. These classifications are called *Diagnosis Related Groups (DRGs)*. Then, the hospital is paid capitation for that patient based on the DRG to which the patient is assigned. DRG-based payments will then be adjusted according to the specifics of a given hospital. For example, hospital A may be paid more for a given DRG than hospital B if hospital A is in a high-cost location and needs more revenue to be able to pay its labor. However, a single hospital will receive the same payment for the same DRG in the same payment-year (as payments are adjusted year to year). This form of payment is sometimes referred to as the "Prospective Payment System" as payments are made based on which patients show up and the amount of resources that they are prospectively expected to use during their stay.

Outpatient Payments

Most outpatient payments are paid based on the Resource Based Relative Value System (RBRVS).[7] Under the RBRVS every service or procedure is assigned a number of Relative Value Units (RVUs). RVUs are meant to capture

---

[7] Say that five times fast.

how resource intensive (both in the sense of physical resources, but also in the sense of time and effort) a particular service or procedure is. So, the more difficult or time intensive the procedure, the more RVUs are assigned. For example, a 15-minute office visit with an established patient is assigned 2.66 RVUs, whereas a CABG surgery for a single artery is assigned 56.78 RVUs.[8]

RVUs are then adjusted based on local conditions. Places with higher resource use (i.e. higher costs for the same service) will be given additional RVUs. Finally, the RVU tally is multiplied by a *conversion factor* to get the payment. The conversion factor for 2021 was 34.8931. So, a service that had a final tally of 10 RVUs would have been paid $348.93, and a service that had a final tally of 25 RVUs would have been paid $872.33.

Quality Incentives

CMS has some programs in place that further adjust payments based on the quality of the care provided. For example, in the case of inpatient hospital spending CMS uses Hospital Value Based Purchasing (HVBP) in which 2 percent of eligible hospital payments are held back and then redistributed based on performance along quality metrics. This creates an incentive for hospitals to improve their quality (or at least to improve their quality in places that will maximize their likelihood of getting additional payments under the program).[9]

Other Public Insurance

There are several other public insurance programs in the United States. Here are some of the biggest other programs and who they cover.

VA and CHAMPVA

US military veterans with a minimum amount of service time, or who were discharged based on certain types of disability are eligible for health benefits from Veteran's Affairs (VA, referred to as "The VA").[10] The VA provides free care for any illness or injury that is connected to prior military service, for veterans with severe service-related disabilities, and for veterans who have no ability to pay. The VA runs its own facilities, and in most cases, care must be provided at such a facility to be paid for by the VA.

---

[8] These are as of the January 2022 CMS Physician Fee Schedule (www.cms.gov/ medicaremedicare-fee-service-paymentphysicianfeeschedpfs-relative-value-files/rvu22a)

[9] Norton et al. (2018) demonstrate that hospitals improve more in places where they are more likely to receive a payment for improvement.

[10] There is no minimum service requirement for veterans who served prior to September 7, 1980.

The VA also runs a health insurance program for dependents of veterans called CHAMPVA. CHAMPVA covers medical expenses for the dependents of permanently disabled veterans, or for dependents of veterans who died while permanently disabled (in both cases provided that said disability is or was a service-related disability).

TRICARE

TRICARE is health insurance for active duty servicemembers and their families. It also covers members of the national guard and their families, survivors of deceased active duty service members, retired service members (this is not the same as discharged service members), as well as Medal of Honor recipients and their families.[11]

CHIP

The Children's Health Insurance Program (CHIP) is similar to Medicaid in that it is a federal-state partnership. In fact, in some states CHIP is part of the state Medicaid program, and in some states, it is its own standalone program. CHIP provides health insurance for children that do not receive coverage under Medicaid but still live in families with low income. When a state has its own standalone CHIP program, then eligibility begins at the upper end of family income used for Medicaid and continues to some higher level of family income.

COBRA

COBRA is an acronym for the Consolidated Omnibus Reconciliation Act of 1985, but everyone calls it COBRA.[12] COBRA is public requirement for private plans to allow individuals to stay enrolled when they normally would not be allowed to be. It is overseen by the Department of Labor and allows workers who lose their employer-provided insurance to extend their insurance coverage (at personal cost) for up to 36 months. This includes individuals who are transitioning between jobs, are fired, or who lose spousal coverage due to death or divorce.

IHS

The Indian Health Service (IHS) provides care for members of recognized tribes who live in one of the IHS service areas. IHS provides numerous services and requires no cost sharing for individuals below 300 percent

---

[11] This is one of the lesser-known benefits of being the recipient of a Medal of Honor.

[12] I've known about this program for a good 15 years, and I just learned the meaning of the acronym while writing this because I had to look it up.

FPL. Though it operates in many ways like an insurance plan, IHS does not count as insurance legally, so individuals who are eligible to obtain services from IHS are also able to enroll in any private or public insurance plans that they are eligible for.

Self-Assessment

1. For each form of public insurance in this chapter, is the eligible population likely to be uninsurable? Why or why not?
2. Can you think of a situation where someone would be better off with Medicare Part B instead of Medicare Advantage? Can you think of a situation where someone would be better off with Medicare Advantage instead of Medicare Part B?
3. Consider the statement "Because everyone over 65 gets Medicare, the system is equal as everyone has the same coverage." Do you agree? Why or why not?
3. The FPL is a single value put out by the federal government for the entire country. Given that different places have different costs of living, does basing Medicaid eligibility off the FPL make sense?
4. One concern with DRGs and RVUs in "upcoding," or the idea that a provider may systematically put patients as more valuable DRGs or systematically list patients as receiving care worth more RVUs than was truly done in order to get larger payments. If you worked for CMS, how would you try to catch "upcoders?"
5. CMS is advised by a panel of medical experts known as the Relative Value System Update Committee (RUC, pronounced "ruck"). The RUC makes recommendations as to which procedures should have their RVU values changed, and by how much. If you were a medical specialty group, how important would it be to try to influence the RUC? Which types of specialties do you think would care the most about influencing the RUC?
6. COBRA is private insurance from your previous employer that you pay for yourself. You pay for 100 percent of the premium of the plan, and sometimes there is also an additional 2 percent administration fee. This is often more expensive than a plan that someone could go out and buy on a health insurance exchange. Even if this is true (COBRA is more expensive than an exchange plan), why would some people still want COBRA rather than a plan from the exchange?

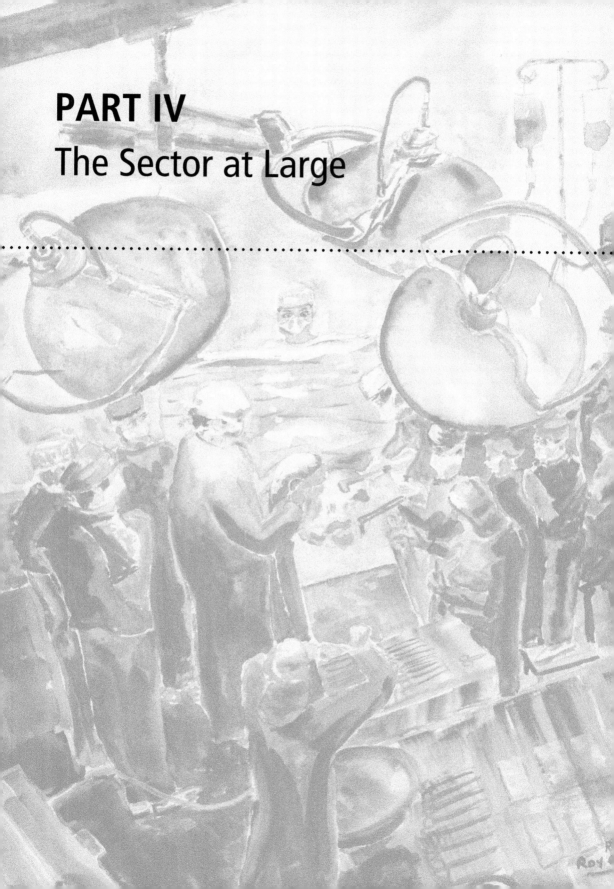

PART IV
The Sector at Large

15 | Pharmaceuticals

In 2020, the United States spent $348.4 billion dollars on pharmaceuticals, this was around 8.5 percent of all healthcare spending for 2020 (Centers for Medicare & Medicaid Services 2022a). There is a lot of variation in the cost of pharmaceuticals. For example, 30 doses of fluoxetine (i.e. Prozac) costs around $12 dollars or somewhere around $0.40 per pill. At the other end of the spectrum is Trikafta, a mix of three gene therapy drugs used to treat cystic fibrosis. Trikafta costs around $26,000 for a course of 84 doses or around $309.52 per pill.[1] A dose of Trikafta is over 650 times more expensive than a dose of fluoxetine.

A natural question is then "why are some drugs so expensive and other drugs so inexpensive?" Part of the answer has to do with the cost of manufacturing, some drugs are just more expensive to make. However, this is only one part of the story. The other part is that some drugs can be and are produced by many pharmaceutical manufacturers, and some drugs can only be and are made by one manufacturer. Fluoxetine is manufactured by numerous producers, each of which competes with the others to sell their product. Trikafta, on the other hand, is manufactured by Vertex Pharmaceuticals and more importantly cannot be manufactured by anyone else without a licensing agreement from Vertex. Why? Vertex holds a *patent*.

Intellectual Property

A patent is a form of intellectual property protection. Intellectual property rights and the associated legal protections are administered by the United States Patent and Trademark Office. A patent gives a party the exclusive rights to an invention, process or chemical compound. Once a party develops an invention, process, or chemical compound, then they can register that new thing with the Patent Office, and if it is sufficiently new, be granted a patent. Patents in the US typically expire 20 years after they are filed.

Patents are different from other forms of intellectual property protection: *copyrights* and *trademarks*. Copyrights protect a created work such

---

[1] I looked up these prices on www.drugs.com, they are at best ballpark figures.

as a book, a song, or a photograph. Copyrights typically expire 70 years after the death of the creator of the work. So, if I were to die, the copyright for this book would be passed to my family and you would have to wait another 70 years before the book became "public domain." Trademarks, on the other hand, are protections for names, logos, and short slogans. Trademarks do not expire so long as the entity using the trademark continues to use it in their business practice.

Why Are Patents Useful?

Patents effectively create a monopoly, granting the patent holder tremendous market power and the ability to charge a much higher price for their product than they would be able to charge if they faced competition. By giving away patents, the US Patent Office is giving away market power and subjecting the public to higher prices. So, why is this something that the government would want to do?

Consider a situation where patents did not exist. You spend several years developing an invention: a drug that cures cancer. You spent millions of dollars inventing your cancer cure. Then, one you release the cure to the market, you start selling it to make back your initial investment in research and development (R&D). Right after this happens, hundreds of chemists will buy your drug and attempt to reverse-engineer it. Some of them will be successful, and start competing against you, driving down the price of the drug. What's worse (for you, not the consumer), is that these new competitors didn't spend nearly as much on R&D (they just copied you). So, these new competitors do not have to make as much money to cover their initial investments and are better positioned to charge lower prices and outcompete you. So, ask yourself, in this situation is it financially worthwhile for you to invent something new?

In the situation I just described, the lack of intellectual property protection has undermined the incentive to innovate. If you invent something and then anyone can copy it and then compete against you with their copy, then it blunts the incentive for you to innovate and create something new. This is not to say that all innovation is done strictly for financial gain. Some innovation is done for more altruistic purposes. Dr. Jonas Salk, the inventor of the polio vaccine famously did not patent the vaccine out of a desire for it to be widely available.[2] However, it is reasonable to claim

---

[2] In a similar manner, when I "invented" a double taco on taco night and named it "The Taconator" I did not patent it, I gave the idea to my children for free. You're welcome, kids.

that with patents, the incentive to create new things is much larger than it would be without patents, perhaps enormously so. There is thus a positive relationship between how strong intellectual property protections are, and how strong the incentive to innovate is, an idea we will return to later in this chapter.

How a New Drug Is Approved in the US

Before getting too deep into the idea of intellectual property and incentives to innovate, I want to take an aside to talk about the drug approval process in the United States. Part of this is to impart institutional knowledge about the process, as the process is interesting in its own right. The other part is to show that this process is involved and takes a long time, and that much of that time is on the 20-year clock for the patent covering the compound seeking approval.

The first step in drug approval is to invent a drug to be potentially approved. This might involve some hefty R&D costs. If, for each successful drug, you also count the cost of unsuccessful drugs developed at the same time (so if a company succeeds twice and fails ten times, then each success' costs includes the cost of five of the failures), then Wouters, McKee and Luyten (2020) estimate these R&D costs to be around $1.1 billion per successful drug.

Now that you've spent your money developing the drug it is time to start the approval process.[3] The goal is to get the Food and Drug Administration (FDA), the entity which decides what can be sold in the United States as a pharmaceutical to approve your compound and allow you to sell it.

Preclinical and Phase 0 Trials

Before moving on to testing the effect of a drug in humans, trials must first be done on non-humans to demonstrate safety and possible benefit. This is done via a *preclinical trial* or a study of the drug *in vitro* (in a bunch of cells) or *in vivo* (in an animal). For example, if I want to know if a drug cures a form of blindness, I could run a preclinical trial on mice that have a similar form of blindness and see if their condition improves. This would not be the definitive proof needed to convince the FDA to let you bring the drug to market but would likely be convincing enough to move on to the next phase of study. If all the mice that were given the drug had their

---

[3] A simplified walkthrough of the FDA approval process can be found at www.fda.gov/patients/learn-about-drug-and-device-approvals/drug-development-process.

blindness cured, but then exploded 6 hours later, then the drug would likely be deemed unsafe, and would not be allowed to proceed.

Before moving to Phase I clinical trials (which are the first "real" clinical trials) a drug goes through Phase 0, which is a quick one-week "weed out" study. A Phase 0 study is used to see if a potential drug does anything to the desired location of the body. To do this, researchers give 10–15 human subjects "microdoses" of the drug: doses that are around 1/100 of the strength that the drug is expected to be given at. This is meant to be so little that it will make no difference in terms of health, but big enough that researchers can look for minute changes in the area in which the drug is supposed to operate biologically. If the drug fails to make any change whatsoever, then it can be quickly weeded out before moving on to the next phase.

Phases I–III

Phase I trials are meant to establish basic safety for a new drug. The main goal of a Phase I study is to make sure that there are no adverse reactions to the drug that are bad enough to scuttle the entire process. In some Phase I studies, multiple groups are used, and the dosage of the drug is ramped up across the groups. Phase I is meant to quickly determine the basic safety of the drug. Everyone who gets the drug dies? That drug is not going to Phase II. Everyone who gets the drug smells bad for 3 hours? That would probably be noted as a side effect and would not be enough to stop future testing (unless the goal of the drug is to make you smell good for 3 hours). Due to the risks, Phase I trials are typically small, using fewer than 100 participants.

Phase II trials establish that a drug is effective and start to establish the correct dosing. These are mostly done via randomized control trial (RCT). Sometimes the objectives of Phase II are done in tandem, and sometimes Phase II is split into Phase IIa, which looks just at dosing, and Phase IIb, which looks just at efficacy. Phase II is larger than Phase I in terms of enrollment, typically using a few hundred participants.

Finally, Phase III is the largest and last round of trials before a drug is put to the FDA for possible approval. Phase III trials use a drug in conditions that mimic clinical use and attempt to further establish efficacy and safety as well as extensively catalog side effects. These trials are large scale RCTs: they can be as large as a few thousand individuals, span multiple sites, and last several years.

New Drug Application

Once Phase III is completed, the sponsors of the drug submit a New Drug Application (NDA) to the FDA. The NDA includes data and results from the prior trials involving the drug, information of the manufacturing process, and proposed labeling and use of the drug.[4] The FDA will then decide based on the information in the NDA whether or not to approve the drug. This can mean a concrete "yes" approval, but a lack of approval does not necessarily mean outright rejection, the FDA may want more evidence of the drug's safety or effectiveness before approving it (which effectively bounces the drug back to Phase III).

Post-market Observation

Once a drug is approved and goes to market it enters "post-market observation" in which the drug is monitored for problems. This can include changes to warnings if a previously unknown drug interaction is discovered but can also include pulling the drug off the market completely if previously unknown dangers are discovered or if previously known dangers turn out to be worse than first realized. For example, Belviq, a weight loss drug approved in 2012 was pulled off the market in 2020 when it was determined that the drug carried an unacceptable cancer risk.

Market Exclusivity

The entire approval process is time consuming, taking 10–15 years from Phase I to approval (Brown et al. 2021). And, during this timeframe, the patent clock is ticking down. The time until the patent expires begins when the patent is filed with the Patent Office, not when the drug enters the market. This means that delays in the clinical trial and approval process are extremely costly for drug companies in terms of lost time during which the patent protects their intellectual property (i.e. lost time during which they are a monopoly).

The FDA often offers additional market exclusivity for newly approved drugs, meaning that it will not allow a competitor to enter for an extra period of time. In some cases, the FDA guarantees exclusivity for a fixed time period after approval, following the pattern "your drug is exclusive for X years post approval." So, if the patent would expire four years after approval, and the FDA guaranteed five years of market exclusivity, then the drug manufacturer gets an extra year.[5] Qualifying "orphan drugs" or drugs treating qualified rare diseases are guaranteed seven years of market exclusivity in this manner. In other cases, the FDA adds additional

---

[4] If a drug is approved, it is approved with a specific set of instructions for use on the label. If a physician prescribes an approved drug to treat a condition other than that which it was approved for, it is known as "off label" use of the drug.

[5] To extend this case, if the patent expired in six years and the FDA guaranteed five years of market exclusivity, then the FDA would take no additional action.

exclusivity to the end of the patent term, following the pattern "after your patent expires, your drug is exclusive for another X months." Qualifying pediatric drugs are given an additional six months of market exclusivity in this manner. These are not the only cases where extra exclusivity is given, there are numerous rules that apply to how additional market exclusivity is granted for a number of classes of drugs.

The Double-Edged Sword of Patents and Market Exclusivity

Patent protections and additional market exclusivity from the FDA say to drug producers "if you invent something new, you will get to be the only seller for a period of time." This is a powerful incentive, because being the only seller allows the producer to charge a high price for their product. The longer the seller is the only player in the market, the stronger the incentive. Five years of market exclusivity is a bigger incentive to innovate than four years of market exclusivity. So, there is a choice to be made as to how long patents should last for and how long the FDA should allow companies to have additional market exclusivity.

This choice is not trivial, because the incentive to invent is costly to the public. Each year of market exclusivity is valuable to drug makers because they can charge a high price but is costly to patients and health insurers because they are the ones who pay that price. There is a tradeoff to be made: the stronger (longer lasting) patents and market exclusivity are, the more innovation is incentivized, but the longer people have to wait before the price comes down. On the other hand, if we weaken patents and market exclusivity (make them shorter lasting), then new drugs will be affordable sooner, but there will be fewer of them invented.

Generic Drugs

Once a drugs patent and market exclusivity have expired competitors are allowed to enter the market selling the same substance. These "generic" versions of the drug must first be approved by the FDA, but the approval process is much shorter as the clinical trials showing safety and effectiveness are not needed. The manufacturer needs to be able to show that the compound that they manufacture behaves the same as its name-brand counterpart. Generics are usually considerably less expensive. The whole point of a generic drug is to compete with the name-brand, and given that quality is similar, the easiest way to do this is to charge a lower price.

Defensive Behavior

When a producer has a monopoly (or any market power), it is extremely profitable for them. It can be so profitable that given the prospect of losing the monopoly, the producer might be well served by spending resources to protect the monopoly. The producer might find behavior that defends their drug's status to be less expensive than the loss of profit from potential competitors.

Evergreening

One way that firms defend market exclusivity is by finding modifications to a drug that are preferable to the original version and patenting the modification. Since potential competitors cannot enter the market for the original drug, it is difficult for the potential competitors to come up with modifications, putting the incumbent firm at an advantage. The incumbent firm could patent the modification at a later date than the original patent and start selling an "improved" version of the drug, effectively extending the life of the patent for the product as a whole. A firm could also patent a process for making a drug, and then later patent a better (more efficient) process, putting any new competitor for the drug at a disadvantage as the drug's patent for the compound might expire but the less costly process for making it would still be under patent.

This practice of finding ways to extend the "overall" patent protection for a product line after the original patent for the main compound has expired is known as *evergreening*. Evergreening presents a challenge because firms will argue forcefully that all improvements represent meaningful changes to drug formulations and production processes, and it is difficult to tell what is truly a meaningful improvement and what is defensive behavior aimed at extending the length of market exclusivity.

Strategic Pricing and Advertising

Once a generic competitor enters a market, an incumbent drug maker may try to segment the market and sell a smaller amount of their drug at a high price rather than substantially lower their prices to compete on price with the newcomer. The idea is to convince patients and providers that there is a meaningful difference between the name-brand drug and the newcomer generic. The higher price serves as a signal of product quality to potential buyers, who will ask the question "if it isn't any better, then why is it more expensive?" High prices can be paired with advertising pushing the name-brand as high quality, with the implication that other versions of the drug are not as high quality.

It is important to note that whether the name-brand drug actually is higher quality is irrelevant to this strategy. It is all about the perception of quality (recall the discussion in Chapter 1). So long as people are convinced that the more expensive drug is worth it, then there may be enough customers to support the higher price name brands even in the presence of lower priced generics.

Self-Assessment

1. What would happen to drug R&D if patents were eliminated for drugs? What would happen in the market for drugs?
2. What would happen to drug R&D if patents were made perpetual (they last forever)? What would happen in the market for drugs?
3. If you oversaw giving market exclusivity to drugs, and could give different lengths of exclusivity to different drugs, how would you decide which drugs to give which length of exclusivity?
4. The Orphan Drug Act of 1983 grants extra exclusivity for drugs that treat rare diseases. The idea is that these diseases might not have a market large enough to spur investment in their research so extra market exclusivity is needed to make the R&D attractive to firms. How does this policy help people with rare diseases? How does this policy harm people with rare diseases?
5. If you are an MCO, how do you feel about generic drugs?
6. If you are a drug manufacturer and invent a faster and less expensive way to make a drug that is under patent, would you want to patent and use this new technique right away? Why might you want to wait to patent and implement the new technique (provided that you can keep it secret)?

Supplement. International Intellectual Property Agreements

Intellectual property laws are nation specific. Just because an item is patented in the United States does not mean that producers in other countries respect that patent. Reciprocal protections for intellectual property are often part of bilateral or multilateral trade agreements but are not universal. This historically has created situations where drugs are patented and produced under patent in places such as the United States or the European Union but are also manufactured as unlicensed (not sanctioned by the patent holder) generics in other countries that are not part of a trade agreement with the country granting the intellectual property protection.

This can create a series of problems for all parties involved. For the patent holder, this is undesirable because they do not receive any revenue from the sale of the unlicensed generic. This can also create problems for the generic manufacturer as they might not have trade knowledge on how to perfectly manufacture the substance, leading to quality differences.

A third problem arises if the countries in which the unlicensed generics are being made have different pharmaceutical needs than the countries in which the drugs are being researched and developed. Drug developers respond to incentives, and if the countries making unlicensed generics have a big need for, as an example, new and powerful antibiotics, and the countries that are part of the trade agreement and respect the patent of the developer have different drug needs, for example blood pressure medication. This creates a strong incentive to invest in drugs that help countries that enforce foreign intellectual property rights, and a paired disincentive to invest in drugs that help countries that do not enforce foreign intellectual property rights. The result is a slow pipeline for drugs that help the populations in countries that are not part of a trade agreement offering reciprocal intellectual property protections.

This issue was addressed via The Agreement on Trade-Related Aspects of Intellectual Property Rights (TRIPS). TRIPS was enacted in 1994 by the World Trade Organization (WTO) and covers all WTO member countries. There are many different parts of the agreement for different types of intellectual property, but for drugs the broad structure was that in countries that were previously allowing unlicensed generics, the generic manufacturers would be given licensing agreements and pay a small amount of royalties back to the patent holder. This allowed the manufacturers to continue to produce reasonably priced drugs for their customers while also creating a larger incentive for drug developers to research drugs that fit the needs of nations that were prior to the agreement allowing the manufacture of unlicensed generics.

16 | Externalities

What Is an Externality?

Humans make decisions by weighing the costs and benefits of the decision. Individuals weigh several factors such as: what will I gain from this? How much time will it take? How much money will I have to spend? Will it be physically uncomfortable? These are all *private* costs and benefits, that is, costs and benefits that accrue to the individual making the choice. There can also be *external* costs and benefits, referred to as *externalities*, which are costs and benefits that accrue to an individual who is not involved in the decision-making process. Externalities are sometimes referred to as *spillovers* as the extra benefits or costs "spill over" onto other parties.

Externalities create problems in decision-making (and in associated markets) because while individuals are fairly good at understanding costs and benefits that impact them directly, they typically do not consider the impact of their choices on others in their private decision-making process. This leads to a situation where people overdo activities that harm others due to not accounting for the additional costs to others, and also underdo activities that help others due to not accounting for the additional benefits to others.

Positive Externalities

Externalities come in two flavors, which depend on the nature of the additional impact on others. When an action carries an additional benefit that accrues to those not involved in the decision-making process the extra benefit is referred to as a *positive externality*. A simple example of an action that carries positive externality is maintaining the exterior of a property. I enjoy gardening.[1] The front of my house is well kept, and I typically have many blooming plants that make the house pleasant to look at. This provides me with happiness, because I like plants, and I like having a nice looking property. My decision to work on the landscaping is based on

---

[1] I actually wanted to be a botanist, but as an undergraduate, freshman biology was early in the morning and economics was in the afternoon, so here we are.

my happiness and the time, money, and effort costs of maintaining the landscaping. However, this activity also generates an additional benefit or positive externality for my neighbors. They can look at my garden and enjoy it too without having spent any time, money, or effort to maintain it. In fact, the quality of the local landscaping also improves their property values somewhat, another positive externality.

Negative Externalities

The other flavor of externality is when there is an additional cost associated with an action which accrues to those not involved in the decision-making process. In this case the additional cost is a *negative externality*. An example of an action that carries a negative externality is using a portable speaker to play music in a public place. The individual who uses the portable speaker gets to enjoy the music of their choosing in the location of their choosing. On the other hand, anyone who is in that location also gets exposed to the music whether they like it or not. If they do not like the music, then the annoyance they suffer is a negative externality.[2]

This happens to me all the time on hiking trails. Someone thinks to themselves "you know what goes great with this nature walk? METAL," and blasts it on the speaker that they've attached to their backpack. I am not here to judge their preferences in music, your favorite artist or genre is for you to decide based on your personal utility function. However, subjecting others to those preferences is often a negative externality (and incredibly inconsiderate).

Risk Externalities

The positive and negative externality examples above are concrete in the sense that the externality is something that you definitively experience. You see the garden, or you don't. You hear the music, or you don't. Both positive and negative externalities can also manifest as a change in the likelihood of something good or something bad happening. In this case, the externality is known as a *risk externality*.

Vaccines carry a positive risk externality. When you get a flu shot you protect yourself against the flu, but others receive an externality benefit in the form of reduced likelihood of catching the flu as you are far less likely to transmit the virus to them. This is a positive risk externality in that you have decreased the likelihood of a bad outcome. A positive risk externality can also be something that increases the likelihood of a good outcome.

---

[2] On the other hand, if they like the music then the music is a positive externality. They can also say "sweet jams" and high five the person with the speaker.

People leaving a baseball game create a positive risk externality for those who remain by increasing the chance that the remaining individuals are able to catch (or pick up) a foul ball.

Driving fast carries a negative risk externality. The faster you are going, the less reaction time you have to steer and the more likely you are to get into a collision. Also, if you are in a collision, the amount of damage done will increase with the speed of the vehicle. So, extra speed creates a negative risk externality on others: you are more likely to hit them and if you do, likely to do more damage. A negative risk externality can also be something that decreases the likelihood of a good outcome. Additional people entering a raffle has a negative risk externality as they decrease the chance of others winning the drawing.

To be precise with semantics, all risk externalities are externalities, but not all externalities are risk externalities. It is also perfectly appropriate to refer to a risk externality as simply an externality, the term "risk externality" is typically only used when drawing specific attention to the risk altering nature of a risk externality.

Correcting Externality Problems

Externalities are a form of *market failure*. One of the reasons why economists like markets so much is that they are good at balancing costs and benefits to get to optimal amounts of production and consumption. This does not happen in the presence of externalities. Actors do not appropriately account for the extra costs or benefits on others and as such overdo activities with negative externalities and underdo activities with positive externalities. As some of these extra benefits and costs are quite large, governments will occasionally intervene in markets to try to correct the externality problem. The main way a government tries to correct externalities is by "internalizing" the externality, or by finding a way for the individual making the decision to "feel" the additional cost or benefit to others. There are three main strategies for correcting externalities.

Taxes and Subsidies
The first is to use taxes and subsidies. An activity has a negative externality that individuals aren't taking into account? Add a tax to it so that the value of the tax approximates the cost imposed on others. The tax makes it so that the private cost to the decision-maker includes the extra external cost and pushes them to make a decision that more correctly reflects both private and public costs. The tax "internalizes" the externality cost. If

an activity has an externality benefit then you can subsidize that activity in the same manner. The subsidy makes it so that the private benefits for the decision-maker include the benefits that accrue to others. The subsidy "internalizes" the externality benefit.

These taxes and subsidies are called *Pigouvian taxes* or *Pigouvian subsidies* after Arthur Cecil Pigou who proposed the idea (Pigou 1920). Pigouvian taxes and subsidies are used in the real world for several types of behavior. Cigarettes which carry a negative externality in the form invasive smell and increased risk of illness due to secondhand smoke are heavily taxed. Similarly, gasoline is also taxed. Gas vehicles create air pollution, a negative externality, and create traffic, which slows down other travelers, another negative externality. One can also view publicly financed education as a Pigouvian subsidy: having additional education in the population carries spillover benefits if the additional education (and associated skills) improves the economy (which is likely felt by everyone).

The difficulty with taxes and subsidies is that while it might be easy to know if a behavior has a positive or negative externality, it is difficult to know exactly how much the tax or subsidy should be. You must accurately measure the external costs and benefits to be able to set the tax or subsidy at the correct amount. This is hard to do. How much does each individual value not being exposed to smoke? That is a difficult question to answer.

Regulation

You can also go after externalities through use of regulation. Regulation is a law or policy that says, "you can't do that" or "you must do this." If a good has a negative externality, then you can regulate it to make it more difficult to do, and if a good has a positive externality, then you can regulate it to make it more necessary to do. For example, lighting campfires during a drought carries a negative risk externality of increased probability of wildfire, so it is illegal to have a campfire during fire bans. Likewise, washing your hands carries a positive externality of decreasing the probability of transmitting illness, therefore health departments require restaurant workers to wash their hands before returning to work after using the bathroom. Regulation carries some of the same difficulties as use of taxes and subsidies: while it might be easy to know if you want to regulate toward more of a behavior or toward less of a behavior, it can be difficult in some cases to know the exact amount to regulate.

Property Rights

A third way to deal with externalities is to clearly assign property rights and then allow people to bargain with each other based on those property rights. The idea that this will solve externality problems was proposed by Coase (1960) and has since been come to be known as the *Coase Theorem*. The bargains that are struck that eliminate the externalities are sometimes referred to as *Coasian bargains*.

Consider a case where you live next door to me and need to study for an exam. I, on the other hand, am blasting music from speakers in my immaculate garden which is making it hard to study. What music? For the purposes of this thought experiment, assume that it's something that you find to be particularly distracting and annoying. In this case let's assume that quiet ahead of the exam is worth $20 to you, and music on my speakers is worth $2 to me. The cost of the action ($20 of broken quiet for you) outweighs the benefit ($2 of musical enjoyment to me), meaning that the correct course of action is to have the music turned off.

So now let's assign property rights and see what happens. The cool part is that it does not matter who we give the property rights to. If you have the right to demand quiet, then you can tell me to shut off my music. I counter with, "can I pay you to keep playing the music?" to which you ask, "how much?" As you value the quiet at $20 and I value the music at $2, I won't be willing to pay enough to get you to relent and let me play the music. The music is turned off, which is the correct outcome. If instead, I have the right to play my music then you can offer to pay me to turn it off. Any amount over $2 will be enough to convince me to do so, and as you are willing pay up to $20 to have quiet, you can buy my quiet. In this case, the correct outcome is also achieved.

The Coase Theorem provides an elegant solution to externality problems: just make who has property rights clear and the problem solves itself. The Coase Theorem has two big drawbacks as a strategy to correct externalities.[3] The first is that the outcome is affected by ability to pay. That means that there could be a situation where you value the quiet at $1,000 (and would need me to pay you $1,000 to let me play my awful music), but do not have that type of money available to pay me off if I have the property rights and value the music at an also high but not as high number, such as $990. The Coase Theorem can fail to provide a solution when the actors are *liquidity constrained*, or do not have enough cash to make the necessary transactions.

The second issue arises when there are prohibitive costs associated with reaching a bargain. For example, if a negative externality impacts many people a small amount, then it is likely too difficult to get them all to band together and demand payment, even if their collective suffering from the

---

[3] There are also some additional wrinkles with the Coase Theorem that are beyond the scope of this book.

externality makes it so that reducing or eliminating the behavior with the negative externality is the correct course of action. Pollution is a problem, but it is difficult to get everyone impacted by it to group together to ask the polluter for $100 apiece.

Examples: Risky Health Behaviors

Risky health behaviors often carry not only risks to self but risks to others. Here are some classic examples of externalities and commonly used interventions that attempt to correct them.

Smoking

Smoking is one of the most commonly used examples of an externality. It is such a good example that I couldn't avoid referencing it earlier, even though I knew I was going to bring it up in its own subsection. There are two main externalities associated with smoking. The first is that others are subjected to the smell which they may not like, I certainly don't, and I also don't like the way it has of sticking to your clothes. The second is that breathing in secondhand smoke increases your risk of various smoking related illnesses. So, if I choose to smoke around others then I would be imposing an additional cost on them.[4]

We try to reduce smoking via taxes and regulation, and in some cases private citizens can try to reduce smoking via Coasian bargains. As mentioned before, tobacco is taxed aggressively in many states. There are also numerous regulations aimed at reducing the amount of smoking, for example, public smoking bans in places such as airplanes and restaurants reduce smoking as well. Finally, it is possible although difficult to strike a Coasian bargain. If I am sitting on a bench and someone is smoking near me, then I could offer them money to stop. There is a transaction cost associated with this: it is super awkward to ask someone to do this, so most people don't.

Drunk Driving

Drunk driving is dangerous, but there are two forms of danger to consider. The first is danger to oneself, which while important, is not an externality.[5]

---

[4] Smoking has a third, rather morbid, but positive externality. Smokers tend to die earlier and thus claim less from programs such as Social Security, lowering the cost of supporting the programs for others.

[5] If you want to get philosophical, you could say that you have two selves, a drunk self and a sober self, and that drunk driving is the drunk self imposing a negative risk externality on the sober self. By that logic, all sorts of negative health behaviors can be seen as one version of you imposing costs on a different version of you.

The second is danger to others on the road or near the road. These people suffer a negative externality created by the drunk driver: they have an increased chance of injury or death as well as an increased chance of suffering vehicle or property damage. This is a risk externality, a drunk driver doesn't hit someone every time they drive drunk, but the increase in risk is large enough and the bad outcome severe enough that law aggressively penalizes drunk drivers. This can be seen as a form of tax. If you are caught driving drunk, then you must pay a large fine and possibly serve jail time (a tax on your time and a tax in the form of lost wages).

Examples: Contagion

Another set of relevant examples of externalities and attempts to correct them revolve around contagious diseases. There are numerous behaviors that carry risk externalities for contagion such as coughing, sneezing, and washing your hands. These activities raise or lower the risk of infection for others, an externality.

Social Stigma as a Tax
One way that we try to reduce negative contagion behaviors (behaviors that potentially spread illness) or induce positive contagion behaviors (behaviors that help prevent illness) is via social norms. If you engage in certain negative health behaviors (like sneezing on others) or fail to engage in positive health behaviors (like washing your hands) then you might be labeled as "gross," and suffer a penalty in social interactions. This is in effect a Pigouvian tax, just one that is paid with social status as opposed to money.

Consider this scenario that may or may not have happened. You are giving a lecture to a class and during that lecture there is a student who is sitting in class eating cheese puffs. From time to time, this student is licking the cheese puff dust off of their fingers. They are doing this aggressively; this student is really going after that delicious cheesy powder. What would your interaction be like at the end of class if that student wanted to ask you a question? If they wanted to shake your hand and thank you for a good class?

Now imagine that you are that student, and while aggressively removing the cheese dust from your fingers with your mouth you lock eyes with the professor and realize that, yes, he is seeing you do this. How does that make you feel? I would expect the answer to be somewhere in the range of "uncomfortable" to "I would feel deep, deep shame." This is the whole point of social stigma around contagion behaviors, the social "grossness" tax helps correct the contagion externality.

Contagion and Severe Illnesses

For more severe contagious illnesses, society has typically used a regulatory approach. The strength of the regulation used depends on the severity of an illness and how easily it spreads, which is just a measure of the size of the negative risk externality carried from a given contagion behavior. If a disease has a worse outcome if you are infected, then you are exposed to a larger negative externality from any given contagion behavior. If a disease is more easily transmitted, then you have a higher chance of catching it from any given contagion behavior, also increasing the size of the negative externality associated with that behavior.

Government officials have the authority to limit some public behaviors in the case of contagion from severe illnesses. The riskier the contagion, the stronger the regulations used. COVID-19 provided numerous examples of this type of government intervention. Travel can increase contagion as illness is moved from one place to another, so the United States federal government limited incoming travelers from countries with known outbreaks. State governors used their authority to limit large gatherings by closing bars, restaurants, and schools. And when state leaders did not impose these types of restrictions, there were cases where local governments did so in their stead. States and localities also imposed masking orders: regulations that required individuals to wear face masks which limit the spread of airborne illnesses such as COVID-19. These types of regulations are often referred to as non-pharmaceutical interventions.[6]

Vaccines

As briefly discussed earlier in the chapter, vaccines carry positive risk externalities. When you get vaccinated, not only are you protecting yourself from illness, but you decrease the likelihood that others will get infected as you can no longer infect others.[7] As such, there are several subsidies and regulations that promote vaccination.

One of the most high-profile versions of subsidizing vaccines occurred during the initial rollout of COVID-19 mRNA vaccines. The US government purchased vaccines directly and provided them without charge, subsidizing the full price. There are other programs that do similar things

---

[6] There is excellent experimental evidence on facemask use reducing transmission of COVID-19 (Abaluck et al. 2022), there is also some nice quasi-experimental evidence on the effectiveness of other non-pharmaceutical interventions at reducing COVID-19 transmission during the initial waves of the outbreak (e.g. Courtemanche et al. 2020; Friedson et al. 2021; Dave et al. 2021, 2022).

[7] In the case of vaccines that reduce infection likelihoods but do not provide complete immunity, you still decrease the likelihood that you infect others.

for other vaccines. For example, the Centers for Disease Control and Prevention administers the Vaccines for Children Program which pays for childhood vaccines for those who would not be able to otherwise afford them. Vaccination is also approached via regulation. Many school districts require specific vaccinations (or an acceptable exemption) in order for children to attend.

What Is the Correct Amount of Intervention? Cost and Benefits

Much of the discussion in this chapter makes the assumption that it is known what the correct amount of intervention is for any given external- ity. This makes the problem of externalities appear deceptively simple. You have a negative externality? Simply tax or regulate it away. Easy.

In reality, externalities are difficult to deal with correctly because when I impose a tax or a regulation, it imposes new costs on actors in the market. When I tax cigarettes, it helps reduce the externality, but it also imposes a cost on those who wish to smoke. When I regulate a firm that is polluting, I reduce the harm to the community, but I also cut into the prof- its of that firm. When I limit travel due to a pandemic, I slow infections but also hamper economic activity. I am not saying that you should not regulate or tax or subsidize in the case of externalities, you often should. What I am saying is that you need to carefully balance the costs and ben- efits of interventions.

There is a systematic way to do this, which is called a "cost–benefit analysis."[8] In a cost–benefit analysis, you count up all of the benefits of doing an action and you count up all of the costs of doing an action. Then, you see which one is bigger. If benefits outweigh the costs, then you do the action. If costs outweigh the benefits, then you don't do the action.

So, if I was considering a complete ban on cigarettes, I would first count up the benefits: I would need to get an estimate of the cost to the popu- lation of being exposed to secondhand smoke. Then, I would need to get an estimate of how much people would be willing to pay to avoid the bad smell from being near smokers. These would be my benefits: the elimina- tion of the externality cost. Next, I would need to count up the costs of my complete smoking ban. How much happiness would smokers lose out on by

---

[8] It's sometimes called a benefit–cost analysis, the order doesn't matter, counting costs and benefits does.

not being able to smoke anymore?[9] I would want to get this in a unit that can be compared to the others, like dollars of value lost. Finally, I would compare the costs and benefits and see which one is bigger. This is not a simple task; these numbers are difficult to pin down. A non-trivial amount of work done by health economists (and by public health and health services researchers as well) tries to get decent estimates of the components needed for cost–benefit analyses.

The process can get even more complicated when the policy in question is adjusted along an intensive margin as opposed to the extensive margin. The example of a complete ban was a change along the extensive margin: all or nothing. What if I raised cigarette taxes? This would be a change along the intensive margin of the policy. We have already decided that we want to use a tax, but what we want to know now is how much should we tax (i.e. should the tax be bigger)? To do a cost–benefit analysis I would need to know how much the change in tax would change smoking behavior along with how that change in smoking would change all of the costs and benefits outlined in the all or nothing example. This is one of the reasons why the Coase Theorem is so attractive (when it is possible to take advantage of, which admittedly is not nearly as often as economists would like), because it sidesteps the whole problem of needing to get accurate estimates of difficult to measure things to craft good policy.

Self-Assessment

1. It's July 7 and my neighbors are shooting off fireworks at 11 pm. What are the private benefits and costs to them from shooting the fireworks? What are the external benefits and costs from shooting of the fireworks?
2. Can you think of a behavior that carries a positive externality for some parts of the population and a negative externality for other parts of the population?
3. Consider the following statement "Negative risk externalities aren't as bad because it isn't a sure thing that the bad outcome will happen." Do you agree? Why or why not?

---

[9] Notice that I did not count the improved health of smokers as a benefit. This is because smokers have in theory already accounted for this in their private decision-making process. The net private benefits and costs (which include their own health risks) are all accounted for in their willingness to pay to be able to smoke. Some economists argue that due to the addictive nature of cigarettes that this is not the correct way to think about the decision. This is a fair point, and worth debating, but also beyond the scope of this book.

4. Why do we not use the Coase Theorem (assigning property rights and allowing people to bargain) to deal with vaccine uptake that is too low?

5. Why do we not use the Coase Theorem (assigning property rights and allowing people to bargain) to deal with contagion of severe illnesses.

6. Suppose that you were in charge of deciding whether or not to shut down a school due to COVID-19. What are the costs and benefits of shutting down the school?

17 | Medical Malpractice

The medical malpractice system serves as a check on risky provider behavior that can lead to bad outcomes. It also serves as a mechanism for getting compensation to those injured by that behavior. However, as this chapter will discuss, the medical malpractice system creates incentives that have the potential to undercut some of its core goals.

Basic Anatomy of a Tort Case

Medical malpractice cases are governed by a state's *tort law*. A tort is an act or omission that causes harm, such as destroying property or physical harm to a person. State tort laws define which types of damages are recoverable in a lawsuit and under what circumstances. An example of a famous tort case is *Liebeck v. McDonald's Restaurants*, in which 79-year-old Stella Liebeck was awarded over $600,000 at trial verdict for third degree burns she suffered when she spilled hot coffee on herself.

During a tort case, the party that suffered the harm is known as the *plaintiff*, so in the *Liebeck v. McDonald's* case, the plaintiff was Stella Liebeck. The party being sued is the *defendant*, so in the same case, the defendant was McDonald's. Tort law lays out the elements that a plaintiff must show in order to establish legal liability. Generally speaking, the plaintiff needs to show that damage has occurred; in *Liebeck v. McDonald's* the damage was burns from spilling hot coffee. The plaintiff also usually needs to show that the defendant was responsible. The bar that needs to be met to establish liability depends on the type of tort case, with medical malpractice being one such type. In *Liebeck v. McDonald's*, the legal argument over responsibility for the damages centered on the question "how hot is too hot for coffee?" with the plaintiff's legal argument boiling down to "this coffee was far too hot."

Goals of the Medical Malpractice System

Damages caused to individuals in the process of receiving medical care are handled through the medical malpractice component of a state's tort law.

Individuals who are harmed can sue providers (physicians, hospitals, etc.) who they believe have harmed them, and attempt to recover restitution through the legal system. This process attempts to accomplish two goals:

1. Provide compensation to injured parties, and
2. Create an incentive for providers to provide care appropriately.

Compensate Injured Parties

The first goal of the system is to provide resources to those who are injured during medical care. A surgery that goes poorly could leave a patient needing additional care, unable to work, or dead. All of these have associated costs to them or to the patient's surviving family, which under some circumstances a society would consider "unfair" for them to be responsible for paying. A successful lawsuit would shift these costs from the plaintiff to the defendant.

This raises a question that we will return to later in the chapter: "Is the injured party receiving the appropriate amount of compensation?" If the answer is yes, then the malpractice system is doing a good job at achieving this goal, if the answer is no, then less so.

Create an Incentive for Providers to Practice Appropriately

The second goal of the system is to provide an incentive for providers to practice appropriately. There are some obvious cases: we do not want surgeons to conduct surgery while intoxicated, and we do want them to wear surgical gloves. So, if surgeons who conduct surgery while intoxicated, or who do not wear gloves get sued and lose, then there is now an incentive for them to practice appropriately.

But most cases are not so cut and dry.[1] Consider a hypothetical situation where there is an additional protection that can be provided by a physician: they can wrap a surgical site in a rare seaweed with healing properties.[2] This seaweed is very expensive and provides a small decrease in the likelihood of a bad outcome (infection) relative to standard bandaging. Should a physician be sued for failing to use the seaweed instead of usual bandages if the patient then gets an infection? How do we evaluate whether this additional care is "appropriate" and thus failing to use it is "inappropriate?"

The economist's answer is to conduct a cost–benefit analysis (which is described in greater detail in Chapter 16). If the benefits of the seaweed (occasional averted infections) are larger than the cost of the seaweed

---

[1] In fact, surgery is rarely cut and dry, as when you cut someone open the inside is usually wet.

[2] To be clear, this is made-up seaweed, to my knowledge this rare seaweed does not exist, and I in no way suggest that you should wrap a surgical site in seaweed.

(which is very expensive), then it is appropriate to use it, and if the costs are larger than the benefits then it is not appropriate to use it.

So, one way to judge the incentives created from the medical malpractice system is to see to what extent providers face consequences for failing to practice appropriately as determined by cost–benefit analyses. If there are practices for which benefits outweigh costs, then we want those to be incumbent upon providers, and if there are practices for which costs outweigh benefits, then we want those to either not be incumbent upon providers (in the case of the very expensive seaweed for example), or actively discouraged (in the case of overtly dangerous practices).

Detailed Anatomy of a Medical Malpractice Case

Medical malpractice cases begin with an adverse event, the party that suffers the adverse event then decides whether or not they would like to file a lawsuit. When filing a suit, the plaintiff will state that the defendant harmed them, and then ask for restitution. Restitution can take on a few forms:

Economic Damages
These are payments meant to restore the plaintiff as best as possible to their original economic condition. Economic damages include payment of medical bills and payment of lost wages. Often, uncertain economic damages, such as "how much would the plaintiff have earned had they not been injured?" are calculated by a *forensic economist.*[3]

Non-economic Damages
These are payments meant to compensate for "pain and suffering." Where economic damages are on the more objective end of the spectrum, non-economic damages are far more subjective. Trying to calculate the correct economic damages may involve questions such as "would your income have grown by 3 percent per year, or by 2 percent per year?" Whereas trying to calculate the correct non-economic damages may involve questions such as "how much would the plaintiff have been willing to pay to have not been set on fire?"

Punitive Damages
Punitive damages are not made to compensate a plaintiff for a loss, but to punish a defendant for bad behavior. These can be added by the court in

---

[3] Forensic economists do economic calculations relating to legal cases, and a common task for a forensic economist is to extrapolate hypothetical income streams for injured parties.

some situations on top of other damages to let the defendant know that they have been especially naughty in the eyes of the law.

Trial

After the plaintiff files a lawsuit, then time will elapse while both parties (the plaintiff and defendant) prepare their legal case, and a trial date will be set. At trial, two different disputed items will be argued:

1. Should the defendant have to pay the plaintiff?
2. If the defendant must pay, then how much should they pay?

To support their arguments, both the plaintiff and the defendant may call witnesses and present evidence. Two types of witnesses may be called. A *fact witness* (sometimes referred to as an eyewitness) is someone with knowledge of the relevant facts of the case, such as someone who saw the surgeon drinking alcohol before a surgery. The other type of witness is an *expert witness*, or someone with professional expertise that can help nail down relevant details of the case. An expert witness may be a physician not directly involved in the case who can speak to whether or not the defendant's actions were within accepted medical practices. Another example is the aforementioned forensic economist, who could testify as to what the plaintiff's lost wages would have likely been had they not been injured.

The final determination in a case is made by a *jury*. The jury will decide in favor of either the plaintiff or the defendant, and if they find in favor of the plaintiff, will decide how much is to be awarded in damages.[4]

Appeal

Once a verdict has been rendered, the case is not necessarily finished. The party that loses can choose to file an *appeal*, which is a request to a higher court to review the case and potentially reverse the decision. Each subsequent court decision can be appealed to an even higher court, all the way up to the Supreme Court of the United States.

Settlement

At any point in the above process the plaintiff and the defendant can reach a *settlement*, which is an agreement to have the defendant make a payment to the plaintiff in exchange for an end to the lawsuit and the cessation of

---

[4] Because torts are a civil proceeding, the potential verdicts are "decision in favor of the plaintiff" and "decision in favor of the defendant." While the much more dramatic, "guilty" and "not guilty" are the potential verdicts for criminal proceedings.

Table 17.1 Medical malpractice cases resolved in Texas in 2012	
Total reported events	460
Was There a Lawsuit?	
No suit filed	54
Suit filed	406
Did It Go to Trial?	
Settled prior to trial	401
Went to trial	5
There Was a Trial. Was There a Verdict?	
Settled prior to verdict	2
Verdict reached	3

Source: Texas Department of Insurance, 2012, *Closed Claims Survey*,
www.tdi.texas.gov/reports/report4.html

any future litigation on the matter. The vast majority of medical malpractice cases are resolved via settlement before trial verdict. There are a few reasons for the popularity of settlements, one of the largest being that trials are both expensive in terms of legal fees, and risky in terms of outcomes, financial and otherwise. As outlined in Chapter 10, in most situations individuals are risk averse, and would be willing to give up some value to eliminate risk – in this case swapping the risky outcome of a trial verdict with the certain outcome of a settlement.

Example: Cases Closed in Texas in 2012

We can observe how medical malpractice cases typically resolve by examining actual data on such cases. Table 17.1 shows how all medical malpractice cases reported to the Texas Department of Insurance as closed (finished) in 2012 resolved. Physicians carry insurance against medical malpractice, so these data were generated any time a medical malpractice insurer was informed of a potential lawsuit and marked as "closed" once the case was complete.

Of the 460 cases that closed in 2012, 54 (or around 12 percent) never had a lawsuit filed. The plaintiff decided for some reason that the case was not worth pursuing further. This shows that the decision to sue is not automatic, many potential plaintiffs may decide that they are unlikely to recover any damages and opt against filing a lawsuit. Of the lawsuits that were filed, 401 (98.7 percent of the filed lawsuits) were resolved out of court before a trial began, and of the five cases that did begin, two of them were settled before a verdict was reached.[5]

This process is not necessarily quick. For the medical malpractice cases that were settled in Texas in 2012, the average time from injury to settlement was 1,290 days (or approximately 3.5 years). That is not to say that every case takes that long, the fastest settlement in the 2012 Texas medical malpractice records was 15 days.[6]

The Heart of a Medical Malpractice Case: Negligence

In a tort case, the goal for the plaintiff is to establish that the defendant carries liability for the harm inflicted. The bar that must be met in a medical malpractice case is to demonstrate *negligence* on the part of the defendant.

Informed Consent

One way that negligence can be established is to show that the defendant did not obtain *informed consent* from the plaintiff before engaging in a procedure. Informed consent means that the patient was fully made aware of the potential risks in the procedure as well as alternative treatment options, and then gave their permission to proceed. In non-emergency cases, failing to obtain informed consent and then cutting someone open for surgery is not terribly different (legally speaking) from stabbing that person.

Legal Test for Negligence: The Learned Hand Rule

The legal test for negligence is called the *Learned Hand Rule*, which is actually a mathematical formula, if $p \times L > C$ then the defendant is negligent for failing to take a given action.[7] Where p is the probability that some damage to the plaintiff occurs if an action is not taken, L is the value of that damage, and C is the cost of taking that action.

This should look familiar because the Learned Hand Rule is based on a cost–benefit analysis. If there was some preventative action for which benefits outweigh costs, then a practitioner can be held legally liable for not taking that action. Likewise, if the action had costs that outweigh the benefits, then the practitioner cannot be held legally liable.

---

[5] Of the cases that resolved out of court, the majority were resolved via traditional settlements, and some were resolved via alternative procedures such as arbitration.

[6] The slowest case to close in 2012 was over 19 years after the original injury.

[7] The Learned Hand Rule is named after Appeals Court Judge Learned Hand, who established the test for negligence in *United States v. Carroll Towing Co.* Billings Learned Hand (who went by Learned Hand) is his actual name.

The Learned Hand Rule for negligence is what is meant to be applied by the jury in a medical malpractice trial. If the defendant did an action that the Learned Hand Rule calculates to be negligent then the jury should find in favor of the plaintiff. What is desirable about this rule is that when it is perfectly applied it creates an incentive for providers to practice "appropriately" as defined earlier in this chapter. Actions that pass a cost–benefit test are rewarded, and actions that fail a cost–benefit test are punished.

Imperfect Application of the Learned Hand Rule

One problem with the Learned Hand Rule is that it is not necessarily applied perfectly by juries. A jury is by definition made up of human beings, and even though you can tell a human being that the case at hand is supposed to be decided solely based on the rule, it is possible to manipulate that human into allowing other factors to influence their decision.

Consider a jury in a hypothetical medical malpractice case. In this case, there was a surgery that went poorly. The jury will be shown two presentations. The defense is going to show the jury evidence that all actions were appropriate based on the Learned Hand Rule. The plaintiff is going to show the jury evidence that the actions were inappropriate, and their evidence is equally compelling – the case is a "toss-up." But in addition, the plaintiff is going to show the jury detailed photographic documentation of the bad outcome from the surgery, in this case some severely mangled genitals.

When the jury goes to deliberate, do you think that these photographs are going to influence the jury in the direction of the plaintiff? How much of the jury's mental capacity will be carefully applying the Learned Hand Rule, and how much will be thinking "DID YOU SEE THAT?!? OWWWWW!" Is the risk of the jury being overly influenced in favor of the plaintiff due to the graphic photographic evidence a risk that you would be willing to take as the defendant? Or, as the defendant, would you be more willing to settle the case, and more willing to settle on terms that are favorable to the plaintiff?

Consequences of Imperfect Application of the Learned Hand Rule

If juries can be manipulated in favor of plaintiffs in certain cases, then there are situations where plaintiffs are disproportionately likely to win even if the case is not meritorious based on strict application of the Learned Hand Rule. There are two implications that follow, (a) there is an incentive for plaintiffs to bring non-meritorious cases when the jury can be swayed in their favor, as plaintiffs are more likely to win and to receive a cash settlement, and (2) providers are no longer incentivized to practice appropriately, they are now have an incentive to be extra careful to avoid non-meritorious (but perhaps close) lawsuits. This overly cautious "inappropriate practice" is referred to as *defensive medicine*, which is performing medical services that have costs greater than benefits to avoid potential malpractice liability.

Evidence

There are a few pieces of evidence that support the above story of jury manipulation and defensive medicine. I will be the first to point out that the pieces of evidence I discuss below do not come from RCTs, and do not conclusively prove the theory that jury manipulation, non-meritorious cases, and defensive medicine all exist. However, they can certainly be read as supportive.

First, a study by Schaffer et al. (2017) analyzes patterns in the National Practitioner Data Bank, which is a repository of all medical malpractice payments made by or on behalf of US physicians. They document that certain specialties are far more likely to pay a medical malpractice claim.[8] For example, per physician, per year, colorectal surgeons, obstetricians, and gynecologists were approximately three times more likely to pay out a claim than emergency medicine physicians, and over 5 times more likely than internal medicine physicians.

The Schaffer et al. (2017) study shows that physicians in certain specialties pay out medical malpractice claims more frequently. These specialties include those that perform procedures that lend themselves to manipulating a jury such as rectal surgery or delivery of a baby – these procedures, when they do not go well, are more likely to play on jury sympathies. But the evidence is merely suggestive, and certainly not conclusive: it is also possible that these specialties do riskier procedures, which have more bad outcomes, or that these specialties attract physicians who commit more errors, which could also account for the pattern of these specialties having a higher frequency of payouts.

The second piece of evidence is a set of quasi-experimental economics studies on defensive medicine. The most famous of these is by Kessler and McClellan (1996).[9] In this study, the authors showed that when state tort

---

[8] These authors are not the first to document such patterns, see for example Jena et al. (2011).

[9] The literature on defensive medicine does not always find evidence in support of defensive medicine's existence. Many studies find a "null" result, or no detectable relationship. As the studies in this literature are quasi-experimental, there is variation in how reliable they are and need to be judged on their individual merits. See Paik et al. (2017) for a recent literature review.

laws were changed to limit liability to physicians, (a) heart disease patients treated under Medicare had fewer services performed, and (b) these same patients did not see different patterns in health outcomes. This evidence is consistent with (but does not conclusively prove) the existence of defensive medicine.

The final piece of evidence comes from the *Harvard Medical Practice Study*, which took records from a hospital in New York State and had them reviewed by a medical panel.[10] The study looked at the hospital records and evaluated independently which records involved an adverse event due to negligence. They also matched the records to actual medical malpractice suits to see which cases resolved in payments. The study found that not every negligent event resulted in a medical malpractice case (they estimated that roughly 1 in 7 negligent events resulted in a case), and that many malpractice cases that paid out did not involve negligence (43 percent of the medical malpractice cases in the study that the panel determined to not involve negligence paid out to plaintiffs).

Taken together, the evidence above fits with a world where juries are imperfect at applying the Learned Hand Rule, and the incentives from imperfect application influence the behavior of both physicians and of potential plaintiffs. That is not to say that this is the only theory that fits the evidence but is certainly a likely one.

Goals of the Medical Malpractice System Revisited

We can now return to the goals of the medical malpractice system:

1. Provide compensation to injured parties, and
2. Create an incentive for providers to provide care appropriately.

Are these goals accomplished? Not always. The Harvard Medical Practice Study showed that not every negligently injured party files suit (and is thus not paid), and that in some cases suits that involved no negligence are paid. It is also very difficult to know if the appropriate amount was paid to compensate the plaintiff, although a failure to pay anything when the case was due to negligence is certainly the incorrect outcome.

---

[10] This large-scale study includes multiple published works, the most widely known being Localio et al. (1991) and Brennan et al. (1996). There have been other studies with similar protocols that have also found mismatch between negligence as evaluated by independent experts and the outcome of the case, see Hyman and Silver (2006) for a review.

Furthermore, to the extent that incentives for defensive medicine exist, providers are not incentivized to provide appropriate care, but to be overly cautious due to legal risk.[11]

Self-Assessment

1. The legal test for negligence in a medical malpractice case is the Learned Hand Rule, which centers on a cost–benefit test. Can you think of an example of a type of precaution that a provider would be negligent for failing to do? Can you think of a type of precaution that a provider would **not** be negligent for failing to do?

2. Imagine that you are a plaintiff's attorney. What type of injury is a case that you would be incredibly eager to take? Why?

3. Imagine that you are a defendant. What type of injury is a case that you would want to settle? Why?

4. Imagine that you are a physician, and someone claims that you are practicing defensive medicine. What would your defense to this accusation be? How would this defense be similar or different to your defense if someone claimed that you were inducing demand?

5. Providers carry insurance against being sued for medical malpractice. Do you think that the presence of this insurance increases or decreases the likelihood of settling cases outside of court? Why?

---

[11] For a deeper dive into the law, economics, and policy surrounding medical malpractice, I recommend the book *Medical Malpractice* by Frank M. Sloan and Lindsey M. Chepke (2008).

18 Inequality

When looking at any outcome, be it in the context of healthcare or the wider world, there is often a focus on single summary measures. If we consider, for example, life expectancy in the United States, the first number you will likely find is average life expectancy. The Centers for Disease Control and Prevention (CDC) reports that the average life expectancy at birth was 76.1 years for 2021 (Arias et al. 2022). But this masks important variation: not every person who is born is going to live for 76.1 years. The average life expectancy is just a summary measure for a larger distribution of how long people live. The same CDC report gives a life expectancy of 79.1 for females and 73.2 for males. These are still summary measures (because it's unwieldy to look at all mortality data at once), but these numbers give us a finer understanding of variation across an important demographic: gender.

When you slice down past summary measures of outcomes, you may (and most often do) see meaningful differences across groups. In other words, you observe inequality. Some of the inequality you observe may be explainable by immutable differences between the groups. For example, there may be some genetic factor that causes females to tend to live longer than males, meaning that the inequality in life expectancy between genders may not be something that society would want to attempt to remedy.[1] But, in other cases, there are meaningful differences in outcomes across groups that are cause for concern.

To return to the example of life expectancy, there is tremendous variation in life expectancy in the United States based on household income. Chetty et al. (2016) report a strong relationship between household income and life expectancy at age 40. Men who were in the top 1 percent of household income lived, on average, more than 14 years longer than men in the bottom 1 percent of household income.[2]

---

[1] There may be other reasons for the differences in outcomes, which have different societal implications. This is why understanding causality between variables (as is discussed in Chapter 5) is so important.

[2] The same comparison for women yields a difference of 10.1 years. For most of the distribution of income, the authors found a roughly linear relationship between household income percentile and life expectancy. Every 5 percentiles a person moves up in household income, they live 0.7–0.9 years longer on average.

Inequality across health outcomes and correlates of health outcomes is interesting for two reasons. The first is that inequality is a valuable area of study on its own. To the extent that inequality is a symptom of systematic features that are "unfair" or "unjust," understanding and trying to remedy inequality is something that many would consider to be a worthy endeavor.

The second is that understanding inequality may help in understanding root causes of health outcomes, and through studying inequality we can help determine what factors matter for improving health. This is connected to the concept of *social determinants of health*, which is the idea that individual environments (both physical and social) may matter tremendously for health outcomes. So, if there is income inequality, and lower-income areas have lower air quality (due to pollution or due to aging building air systems), which leads to respiratory illness and shorter life expectancy, then understanding this chain of causality is helpful from both a medical treatment and from a policy perspective. Treating individual respiratory symptoms directly may not be nearly as effective (or as cost-effective) as upgrading air quality, something that we may not have learned without a broader view of income, environment, and health.

The Veil of Ignorance

To dig a little deeper into the idea of "fairness" I want to step out of economics for a second and into philosophy. Don't worry, I'm not a philosopher, so you won't wink out of existence from reading this section.[3] I just want to bring some philosophy ideas into the mix because they help organize thinking about fairness and how we design a society. The concept I want to bring in is of the "veil of ignorance" a term coined by John Rawls in his 1971 book *A Theory of Justice*.

The veil of ignorance is a metaphysical barrier that everyone in a society can exist behind. Behind the veil of ignorance all individuals within a society can see the features of the society but cannot tell who they are within that society. Individuals exist behind the veil, make decisions about how their society is to be set up, and then pass through the veil of ignorance and into that society, only then learning who they are. The argument made by Rawls is that this eliminates people's biases when designing societies and allows for a fairer societal organization. Obviously, we don't have a way to

---

[3] I think.

actually do this, but it provides a useful thought experiment that can serve as a framework for deciding what is fair and what isn't.

A useful feature of the veil of ignorance is that it allows us to think through the difference between desirable and undesirable forms of inequality. Behind the veil of ignorance, I may not know what my personal ability (and productivity) is, but I may still wish to live in a society where higher productivity workers are paid more than lower productivity workers. There may be an amount of inequality along certain characteristics that I would want to exist, even when I do not know which place in the society I would inhabit. On the other hand, there are also forms of inequality that I would almost certainly not want to exist if I was behind the veil of ignorance, such as inequality explicitly due to race or gender. A useful (but also sometimes difficult) question to ask yourself when considering possible policies, and in particular policies that involve inequality, is "would I want this if I was behind the veil of ignorance?"[4]

Income, Race, Gender, and Health Outcomes in the United States

For the next chunk of this chapter, I want to lay out a few stylized facts about inequality with regards to demographics and health outcomes. The idea is to first get a sense of the "facts on the ground" and then try to find some theories (and some evidence as well) that help to explain those facts. None of this is meant to be exhaustive. Inequality is a large and growing area of research in both health economics and economics in general, and this chapter is meant to give an introductory, but certainly not a complete, tour of its relevance.

To return to the idea that there is inequality in health outcomes based on demographics, we can again look at life expectancy as reported by the CDC (Arias et al. 2022). Not only are there meaningful differences based on gender as discussed at the start of the chapter and based on income (as discussed by Chetty et al. 2016), but there are also differences based on race and ethnicity. The life expectancy for a Hispanic

---

[4] There are some interesting implications (which are way outside the scope of this book) with regards to who is placed behind the veil of ignorance (and who is not) when deciding on societal features. For example, the decisions made about pollution and resource usage might be different if the parties placed behind the veil do or do not include future generations.

individual in 2021 was 77.7 years, this is compared to 76.4 years for non-Hispanic Whites, 83.5 years for non-Hispanic Asians, and 70.8 years for non-Hispanic Blacks.

Life expectancy is not the only relevant measure of health outcomes. We can also look at differences in other health outcomes (as well as other measures related to health) based on the 2018 National Health Interview Survey (NHIS). Table 18.1 collates results from the 2018 NHIS public reports. There are also public use files that can be used to do your own analyses if you want to explore the data yourself (National Center for Health Statistics 2019). The numbers in the table are the percent of each group (in the NHIS) that reports having the outcome listed on the leftmost column of the table. So, for the first group, males, 2.0 percent reported having poor health, and 37.2 percent reported having excellent health.

Remember, these numbers are still summary measures, and even though they are more finely delineated than averages for the entire population, they still hide a considerable amount of variation. Also, as summary measures, these numbers don't tell us what causes any of the observed differences, just that those differences exist. Finally, this is a limited set of measures, there are many other outcomes across which meaningful differences might exist.

The top part of the table deals with what can be considered health outcomes: self-reported health and self-reported incidence of various diagnoses. The bottom part of the table deals with self-reported access to care and ability to afford care. Take a little time and look at the table for yourself, I'm not going to discuss every data point, just few things that jump out to me.

The most noticeable set of differences are based on income. Higher-income individuals uniformly have better outcomes than lower-income individuals. This is true both for health outcomes, but also for access and ability to afford care. There are also differences by race and gender, although the patterns are not as uniform as when looking across income. In general, the White population tends to have better outcomes than other demographics, although the magnitude of these differences varies considerably from outcome to outcome. For example, the Black–White difference in the rate of diabetes is much bigger than the Black–White difference in the rate of severe psychological distress. Some of the smallest differences are across gender, although there are still some rather large differences across gender for some variables. Females are much more likely than males to have a usual place of care, they are also more likely than males to report having cancer.

Table 18.1 Demographics of selected health and care outcomes from the 2018 NHIS

Measure	Male	Female	White	Black	Hispanic	Income Under $35,000	Income Over $35,000
Poor health	2.0	2.0	1.8	2.9	2.5	4.7	1.2
Excellent health	37.2	36.6	37.5	33.5	34.2	28.2	39.5
Heart disease	12.6	10.1	11.5	10.0	8.2	13.4	10.8
Cancer	7.6	9.1	9.1	5.1	4.2	7.6	8.8
Diabetes	10.2	8.9	8.6	13.1	13.2	13.4	8.3
Obesity	30.9	31.2	31.0	38.0	34.9	34.9	30.1
Missing teeth	6.8	7.0	6.6	9.1	7.7	11.2	5.4
Serious psychological distress	2.9	4.8	3.9	3.8	4.6	8.1	2.6
Had a usual place of care	81.4	89.3	85.4	85.3	79.3	79.2	87.6
Delayed care due to cost	6.9	7.4	7.3	7.5	6.8	12.8	5.7
Did not get care due to cost	4.4	5.0	4.5	6.1	5.0	10.3	3.2

Source: National Health Interview Survey Public Reports, www.cdc.gov/nchs/nhis/shs/tables.htm

Why Do We See Inequality in Health Outcomes?

To think about why health outcomes are unequal across groups we can bring back a tool from Chapter 2: the health production function. If something influences health, then it is in the health production function. So, by that logic, if there is a difference in a health outcome across groups, then the root of that difference is in the health production function as well.

Some of these differences may be immutable based on genetics (recall that genetics are something that enters into the health production function). For example, there is a gender difference in rates of ovarian cancer (as you have to have ovaries to get ovarian cancer, and women are much more likely than men to have ovaries). So, there is gender inequality in the prevalence of this form of cancer, and we can largely (but perhaps not completely, I'm not an oncologist) chalk that one up to due to genetic differences.

On the other hand, some differences in health outcomes may be due to differences in other variables in the health production function, such as the amount of medical care consumed, lifestyle choices, or environmental factors. Inequality in these inputs in the health production function could cause inequality in health outcomes. A meaningful difference in dental care used across groups could lead to some of the observed differences in missing teeth recorded in Table 18.1. Similarly, differences in diet could lead to the observed differences in diabetes.

Just because in some cases we can isolate what part of the health production function is the likely source of inequality does not mean that we always know the full "why" of that inequality. For example, we might observe a population that eats nothing but fast food, leading to a health disparity relative to the rest of the population. This alone does not mean that we understand the full story.

"Group A," that chooses to eat nothing but fast food because they prefer it over healthier options is not the same as a "Group B" that eats only fast food because that is the only food locally available. If the goal is to remedy the health disparity (i.e. close gaps in health outcomes) created by the difference in lifestyle choices, then different policies would be effective or ineffective for Group A vs. Group B. Even though for both groups the cause of the health outcome is likely diet, the reason for the dietary choice is different across groups.

Inequality in Medical Care

One reason why we might see differences in health outcomes across demographic groups is that those groups may have different patterns of consuming medical care. The simplest way to see this is by looking at income. Medical care is a normal good (meaning you purchase more of it as you have more income), and if we have not yet hit the flat of the curve, we would expect additional medical care to improve health outcomes. In Table 18.1, higher income individuals were more likely to have a usual source of care and less likely to have not gotten care due to cost, so ability to pay for care could directly influence health outcomes (this is something that is predicted by the Engel curves in Chapter 3).

This also means that any source of income inequality can turn into health inequality if the medical care being consumed is prior to the flat of the curve. There is a tremendous amount of evidence in economics (as well as in social science more broadly) that there are large and persistent income inequalities based on demographics such as gender (see Blau and Khan 2017 for a review) or race and ethnicity (see Carniero et al. 2005 for a review). Some (but not all) of this gap has been shown experimentally to be due to overt discrimination in the labor market (for an example of this type of study see Bertrand and Mullainathan 2004, or see Neumark 2018 for a review).

This does not mean that all differences in medical care consumed are due to differences by group in terms of income. There is also the possibility that preferences with regards to medical care play a role as well. Survey evidence shows striking differences in trust in medical providers based on race, which suggests that groups with less trust in providers would be less likely to choose to consume medical care all else being equal (Boulware 2003).[5]

It is also possible that there are differences in the effectiveness of medical care across demographic groups. Medical care improves over time due to research and development of new technologies. If there is under- or over-investment in technologies that help one group more than another, then a gap in health outcomes could arise as one group gets better return in terms of health outcomes for each dollar they spend on medical care. This is demonstrated by Michelman and Msall (2022) who show that FDA guidance to avoid testing on "women of childbearing potential" led to a gap in the number of new drugs developed that aid women relative to the number of new drugs developed to aid men.

---

[5] The differences in the Boulware (2003) survey are between Black and White respondents. The authors, as well as a larger literature suggest that these differences in attitudes may be due to historical mistreatment of the Black population by the medical profession, citing the Tuskegee syphilis experiments as a moment of particular historical significance, see Gamble (1993) for a deeper discussion. Economists estimate that the revelation of the abuses during the Tuskegee experiments account for around 35 percent of the Black–White life expectancy gap for males (Alsan and Wanamaker 2018).

To give another example, cancer clinical trials tend to disproportionally study young White males, which could lead to an innovation gap if there are meaningful differences in what treatments are effective based on race, gender, or age (Murthy et al. 2004).

Inequality in effectiveness of care could also be due to discrimination in the health care system itself. For example, many hospitals in the United States were overtly segregated based on race. It was only during the 1960s, due to the federal government's threat to withhold funding under the Civil Rights Act of 1964 that segregated hospitals integrated (Reynolds 1997).

Inequality in the Local Environment

Environmental factors also play a role in determining health outcomes. So, to the extent that there is inequality in access to good environments (or inequality in who is exposed to bad environments) this can also create inequality in health outcomes. As with access to and use of medical care, these environmental differences could be due to differences in income as many environmental features are paid for as part of the cost of housing. Housing that has access to parks tends to cost more, and housing that is near heavily polluted areas tends to cost less.

It is also possible that differences in local environment are due to discrimination in the housing market. This can come in many forms, from discrimination with regards to who is shown which homes to purchase or rent, known as "redlining" (Ondrich et al. 2003), to discrimination with regards to who is given a loan and under what terms (Ross and Yinger 2002).

Regardless of how inequality in local environment comes about, to the extent that the environment influences the health production function, it will create inequality in health outcomes. Work by Breen et al. (2022) shows that measures of racial isolation (a single demographic group packed into a local area) and the confluence of racial isolation and poverty are strongly associated with increased mortality for the isolated group.

Intergenerational Persistence

When thinking about inequality and in particular inequality with regards to income, it is important to realize that a large part of an individual's place within the income distribution comes from their parents. Parental income is a strong predictor of eventual child income. The extent to which a child can move up in the income distribution relative to their parents or their *intergenerational mobility* is also not random (Solon 1999 provides a review of this literature). Chetty et al. (2014) show that individuals who grow up in areas with less racial segregation, less income inequality, and with better schools have better intergenerational mobility.

Urban and Rural Differences

Another place where there is inequality in health outcomes is between urban and rural locations. Mortality rates are higher in rural areas, a phenomenon known as the "rural mortality penalty" (Cosby et al. 2019). Interestingly, the inequality hasn't arisen due to rural areas seeing increasing mortality over time: mortality has been falling in both urban and rural areas in the United States in recent decades, it has just been falling faster in urban areas than in rural areas (Cosby et al. 2008).

In addition to the sources of inequality discussed earlier in the chapter, rural areas are more sensitive to disruptions in their supply of medical care. The closure of a hospital in a rural area creates a much larger change in travel time to the nearest hospital than a closure of a hospital in an urban area. Rural areas have had a large number of hospital closures in recent years (Kaufman et al. 2016), and closures when there was no other local hospital were associated with negative changes in the local economy such as decreases in local income and increases in the local unemployment rate (Holmes et al. 2006). All of these factors could impact health outcomes.

Inequality for the Healthcare Workforce

To this point, we have discussed inequality in health outcomes, but there is also documented inequality with regards to pay within the healthcare workforce (World Health Organization 2022). Pay inequality can be tricky to nail down as there can be differences in worker characteristics, such as experience, that explain some of the observed differences in pay. For example, females may choose to exit the labor force when they have children and re-enter later in life, missing out on work experience that could account for some of the observed pay differences. Lo Sasso et al. (2011) demonstrate that there are still large pay gaps that cannot be accounted for by these types of differences. They show that in 2008, newly trained female physicians made over $16,000 less than newly trained male physicians with the same specialties and practice type.

Self-Assessment

1. In this chapter, you were provided with summary measures that show demographic differences in health outcomes across race, gender, and income. Can you think of a possible further difference that could exist **within** one of these groups that is not observable with the summary data given?

2. Can you think of an example of a situation where treating the symptoms of an illness would not be as effective as intervening to change the social determinants of that illness?
3. Can you think of a type of inequality that you would choose to put into a society from behind the veil of ignorance?
4. Consider the following statement "If we just got rid of income inequality then there would be no health inequality." Do you agree? Why or why not?
5. What would you hypothesize would be the relationship between an increase in income for parents and the eventual health outcomes for their children later in life? What role does intergenerational mobility play?

19 | International Comparisons

This book has been an introduction to the economics of healthcare with a specific focus on the healthcare system in the United States. In this final chapter, we're going to discuss how the United States compares to other countries. I'll save you a little bit of time here if you don't want to actually read the whole chapter: the United States spends more per capita than any other country in the OECD but performs solidly middle of the pack in terms of health outcomes.[1]

The question that remains is "why?" Again, to save you some time, here's the long and short of it: we're not completely sure. There are several possible explanations: differences in lifestyle choices, differences in costs, differences in how much spending is on the flat of the curve to name a few. Each of the explanations that follow later in the chapter are plausible, but no single one of them has been definitively shown to be "the reason" for the difference between the United States and the rest of the OECD. My personal opinion is that each of them is likely a contributing factor, and no single explanation accounts for the full difference.

Comparing OECD Countries

The first fact that we'll establish is that the United States spends more than any other OECD country. This is simple to show. Table 19.1 shows the top 25 OECD countries in terms of healthcare spending per capita.[2]

The United States spends more per capita than anyone else, and it isn't even close. The United States spends over one-and-a-half times what Switzerland, the next biggest spender, spends per person on healthcare.[3]

---

[1] You've almost made it to the end of the book and you're seriously considering not reading the final chapter? What if there's a big twist at the end?

[2] These data come directly from the OECD, you can download them yourself here: https://data.oecd.org/healthres/health-spending.htm, the website's dashboard will also let you download all of the OECD health outcome data in the discussion to follow.

[3] The United States spent 1.65 times what Switzerland spent per capita on healthcare in 2020, but I didn't want you to worry about how much of the difference was due to

Table 19.1 Top 25 OECD countries healthcare spending		
Country	Healthcare Spending per Capita 2019 (US Dollars)	US Spent This Much More
United States	10,856	
Switzerland	6,942	×1.56
Norway	6,476	×1.68
Germany	6,408	×1.69
Netherlands	5,649	×1.92
Austria	5,624	×1.93
Sweden	5,388	×2.01
Denmark	5,360	×2.03
Luxembourg	5,360	×2.03
Belgium	5,353	×2.03
Canada	5,190	×2.09
France	5,168	×2.10
Australia	5,130	×2.12
Ireland	4,947	×2.19
Japan	4,611	×2.35
United Kingdom	4,385	×2.48
Finland	4,382	×2.48
Iceland	4,318	×2.51
New Zealand	4,250	×2.55
Italy	3,565	×3.04
Spain	3,523	×3.08
South Korea	3,277	×3.31
The Czech Republic	3,272	×3.32
Portugal	3,224	×3.37
Slovenia	3,222	×3.37

Source: OECD, https://data.oecd.org/healthres/health-spending.htm

COVID-19, so the table shows the 2019 numbers. The United States spent 1.51 times what Switzerland spent per capita on healthcare in 2018. No matter which recent year you pick, the answer is that the United States spent a lot more.

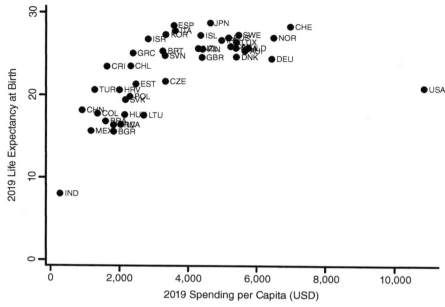

Figure 19.1 Life expectancy at birth and per capita healthcare spending 2019
Source: Created by author from OECD spending and health risks data, https://data.oecd.org/
healthres/health-spending.htm and www.oecd-ilibrary.org/social-issues-migration-health/
health-risks/indicator-group/english_1c4df204-en

If we want to look at bigger discrepancies, the United States spent over 12 times what China spent per capita on healthcare in 2019, and over 47 times what India spent per capita.

Next, let's compare spending on healthcare in OECD countries to some health outcomes for those countries. For example, we can look at life expectancy at birth. Data for 2019 are shown in Figure 19.1. Each country is labeled, with its three letter OECD country abbreviation, the United States is labeled "USA" and is way over on the right. The United States is a clear outlier in terms of spending but is middle of the pack in terms of life expectancy for the OECD (although among the top spenders in Table 19.1, the United States is dead last). There is a slightly visible association in the non-United States countries: better outcomes are associated with more spending per capita, but the United States completely breaks out of the pattern.

Figure 19.2 shows the same picture but for the outcome of infant mortality. Again, the United States spends more than anybody else and gets middle of the pack health outcomes. Figure 19.3 is the same picture for deaths due to cancer.

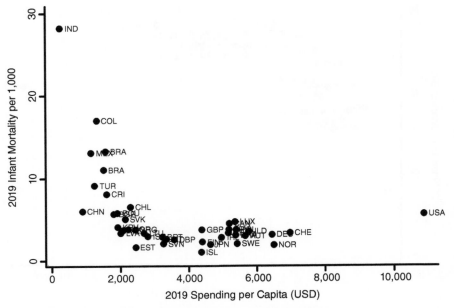

Figure 19.2 Infant mortality and per capita healthcare spending 2019
Source: Created by author from OECD spending and health risks data, https://data.oecd.org/
healthres/health-spending.htm and www.oecd-ilibrary.org/social-issues-migration-health/
health-risks/indicator-group/english_1c4df204-en

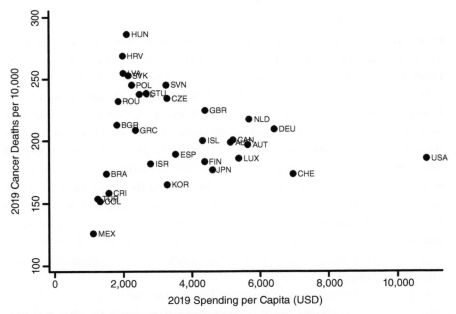

Figure 19.3 Cancer deaths and per capita healthcare spending 2019
Source: Created by author from OECD spending and health risks data, https://data.oecd.org/
healthres/health-spending.htm and www.oecd-ilibrary.org/social-issues-migration-health/
health-risks/indicator-group/english_1c4df204-en

There are fewer data points in Figure 19.3 than in Figure 19.2 or Figure 19.1 because fewer countries have complete OECD data for cancer mortality, but even with the smaller sample the pattern is the same as the other figures. Once again, the United States spends the most money per person on healthcare but gets middle of the road health outcomes. Pretty much any health outcome that you collect, the United States performs mediocrely relative to its OECD counterparts.

Theories That Fit the Facts

Given that the United States spends the most on healthcare but does not get the best health outcomes, we are left to ask the question "why?" There are several explanations that potentially fit the facts.

Lifestyle Choices

One possible explanation for the patterns in the figures is that despite the United States spending much more on medical care, the health gains from care consumption are more than offset by lifestyle choices of the population. The idea is that the amount of medical care consumed is not going to matter much if your population is a bunch of chain-smoking, beer-guzzling, burger-slamming couch potatoes.

There may be a role for lifestyle choices in the United States' place as an outlier in the figures, but it seems unlikely that this is the whole story. For example, using the same data source as used in the tables and figures earlier in this chapter, in terms of alcohol consumption, the United States population was 24th out of OECD countries, with the top 18 countries consuming at least 10 percent more alcohol per capita than the United States. The United States was also 36th out of OECD countries in terms of daily smokers, solidly in the bottom third in terms of smoking rate.[4] On the other hand, the United States had the second highest rate of the population that was overweight or obese, second only to Mexico. If the story for why the United States gets worse outcomes is lifestyle choices, then it is only certain lifestyle choices (such as those that lead to obesity) and not others (such as smoking).

The Flat of the Curve

Another possible explanation for its poor performance is that the United States consumes a larger proportion of medical care that is on the flat of

---

[4] Where being in the bottom means fewer people smoke.

the curve. The United States may be bad at getting individuals to purchase effective care, and would thus be a place where (a) a lot of money is spent, and (b) a lot of that money is spent on care that does little to improve health outcomes. There are a few potential culprits that could cause this type of spending.

First, physicians could be demand inducing. The type of care that a physician would want to demand induce would be care that does no harm to health (it may improve health but doesn't have to) but is not worth the cost. This could be medical care such as extra follow-ups, extra diagnostics, or more expensive pharmaceuticals when cheaper versions are available. To the extent that the additional medical care did not improve health, induced demand would be on the flat of the curve.

A similar story, at least for diagnostics and follow-ups can be told for defensive medicine: in this case providers would be generating additional care that does not necessarily improve health but instead helps protect them from legal liability. Defensive medicine seems unlikely to explain the poor returns on health spending in the United States relative to the OECD as the entire medical liability system accounts for less than 2.5 percent of United States medical spending (Mello et al. 2010).

Another source of spending on the flat of the curve could be simple overconsumption of care without any direction from providers. Individuals with health insurance tend to consume more care and the features of that insurance influences the degree to which they increase consumption. These features of a plan can also steer patients toward or away from different types of care. This is something that we saw theoretically in Chapter 4, and that has shown up in empirical studies of health insurance and care utilization (recall for example the RAND and Oregon experiments discussed in Chapter 5). It is then possible that the structure of health insurance in the United States pushes individuals to purchase care that is less cost-effective (i.e. on the flat of the curve) relative to its OECD contemporaries.

Cost Differences

A third possibility is that healthcare in the United States simply costs more. People in the United States could be spending more per unit and thus have larger per capita expenditures but get less in terms of bang for the buck. An extreme version of this would be where the average American spends more on medical care in terms of dollars than their international counterparts, but actually gets fewer units of care.

Himmelstein et al. (2020) estimate that the United States spends over twice as much on overhead (i.e. administration of health plans) as Canada. Their estimates were quite large for both countries but much larger for the

United States: they found that over 34 percent of US health expenditures could be counted as overhead as compared to 17 percent for Canada. This is just the difference in the cost of running the healthcare systems and does not account for any differences in the cost of inputs.

The United States might also have higher input costs. For example, according to an OECD report by Fujisawa and Lafortune (2008), in 2003, a general practitioner in the United States was paid around 20 percent more than a general practitioner in the next highest paid OECD country (the UK). The United States is not, however, the highest salary location in all situations, the same report showed that in 2004, a specialist in Norway was paid over 22 percent more than a specialist in the United States.

For pharmaceuticals, the story is a bit more uniform, with the United States having unambiguously higher costs. A 2021 RAND report by Mulcahy et al. found prices of pharmaceuticals in the United States to be over 250 percent higher than the OECD average. Prices were over 340 percent higher for branded drugs and just under 85 percent higher for generics.

Systemwide Differences

Another way to think about the differences across countries is to look at the overall structure of the healthcare system. To some extent, trying to compare spending and outcomes across countries (even within the OECD) is a bit like comparing apples and oranges. There are many differences between any two countries in terms of the organization of their healthcare sector and a large number of these differences could potentially be important for determining spending and health outcomes. So, let's take a moment and discuss, in broad strokes, some of the different types of systems that are out there.

The Bismarck Model

The Bismarck model is named after Otto Von Bismarck, the chancellor of the German Empire who instituted the first version of this system in 1883. The Bismarck model centers around well-regulated not-for-profit health insurers who provide health insurance to the population for a fee. The fee can be paid by enrollees but is often paid in part by employers and can be offset or fully covered in some cases by public funds. Under some versions of the Bismarck model there is also an optional private health insurance sector where individuals can choose to purchase more generous health insurance with a greater degree of choice across providers. This is done, for example, in Switzerland. Examples of other countries with Bismarck model healthcare sectors are Belgium, France, Germany, and Japan.

The Beveridge Model

The Beveridge model is named after Lord William Beveridge (a UK economist), who was one of the leading forces behind the establishment of the British NHS (which was discussed in the supplement to Chapter 11). Under the Beveridge model, the entire population is covered by government insurance paid for by taxes, and most (if not all) health services are provided directly by government providers. In many ways, the Beveridge model is like a single large HMO run by the government. Examples of countries with Beveridge model healthcare are New Zealand, Spain, and the UK.

Nationalized Health Insurance

Under nationalized health insurance there is a single health insurance plan run by the government and financed by taxes. Unlike the Beveridge model, providers are largely independent and accept payment from government insurance for their services but are not employed by the government directly. It is still possible for there to be some publicly owned providers under this system (much as there can be some private providers under a Beveridge model), but this is not the majority of cases. Some countries with nationalized health insurance have small private health insurance markets for certain types of care not covered fully by the government, for example Canada has a private market for dental insurance. Examples of countries with nationalized health insurance are Canada and South Korea. Both the Beveridge model and nationalized health insurance can be considered "single payer" systems, as in both cases there is a single dominant health insurance company in the market: the government.

You're on Your Own Model

This model is also known as a strict fee-for-service system. Under this system there is little to no health insurance market (public or private) and individuals largely purchase medical care directly from providers with out-of-pocket payments (when they can afford them). This is the healthcare system for low-income countries where healthcare and health insurance markets are still developing.

The United States

If you want to fit the United States into these frameworks you can do it, but in a patchwork sense. Employer-sponsored health insurance has many similarities to the Bismarck model, the key difference being the profit motive for health insurers is present in the United States but not in countries where health insurers are regulated not-for-profits. Nationalized health insurance is analogous to Medicare, or at least the government administered insurance portions of Medicare (i.e. not Medicare Advantage which involves the private health insurance market). The Beveridge model is similar to care under the United States Veteran's Administration which runs its own hospitals to provide care for those it covers. And, of course, the you're on your own model is what Americans who do not have health insurance deal with.

Final Thought: The Devil Is in the Details

To conclude, I want to bring back a point that I brought up in Chapter 11. A healthcare system broadly defined is a set of institutions upon which policies (public and private) are layered. These policies or institutional details create incentives which help push the behavior of firms, providers, and patients. Though systemwide choices will make some outcomes easier or more difficult to attain, the devil really is in the details. Small changes to how incentives are structured can cause wildly different choices by economic actors. A different type of insurance cost sharing, or a different payment scheme for a physician, or a different set of regulations to try to curb spread of an illness could have wildly different outcomes as they influence human decision-making in different ways.

Hopefully, here at the end of this book, you now have the tools to think through how these incentives will influence human behavior and to start to think about how to design incentives that will push individuals to make desirable choices. Healthcare is a sector that is messy and complicated and difficult to manage, but that also means that it is a sector full of opportunity to make things better.

Self-Assessment

1. Go to https://data.oecd.org/ and find a measure of health. Plot it against national spending on healthcare (https://data.oecd.org/healthres/health-spending.htm). Which country is an outlier? (HINT: It's the United States).

2. Consider the statement "The United States gets worse health outcomes than other OECD countries despite its high level of spending because Americans have poor lifestyles." Do you agree? Why or why not?

3. Consider the statement "The United States can't be on the flat of the curve because of the high level of managed care in the US healthcare system." Do you agree? Why or why not?

4. Consider the statement "If drug prices are so much higher in the United States, then the US government should just refuse to pay high prices for drugs, they have the bargaining power to do it, and it would make everyone better off." Do you agree? Why or why not?

5. Which structures of a national healthcare system (i.e. the Bismarck model, the Beveridge model, etc.) would you expect to have higher administrative costs systemwide? Why?

6. What is one advantage of the United States' healthcare system compared to a Beveridge system? What is one disadvantage of the United States' healthcare system compared to a Beveridge system?

References

Abaluck, J., Kwong, L.H., Styczynski, A., et al. 2022. Impact of community masking on COVID-19: a cluster-randomized trial in Bangladesh. *Science*, 375(6577), eabi9069.

Aiken, L.H., Buchan, J., Sochalski, J., Nichols, B. and Powell, M. 2004. Trends in international nurse migration. *Health Affairs*, 23(3), 69–77.

Alsan, M. and Wanamaker, M. 2018. Tuskegee and the health of black men. *The Quarterly Journal of Economics*, 133(1), 407–455.

American Medical Association. n.d. *Code of Medical Ethics Opinion 11.3.4*. Chicago, IL: AMA. Available at: www.ama-assn.org/ delivering-care/ethics/fee-splitting

Angrist, J.D. and Pischke, J.S. 2008. *Mostly Harmless Econometrics*. Princeton, NJ: Princeton University Press.

Arias, E., Tejada-Vera, B., Kochanek, K.D. and Ahmad, F.B. 2022. Provisional life expectancy estimates for 2021. *NVSS Vital Statistics Rapid Release*, 23.

Artiga, S., Hinton, E., Rudowitz, R. and Musumeci, M. 2017. *Current Flexibility in Medicaid: An Overview of Federal Standards and State Options*. San Francisco, CA: Henry J. Kaiser Family Foundation. Available at: www .kff.org/report-section/current-flexibility-in-medicaid-issue-brief

Association of American Medical Colleges. 2022. *Data and Analysis, Total Graduates by U.S. Medical School and Sex, 2002–2021*. Washington, DC: AAMC. Available at www.aamc.org/data/facts/ enrollmentgraduate/

Baicker, K., Taubman, S.L., Allen, H.L., et al. 2013. The Oregon experiment: effects of Medicaid on clinical outcomes. *New England Journal of Medicine*, 368(18), 1713–1722.

Bertrand, M. and Mullainathan, S. 2004. Are Emily and Greg more employable than Lakisha and Jamal? A field experiment on labor market discrimination. *American Economic Review*, 94(4), 991–1013.

Blau, F.D. and Kahn, L.M. 2017. The gender wage gap: extent, trends, and explanations. *Journal of Economic Literature*, 55(3), 789–865.

Boulware, L.E., Cooper, L.A., Ratner, L.E., LaVeist, T.A. and Powe, N.R. 2003. Race and trust in the health care system. *Public Health Reports*, 118(4), 358.

Breen, N., Andres, J., Fossett, M., Gomez, M.M. and Moy, E. 2022. The effects of residential segregation on black and white mortality in the United States. *The Review of Black Political Economy*, September 4 (online).

Brennan, T.A., Sox, C.M. and Burstin, H.R. 1996. Relation between negligent adverse events and the outcomes of medical-malpractice litigation. *New England Journal of Medicine*, 335(26), 1963–1967.

Brill, S. 2013. "Bitter Pill." *Time Magazine,* March 4, 2013.

Brown, D.G., Wobst, H.J., Kapoor, A., Kenna, L.A. and Southall, N. 2021. Clinical development times for innovative drugs. *Nature Reviews: Drug Discovery*, 10 November.

Cadena, B.C. and Smith, A.C., 2022. Performance pay, productivity, and strategic opt-out: evidence from a community health center. *Journal of Public Economics*, 206, Article 104580.

Carneiro, P., Heckman, J.J. and Masterov, D.V. 2005. Understanding the sources of ethnic and racial wage gaps and their implications for policy. In L.B. Nielsen and R.L. Nelson, eds., *Handbook of Employment Discrimination Research*. Dordrecht, The Netherlands: Springer, pp. 99–136.

Centers for Medicare & Medicaid Services. 2022a. *National Health Expenditure Data, National Health Expenditure Accounts.* Baltimore, MD: CMS. Available at: www.cms.gov/Research-Statistics-Data-and-Systems/Statistics-Trends-and-Reports/NationalHealthExpendData/NationalHealthAccountsHistorical

Centers for Medicare & Medicaid Services. 2022b. *NHE Fact Sheet.* Baltimore, MD: CMS. Available at: www.cms.gov/Research-Statistics-Data-and-Systems/Statistics-Trends-and-Reports/NationalHealthExpendData/NHE-Fact-Sheet

Chetty, R., Hendren, N., Kline, P. and Saez, E. 2014. Where is the land of opportunity? The geography of intergenerational mobility in the United States. *The Quarterly Journal of Economics*, 129(4), 1553–1623.

Chetty, R., Stepner, M., Abraham, S., et al. 2016. The association between income and life expectancy in the United States, 2001–2014. *JAMA*, 315(16), 1750–1766.

Clemens, J. and Gottlieb, J.D. 2017. In the shadow of a giant: medicare's influence on private physician payments. *Journal of Political Economy*, 125(1), 1–39.

Coase, R.H. 1960. The problem of social cost. *The Journal of Law and Economics*, 3, 1–44.

Cosby, A.G., McDoom-Echebiri, M.M., James, W., et al. 2019. Growth and persistence of place-based mortality in the United States: the rural mortality penalty. *American Journal of Public Health*, 109(1), 155–162.

Cosby, A.G., Neaves, T.T., Cossman, R.E., et al. 2008. Preliminary evidence for an emerging nonmetropolitan mortality penalty in the United States. *American Journal of Public Health*, 98(8), 1470–1472.

Courtemanche, C., Garuccio, J., Le, A., Pinkston, J. and Yelowitz, A. 2020. Strong social distancing measures in the United States reduced the COVID-19 growth rate: study evaluates the impact of social distancing measures on the growth rate of confirmed COVID-19 cases across the United States. *Health Affairs*, 39(7), 1237–1246.

Cunningham, S. 2021. *Causal Inference: The Mixtape.* London: Yale University Press.

Currie, J., Lin, W. and Meng, J. 2014. Addressing antibiotic abuse in China: an experimental audit study. *Journal of Development Economics*, 110, 39–51.

Darden, M.E., Hotchkiss, J.L. and Pitts, M.M. 2021. The dynamics of the smoking wage penalty. *Journal of Health Economics*, 79, 102485.

Datta, A. and Dave, D. 2017. Effects of physician-directed pharmaceutical promotion on prescription behaviors: longitudinal evidence. *Health Economics*, 26(4), 450–468.

Dave, D., Friedson, A., Matsuzawa, K., Sabia, J.J. and Safford, S.,2022. JUE Insight: Were urban cowboys enough to control COVID-19? Local shelter-in-place orders and coronavirus case growth. *Journal of Urban Economics*, 103294.

Dave, D., Friedson, A.I., Matsuzawa, K. and Sabia, J.J. 2021. When do shelter-in-place orders fight COVID-19 best? Policy heterogeneity across states and adoption time. *Economic Inquiry*, 59(1), 29–52.

Dave, D., Friedson, A., Matsuzawa, K., Sabia, J.J. and Safford, S. 2022. JUE insight: were urban cowboys enough to control COVID-19? Local shelter-in-place orders and coronavirus case growth. *Journal of Urban Economics*, 103294.

DeJong, C., Aguilar, T., Tseng, C.W., et al. 2016. Pharmaceutical industry-sponsored meals and physician prescribing patterns for Medicare beneficiaries. *JAMA Internal Medicine*, 176(8), 1114–1122.

Department of Health and Human Services 2020. *Medicare and Medicaid Programs: CY 2020 Hospital Outpatient PPS Policy Changes and Payment Rates and Ambulatory Surgical Center Payment System Policy Changes and Payment Rates. Price Transparency Requirements for Hospitals to Make Standard Charges Public.* 84 FR 65524. Washington, DC: DHHS.

Doyle, A.C. 1975. *The Adventures of Sherlock Holmes.* New York: A & W Visual Library.

Friedson, A.I. 2018. Medical scribes as an input in health-care production: evidence from a randomized experiment. *American Journal of Health Economics*, 4(4), 479–503.

Friedson, A.I., McNichols, D., Sabia, J.J. and Dave, D. 2021. Shelter-in-place orders and public health: evidence from California during the COVID-19 pandemic. *Journal of Policy Analysis and Management*, 40(1), 258–283.

Fujisawa, R. and Lafortune, G. 2008. The remuneration of general practitioners and specialists in 14 OECD countries: what are the factors influencing variations across countries? *OECD Health Working Papers*, No. 41. Paris: OECD Publishing.

Gallagher, E.A., Gopalan, R., Grinstein-Weiss, M. and Sabat, J. 2020. Medicaid and household savings behavior: new evidence from tax refunds. *Journal of Financial Economics*, 136(2), 523–546.

Gamble, V.N. 1993. A legacy of distrust: African Americans and medical research. *American Journal of Preventive Medicine*, 9(6), 35–38.

Godlee, F., Smith, J. and Marcovitch, H. 2011. Wakefield's article linking MMR vaccine and autism was fraudulent. *BMJ* 342, c7452.

Goldin, J., Lurie, I.Z. and McCubbin, J. 2021. Health insurance and mortality: experimental evidence from taxpayer outreach. *The Quarterly Journal of Economics*, 136(1), 1–49.

Grossman, M. 1972. On the concept of health capital and the demand for health. *Journal of Political Economy*, 80(2), 223–255.

Guzman, G.G. 2018. Household income: 2017. *American Community Survey Briefs*, ACSBR/17-01.

Hemmingson, G., Lynch, S., Mason, N.F. and Ewing, E.T. 2015. Radam's microbe killer: advertising cures for tuberculosis. *Circulating Now*, October 9. Available at: https://circulatingnow.nlm.nih .gov/2015/10/09/radams-microbe-killer-advertising-cures-for-tuberculosis/

Hickson, G.B., Altemeier, W.A. and Perrin, J.M. 1987. Physician reimbursement by salary or fee-for-service: effect on physician practice behavior in a randomized prospective study. *Pediatrics*, 80(3), 344–350.

Himmelstein, D.U., Campbell, T. and Woolhandler, S. 2020. Health care administrative costs in the United States and Canada, 2017. *Annals of Internal Medicine*, 172(2), 134–142.

Holmes, G.M., Slifkin, R.T., Randolph, R.K. and Poley, S. 2006. The effect of rural hospital closures on community economic health. *Health Services Research*, 41(2), 467–485.

Hotchkiss, J.L. and Pitts, M.M. 2013. Even one is too much: the economic consequences of being a smoker. *Federal Reserve Bank of Atlanta Working Paper 2013-3*. Atlanta, GA: Federal Reserve Bank of Atlanta.

Huntington-Klein N. 2021. *The Effect, An Introduction to Research Design and Causality*. Boca Raton, FL: CRC Press.

Hyder, A.A., Puvanachandra, P. and Morrow, R.H. 2012. Measuring the health of populations: explaining composite indicators. *Journal of Public Health Research*, 1(3), 222.

Hyman, D.A. and Silver, C. 2006. Medical malpractice litigation and tort reform: it's the incentives, stupid. *Vanderbilt Law Review*, 59, 1085.

Jena, A.B., Seabury, S., Lakdawalla, D. and Chandra, A. 2011. Malpractice risk according to physician specialty. *New England Journal of Medicine*, 365(7), 629–636.

Kaufman, B.G., Thomas, S.R., Randolph, R.K., et al. 2016. The rising rate of rural hospital closures. *The Journal of Rural Health*, 32(1), 35–43.

Keisler-Starkey, K. and Bunch, L.N. 2020. *Health Insurance Coverage in the United States: 2019*. Washington, DC: US Census Bureau.

Kessler, D. and McClellan, M. 1996. Do doctors practice defensive medicine? *The Quarterly Journal of Economics*, 111(2), 353–390.

Kurani, N., Ortaliza, J., Wager, E., Fox, L. and Amin, K. 2022. How has US spending on healthcare changed over time? *Peterson-KFF Health System Tracker*. New York: Peterson Center on Healthcare. Available at: www.healthsystemtracker.org/chart-collection/u-s-spending-healthcare-changed-time

Liebeck v. McDonald's Restaurants 1994. PTS, Inc., 1995 W.L. 360309.

Lo Sasso, A.T., Richards, M.R., Chou, C.F. and Gerber, S.E. 2011. The $16,819 pay gap for newly trained physicians: the unexplained trend of men earning more than women. *Health Affairs*, 30(2), 193–201.

Localio, A.R., Lawthers, A.G., Brennan, T.A., et al. 1991. Relation between malpractice claims and adverse events due to negligence: results of the Harvard Medical Practice Study III. *New England Journal of Medicine*, 325(4), 245–251.

Mahoney, N. 2015. Bankruptcy as implicit health insurance. *American Economic Review*, 105(2), 710–46.

Manning, W.G., Newhouse, J.P., Duan, N., Keeler, E.B. and Leibowitz, A. 1987. Health insurance and the demand for medical care: evidence from a randomized experiment. *The American Economic Review*, 77(3), 251–277.

Meeker, D., Linder, J.A., Fox, C.R., et al. 2016. Effect of behavioral interventions on inappropriate antibiotic prescribing among primary care practices: a randomized clinical trial. *Journal of the American Medical Association*, 315(6), 562–570.

Mello, M.M., Chandra, A., Gawande, A.A. and Studdert, D.M. 2010. National costs of the medical liability system. *Health Affairs*, 29(9), 1569–1577.

Michelman, V. and Msall, L. 2022. *Sex, Drugs and R&D: Missing Innovation from Regulating Female Enrollment in Clinical Trials*. Working paper. Cambridge, MA: NBER.

Mitchell, J.M., 2008. Do financial incentives linked to ownership of specialty hospitals affect physicians' practice patterns? *Medical Care*, 46(7), 732–737.

Moseley, J.B., O'Malley, K., Petersen, N.J., et al. 2002. A controlled trial of arthroscopic surgery for osteoarthritis of the knee. *New England Journal of Medicine*, 347(2), 81–88.

Mulcahy, A.W., Whaley, C.M., Gizaw, M. et al. 2021. International Prescription Drug Price Comparisons: Current Empirical Estimates and Comparisons with Previous Studies. Santa Monica, CA: RAND Corporation. Available at: www.rand.org/pubs/research_reports/RR2956.html

Murthy, V.H., Krumholz, H.M. and Gross, C.P. 2004. Participation in cancer clinical trials: race-, sex-, and age-based disparities. *JAMA*, 291(22), 2720–2726.

National Advisory Committee on Rural Health and Human Services. 2011. *The 2010 Report to the Secretary: Rural Health and Human Services Issues*. Rockville, MD: HRSA.

National Center for Health Statistics 2019. *Survey Description, National Health Interview Survey, 2018*. Hyattsville, MD: NCHS.

Neumark, D. 2018. Experimental research on labor market discrimination. *Journal of Economic Literature*, 56(3), 799–866.

Nguyen, T.D., Bradford, W.D. and Simon, K.I. 2019. Pharmaceutical payments to physicians may increase prescribing for opioids. *Addiction*, 114(6), 1051–1059.

Norton, E.C., Li, J., Das, A. and Chen, L.M. 2018. Moneyball in Medicare. *Journal of Health Economics*, 61, 259–273.

NPR/Robert Wood Johnson Foundation/Harvard T.H. Chan School of Public Health. 2019. *Life in Rural America Part II*. Princeton, NJ: Robert Wood Johnson Foundation.

OECD. 2022. *"Health Status", OECD Health Statistics (Database)*. Paris: OECD. https://doi.org/10.1787/data-00540-en

OECD. 2022. *Alcohol Consumption (Indicator)*. Paris: OECD. https://doi.org/10.1787/e6895909-en

OECD. 2022. *Daily Smokers (Indicator)*. Paris: OECD. https://doi.org/10.1787/1ff488c2-en

OECD. 2022. *Health Spending (Indicator)*. Paris: OECD. https://doi.org/10.1787/8643de7e-en

OECD. 2022. *Overweight or Obese Population (Indicator)*. Paris: OECD. https://doi.org/10.1787/86583552-en

Ondrich, J., Ross, S. and Yinger, J. 2003. Now you see it, now you don't: why do real estate agents withhold available houses from black customers? *Review of Economics and Statistics*, 85(4), 854–873.

Paik, M., Black, B. and Hyman, D.A. 2017. Damage caps and defensive medicine, revisited. *Journal of Health Economics*, 51, 84–97.

Parascandola, J. 1999. Patent medicines and the public's health. *Public Health Reports*, 114(4), 318.

Perlis, R.H. and Perlis, C.S. 2016. Physician payments from industry are associated with greater Medicare Part D prescribing costs. *PloS One*, 11(5), e0155474.

Perraillon, M.C., Konetzka, R.T., He, D. and Werner, R.M. 2019. Consumer response to composite ratings of nursing home quality. *American Journal of Health Economics*, 5(2), 165–190.

Pigou, A.C. 1920. *The Economics of Welfare*. London: Macmillan.

Proctor, B.D. 2016. *Income, Poverty, and Health Insurance Coverage in the United States: 2010*. Report P60-256. September. Washington, DC: Census Bureau.

Rawls, J. 1971. *A Theory of Justice*. Oxford: Oxford University Press.

Reynolds, P.P. 1997. The federal government's use of Title VI and Medicare to racially integrate hospitals in the United States, 1963 through 1967. *American Journal of Public Health*, 87(11), 1850–1858.

Rhee, T.G. and Ross, J.S. 2019. Association between industry payments to physicians and gabapentinoid prescribing. *JAMA Internal Medicine*, 179(10), 1425–1428.

Roback, J. 1982. Wages, rents, and the quality of life. *Journal of Political Economy*, 90(6), 1257–1278.

Ross, S.L. and Yinger, J. 2002. *The Color of Credit: Mortgage Discrimination, Research Methodology, and Fair-Lending Enforcement*. Cambridge, MA: MIT Press.

Rudowitz, R., Orgera, K. and Hinton, E. 2016. *Medicaid Financing: The Basics*. Menlo Park, CA: Kaiser Commission on Medicaid and the Uninsured.

Schaffer, A.C., Jena, A.B., Seabury, S.A., et al. 2017. Rates and characteristics of paid malpractice claims among US physicians by specialty, 1992–2014. *JAMA Internal Medicine*, 177(5), 710–718.

Schwartz, M.S. 2020, March 11. *Missouri Sues Televangelist Jim Bakker for Selling Fake Coronavirus Cure*. Washington, DC: NPR.

Seuss, Dr. 1973. *Did I Ever Tell You How Lucky You Are?* New York: Random House.

Sloan, F.A. and Chepke, L.M., 2008. *Medical Malpractice*. Cambridge, MA: MIT Press.

Solon, G. 1999. Intergenerational mobility in the labor market. In *Handbook of Labor Economics* (Vol. 3). Amsterdam: Elsevier, pp. 1761–1800.

Texas Department of Insurance. 2012. *Closed Claims Survey*. Austin, TX: Texas Department of Insurance. Available at: www.tdi.texas.gov/reports/report4.html

Thaler, R.H. and Sunstein, C.M. 2008. *Nudge: Improving Decisions about Health, Wealth and Happiness*. New Haven, CT: Yale University Press.

Trish, E.E. and Herring, B.J. 2015. How do health insurer market concentration and bargaining power with hospitals affect health insurance premiums? *Journal of Health Economics*, 42, 104–114.

US Congress. 1989. *United States Code: Social Security Act, 42 U.S.C. §§ 1877*. Washington, DC: US Congress.

United States v. Carroll Towing Co., 159 F.2d 169 (2d Cir. 1947)

Varkevisser, M., van der Geest, S.A. and Schut, F.T. 2012. Do patients choose hospitals with high quality ratings? Empirical evidence from the market for angioplasty in the Netherlands. *Journal of Health Economics*, 31(2), 371–378.

Wakefield, A.J., Murch, S.H., Anthony A., et al. 1998. Ileal lymphoid nodular hyperplasia, non-specific colitis, and pervasive developmental disorder in children [retracted]. *Lancet*, 351, 637–641.

Whaley, C.M. 2019. Provider responses to online price transparency. *Journal of Health Economics*, 66, 241–259.

World Health Organization. 2022. *The Gender Pay Gap in the Health and Care Sector a Global Analysis in the Time of COVID-19*. Geneva: WHO. Available at: www.who.int/publications/i/item/9789240052895

Wouters, O.J., McKee, M. and Luyten, J. 2020. Estimated research and development investment needed to bring a new medicine to market, 2009–2018. *JAMA*, 323(9), 844–853.

Yinger, J. 1986. Measuring racial discrimination with fair housing audits: caught in the act. *The American Economic Review*, 75(5), 881–893.

Young, A., Chaudhry, H.J., Pei, X., et al. 2019. FSMB census of licensed physicians in the United States, 2018. *Journal of Medical Regulation*, 105(2), 7–23.

Index